# Personal, Social and Moral Education in a Changing World

# Personal, Social and Moral Education in a Changing World

Edited by
John Thacker, Richard Pring
and David Evans

NFER-NELSON

Published by The NFER-NELSON Publishing Company Ltd.,
Darville House, 2 Oxford Road East,
Windsor, Berkshire SL4 1DF, England

First Published 1987
© 1987, Thacker, Pring, Evans

Phototypeset by David John Services Ltd.,
Maidenhead, Berkshire
Printed by Antony Rowe Ltd, Chippenham, Wiltshire

ISBN 0 7005 1157 1
Code 8288 02 1

# Contents

# Notes on Contributors

*john Balding* is a Senior Lecturer in Education at Exeter University and Director of the Schools Health Education Unit which is funded by the Health Education Council and based at the School of Education. He is the designer and developer of Just One Minute, Just a Tick and a General Health-Related Behaviour Survey Method which are curriculum planning methods in Health Education widely used in UK schools. He is also managing editor of *Education and Health,* a journal which is available in most secondary and many primary schools in the UK.

The late *Leslie Button* was a Research Fellow at the University of Exeter. Prior to this, he was a Senior Lecturer at the University College of Swansea and his research interests in developmental group work were published in *Discovery and Experience* (1971) and *Developmental Group Work with Adolescents* (1974). He later incorporated this approach into materials for use with secondary schools entitled *Group Tutoring for the Form Tutor* (1981, 1982).

*David Evans* is presently Honorary Lecturer in Education at Exeter University after 21 years, first, as Lecturer, and then as Senior Lecturer in the School of Education. His primary teaching and research interests are in the fields of individual differences and child development with particular reference to development of language in the mentally handicapped. Of late he has become interested in PSMEd. He has written on the theme of individual differences in moral development.

*Robert Hannaford* is an Anglican priest, presently employed as St Luke's Foundation Chaplain at the University of Exeter. He taught RE in a comprehensive school before becoming a priest and now lectures in philosophy at the University of Exeter.

*Peter Kutnick* is Senior Lecturer in Educational Psychology at the University of the West Indies. He was formerly a lecturer in Education at Sussex University with research interests in the social and moral development of young children and the effects of schooling on pupils in various cultural settings. His publications include *Relating to Learning* (1983).

*Alan Morrison* is a freelance writer on Peace Education. He was formerly a social worker in a Child Guidance Clinic and a member of the Avon Peace Education Project.

*Sue Plant* is Senior Advisory Teacher in Health Education for Devon LEA. She is a qualified School Counsellor and was formerly a deputy head responsible for co-ordinating PSMEd in a secondary school.

*Jack Priestley* is Lecturer in Education at Exeter University with special responsibility for the secondary postgraduate course in religious education there which has always contained significant elements of personal, social and moral education. He has published widely in Britain, Canada and the USA and at all levels from academic papers to secondary and primary textbooks. The Living Festivals series which he initiated and edits is increasingly used in multicultural classrooms. He would like to acknowledge with gratitude a small grant from the Hibbert Trust which made possible a study visit to the United States when this chapter was researched.

*Richard Pring* is Professor of Education at the University of Exeter. He has written extensively in the field of PSMEd, including *Personal and Social Education in the Curriculum* (1984). He is involved in the new educational initiatives for the 14–18 age-group and is currently director of the Centre for TRIST 14 to 18 Inservice Development.

*Peter Scrimshaw* is a Lecturer at the Open University where his recent work has included membership of the team that produced the INSET materials prepared for the GCSE. His publications include *Community Service, Social Education and the Curriculum* (1981) and his current interests centre upon the potential use of computers in improving the quality and effectiveness of education.

*Geoff Stanton* is Vice Principal at Richmond upon Thames College. He has been a member of the Further Education Unit and is interested in the impact of curriculum changes on the relationship between teachers and students.

*Bryan Stephenson* is a Lecturer in Education at the University of

Exeter, with special reference to the teaching of geography. He is involved in curriculum development in World Studies and has contributed to various publications on these subjects and also to studies of classroom language.

*John Thacker* is a Lecturer in Education at the University of Exeter, with particular responsibility for the professional training course for Educational Psychologists at the School of Education. He has carried out research in interpersonal problem-solving and has published curriculum materials in this area entitled *Steps to Success* (1982). Current interests include work with a team of junior and middle school teachers investigating the contribution of developmental group work to PSMEd and pastoral care with younger children.

*Helen Weinreich-Haste* is Senior Lecturer in Psychology at the University of Bath. Her main research interests are in the development of moral, social and political reasoning, and in the development of sex roles. Both these fields have direct implications for education, and she has published in both psychology and education.

# Preface

The contents of this book originate in a series of three weekend seminars held at the University of Exeter between February and May 1984. The seminars were organized by the editors of this book and sponsored by the St Luke's Trust. The seminars were attended by some 25 persons representing a wide range of interests in personal, social and moral education, including academic and research workers, as well as teachers and LEA advisers responsible for designing and implementing programmes in this area for schools. This enabled the seminar participants to review the conceptual issues involved in the area and to examine the interrelationships between these issues and some practical attempts to introduce personal, social and moral concerns into the organization, teaching approaches and curriculum content of schools. This proved to be an enriching experience for the participants, and the contents of this book reflect the breadth of perspectives represented in the seminars. The final versions of the chapters were produced as a result of the thinking and discussions which began at the seminars. Section A comprises three chapters which raise a wide range of issues which need to be considered by people concerned with personal, social and moral education. In Section B there are two chapters which examine the contribution of psychology to the area, while Section C examines the role of values and a religious perspective on the field. In Section D attention is turned to two attempts to construct and implement programmes in schools aimed directly at the personal, social and moral education of young people, while Section E examines the contribution of other curriculum approaches to this area.

Each section has a brief factual introduction and concludes with a discussion by the editors. In the Epilogue the editors draw together the issues raised by the book as a whole.

## Acknowledgements

Acknowledgement is due to the St Luke's Trust without whose considerable financial support and encouragement the seminars and this book would not have been possible; to Exeter University School of Education; and to all the contributors to this book, and especially the late Leslie Button who completed his paper only a few weeks before he died.

# Section A
# Issues

# INTRODUCTION

These first three chapters are 'introductory' in the sense that between them they raise the very wide range of issues with which a book with the title *Personal, Social and Moral Education in a Changing World* might be expected to concern itself.

Richard Pring, first, sets the context within which has developed the present self-conscious approach to personal, social and moral education (PSMEd), and then points out the various pressures on schools to develop such approaches. This is followed by a detailed analysis of the problems that educators must face in this task – ethical, conceptual, political and social. Finally, he suggests a possible way forward through a shift from the impersonal to the personal.

Geoff Stanton analyses the social changes which have affected educational and personal values and the political developments intended to control and effect these changes.

Peter Scrimshaw attempts the difficult task of analysing ways in which we might, as educators, cope with the unpredictability of the future in a time of very rapid change. He points out some of the information we would need to attempt this task and, from this, some possible features of our future world. We would probably all guess at different scenarios, and probably would all agree that the task is a virtually impossible one. Given the difficulty of this task, Scrimshaw then suggests that an alternative strategy is to see schools and teachers as agents of change, playing an important part in choosing goals as well as in bringing about their realization.

In all three chapters the main emphasis, in accord with the briefs given by the editors, is on the education of the secondary school child. Geoff Stanton goes a little beyond this in his emphasis on the 14–18 curriculum and Richard Pring also pays some attention to this age-group.

# 1 Implications of the changing values and ethical standards of society

*Richard Pring*

## Context

The HM Inspectorate say in their survey of secondary schools (DES/HMI, 1979a) that, in recent years, the provision of opportunities and experiences that will help the personal development of pupils as well as preparing them for the next stage in their lives 'have assumed a more significant and conscious place in the aspirations of schools in response to external pressures and to changes in society, and within the schools themselves' (p.206) and, in concluding the curriculum section of the chapter on personal and social development, they indicate the wide front on which these objectives must be pursued: 'It is clear that there is a need for many schools to reconsider curricula, methods of teaching, use of resources and methods of grouping pupils with regard to their impact on pupils' personal development' (p.218).

The HMI do not spell out the external pressures or the changes in society and in the school itself which give personal and social education a more significant place in the curriculum. But other HMI and DES reports are more forthcoming. The consultative document *Education in Schools* (1977a) places among its list of educational aims 'to instil respect for moral values, for other people and for oneself, and tolerance of other races, religions, and ways of life'. This is reiterated in the DES (1979b, 1981) papers *A Framework for the Curriculum* and *The School Curriculum,* which say schools should aim 'to instil respect for religions and moral values, and tolerance of other races, religions and ways of life'.

**Pressures**

Briefly, the pressures upon children and upon society that, for the authors of these documents, make necessary a more self-conscious approach to personal and social development are of the following kinds.

*Behaviour*

There is a popular anxiety about what some young people do and about the obligation of schools to do something about it. This can cover such a wide range of behaviours as racial remarks or violence, vandalism, football hooliganism, stealing and sexual relationships in early adolescence.

*Values*

These are not the same as behaviour, but obviously closely related. It is expected that schools will not only insist upon 'right behaviour', but will inculcate certain values, particularly those related to achieving efficiency in the world of work. For example, early in 1982 Sir Keith Joseph told the Institute of Directors that schools should 'preach the moral virtues of free enterprise and the pursuit of profit'.

*Forming a set of values*

There is an uneasy tension between this and the above sub-section, namely the teaching of specific values. And yet helping young people to form 'an acceptable set of values' is high on the agenda, as though there is no 'off the peg' set of values to be handed on. This, of course, reflects changes that are occurring outside the school – in family life or in the conduct of public affairs. Old certainties disappear, moral traditions are weakened and the individual cannot easily find consensus within society on standards of behaviour on many matters of profound personal concern. Greater responsibility therefore rests on the individual to establish a set of values which can provide an adequate guide in a rather unpredictable future and which, at the same time, are socially ameliorative. Such a responsibility does, of course, relate to a shifting attitude in society towards authority. Certainly at school, but elsewhere too, it is increasingly difficult to resolve disputes by the use of power rather than through co-operation and the achievement of consensus.

## Resisting undesirable pressures

Pupils are increasingly under pressure from the hard-sell techniques of those who see them as sources of profit, for example, in fashion, in music and now in video film. There is an increasing contradiction between such pressures, justified under free enterprise, and the extra resources required to counteract or to resist them.

## Resolving cultural differences

The school is a forum in which not only are there important individual differences in values (arising out of different family experiences and social traditions), but also cultural differences between groups of pupils, especially groups from different ethnic backgrounds. It is not easy to find a way of respecting, while at the same time bridging, these differences in establishing a common cultural and educational experience.

## Facing an unpredictable future

The collapse of the traditional time-serving apprenticeship system is symbolic of more profound social changes. Gone are the days when young people could enter training programmes that would give them skills for life and assurance of a future very like that of their mothers and fathers before them. They do not know what the future holds in store for them. They do know that employment (a long established symbol of adulthood) is being postponed in effect until 18 at the earliest and that, even then, such employment may be intermittent or (in some parts of the country) unavailable. To face such an unpredictable future requires a psychological strength – an inner sense of one's importance – that in the past has been left to chance, certainly not to the school or its curriculum as a major goal.

*Preparation for adult life*

This is a glib phrase that, of course, means quite different things to different people. It is sometimes interpreted narrowly in the sense of providing those values and skills that enable young people to slot into the world of work as it is or is likely to be. It is at other times interpreted much more broadly in the sense of providing those qualities of independent judgement, resistance to pressure and fashion, personal strength and critical appraisal that are the fruit of education at its best. But there are difficulties in reconciling these different interpretations, as the HMI have noted:

> the educational system is charged by society . . . with equipping young people to take their place as citizens and workers in adult life . . . Secondly, there is the responsibility for educating 'the autonomous citizen', a person able to think and act for herself or himself, to resist exploitation, to innovate and to be vigilant in defence of liberty. These two functions do not always fit easily together. (DES/HMI, 1977a, p.9)

One aspect of this preparation for adult life will be some form of political education – enabling young people to internalize those values which are essential to the maintenance of the democratic form of life and to contribute constructively to those social institutions which affect their welfare.

These, very briefly, are some of the pressures upon schools to take more seriously and systematically a concern for personal and social development, and this concern contains at its centre moral values. But there are, as pointed out, paradoxes within these demands upon schools: the apparent contradictions between, first, getting young people to behave in a preordained way and at the same time encouraging them to take responsibility for their own behaviour; secondly, between handing on a specific set of values and enabling them 'to form an acceptable set of values of their own'; thirdly, between permitting within society the sophisticated exploitation of young people as potential sources of profit and yet expecting schools to resist this exploitation; and fourthly, between preparing young people for specific roles in society and yet encouraging an independence of thought and a critical stance towards the adult world they are entering into.

The tensions that make it difficult for schools to respond to the demands made upon them are exacerbated by the rather ambivalent role into which adolescents are placed. On the one hand, they are being kept for longer periods in a state of economic and psychological dependence – in 50 years the normal age for entering into employment has changed from 12 to 18. On the other hand, they need to be treated in an increasingly adult way – the average age of the onset of puberty has shifted in the other direction. Such changes make demands upon teacher–student relationships, especially the exercise of authority, which affects how the schools can and should take on the challenges briefly outlined above. Indeed I want to argue that, in the light of changes in the moral and social climate outside the school and of what we know about adolescent development, the way ahead must lie not so much in teaching a set of values or behaviours, but in helping young people to cope with a situation in which there is less respect for authority in almost every aspect of our social life and less consensus over what are worthwhile ends to pursue. However, before this line of argument is developed, we shall attend further to the kinds of problem that any such task must confront.

## Problems

### Ethical

Personal and social development raises questions not only about the sort of society one wishes to foster, but also about the kind of person one wishes to live within that society. But there are large areas of disagreement over what that society should be and over what counts as the virtuous citizen, so that the teacher cannot engage with confidence in promoting social or personal values. Furthermore, there do not on the surface appear to be agreed procedures for resolving the differences that separate people even within the teaching profession. With what authority, therefore, can teachers assume responsibility for personal and social development, in the way they can in areas such as mathematics or science?

The consequences of this ethical scepticism is reflected in various programmes, especially in North America, of 'values clarification' – avoiding any specific value position, but helping the pupils to clarify their own minds on what they do (and want) to commit themselves to (see Simon, 1972).

*Conceptual*

We have seen from our brief account in the first section of this chapter how different, and indeed contradictory, are the pressures upon schools that make the personal and social preparation of young people for the future important. It is not at all easy to make sufficient sense of the personal development that lies behind these social pressures such that they can be translated into manageable curriculum terms. They refer to knowledge about society and the place of the individual within it, knowledge how to behave in appropriate situations ('social and life skills'), attitudes towards both society and particular individuals, dispositions (moral virtues of various kinds) and a range of socially desirable habits. It includes, too, qualities of personal well-being – self-confidence and self-respect, perseverance and determination. Furthermore, once this complex picture of personal and social development is applied to the wide range of social contexts in which the adolescent lives, the contexts of employment (or indeed of unemployment), of raising a family, of sexual relationships and of political involvement, the area seems too vast and amorphous for coherent analysis and for formulating clear curriculum policies.

*Political*

Personal and social development cannot avoid political questions. It is concerned with the quality of personal life certainly, but the quality of that life depends upon the sort of society one lives in and upon the social relationships created within it. On the other hand, the society we live in will be formed in part by the personal qualities of the young people prepared for entry into it. It is, needless to say, a two-way process of individuals affecting social values and relationships, and society in turn shaping the personal values, habits and understanding of each individual. This does inevitably create problems because it would clearly be wrong for teachers to use their positions of authority to promote a particular political viewpoint. And we have seen how attempts have been made to prevent the introduction of controversial issues into the educational component of certain YTS courses. How, then, might one prepare young people for a future, in which they are to participate politically, without abusing the trust which people of different political persuasions place in the schools?

*Social*

David Hargreaves states in his recent book on comprehensive schools:

> our present secondary school system, largely through the hidden curriculum, exerts on many pupils, particularly but by no means exclusively from the working class, a destruction of their dignity which is so massive and pervasive that few subsequently recover from it. (Hargreaves, 1982, p.17)

Hargreaves's is a devastating attack upon the pretensions of schools to be fostering personal and social development where the sense of personal worth is near destroyed through the constant experience of failure and through the lack of respect felt for those values which they prize most dearly and which they bring with them into schools. I say 'near destroyed' because Hargreaves points to the various ways in which youngsters preserve a sense of dignity, often finding refuge in a shared opposition to what the school offers, or in a rebellion against authority, or in an assertion of their cultural values (in their style, dress, language, music, etc.).

This sense of personal worth and of dignity is threatened further by the prospect and experience of unemployment – by no longer seeing the courses and examinations taken in school as a means to a decent economic future. Furthermore, in a world where the rich and the professional classes get richer while the poor both increase and get poorer, one can see how a disenchanted group of school-leavers will eventually become alienated from the values and the social institutions that determine in large measure our national form of life.

These, then, seem to be the main kinds of problem that make it difficult for the educational service to meet satisfactorily the pressures to prepare young people adequately for a rather unpredictable future where there is little social consensus over the values that should guide personal choices and should help develop appropriate social forms of life. What values should teachers and others promote, where there is so much disagreement over what is right or wrong or over what is a worthwhile form of life? How to translate these personal and social concerns into curriculum terms when they cover so wide and diffuse a territory? How to reconcile such curriculum involvement in an area which is so politically sensitive? And how to ensure a sense of relevance to a growing number of young people who will look anywhere but to school in order to preserve a sense of dignity?

**A possible way forward**

Derek Morrell, who with Jocelyn Owen formed the first joint secretariat of the Schools Council, did, in a Joseph Payne Memorial Lecture, give some indication of how the educational and connected services might give the pupils 'the strength they need to respond to change in their own lives without too much anxiety', and how they might be helped 'to be rather better at solving their problems, the nature of which we cannot predict with any certainty, than we have been at solving ours':

> Only, I would suggest, by shifting the emphasis from the impersonal to the personal. A bureaucratical, impersonal approach is valid only if it can be assumed that the future is likely, in most important respects, to resemble the past: support is then provided by precedent, by traditions and procedures which draw their validity from past experience, and which have future validity only if it can be assumed that that experience is likely to be replicated, at least in large measure. And if this cannot be assumed in any important area of human activity, there is only one alternative approach which possesses validity. It is to use

past and present experience as a source of knowledge of, or of judgments about, those personal qualities which appear to be helpful in solving problems as they arise, and then to help the pupils to acquire those qualities. We must, in other words, make new educational choices, and go on doing so for so long as our condition remains one of change. (Morrell, Joseph Payne Memorial Lectures, 1965–6)

Morrell argues that in making new educational choices we, too, are pushed back into re-examining social and educational values where there is no tradition upon which one can draw for clear and certain answers. And indeed it is this which he saw to be the main purpose of the Schools Council – to provide a framework in which tradition might be examined for finding solutions to new problems and in which professionals might find support in responding, to the very difficulties that have been made explicit in this chapter. It was to be

first and foremost, an attempt to democratise the processes of problem solving as we try, as best we can, to develop an educational approach appropriate to the permanent condition of change . . . and are all seeking to respond to change without adequate knowledge of its characteristics, and without adequate means of harmonising our own response with the responses made by others whose perspective is different. (ibid.)

For Morrell, therefore, the educational crisis he spoke about was 'fundamentally part of a general crisis of values', and the curriculum, rather than simply drawing upon past knowledge for present understanding, must contribute to a solution of the crisis of values. To that end, there must be a shift from the impersonal to the personal – a central focus upon the feelings, concerns and self-perceptions of young people together with an enhancement of those powers of problem-solving, of self-transcendence, of sensitivity and of imagination that will enable them to form a set of values that are both 'personally and socially ameliorative'. The only possible basis for true moral discourse is, as Morrell argued, 'the objectification of self' – the coming to grips with, the imaginative understanding of, and the reasoning about those matters which are of deep personal significance. But this 'objectification', it must be pointed out, signifies the shifting away from purely egoistical preoccupations to the establishment of positions which are objectively defensible.

Twenty years later we can see these sentiments reflected in not a few curriculum developments which have had, and are still having, an impact upon what is taught in schools and colleges, but above all upon the styles of teaching and the relationships that exist in classrooms – for example, the much more systematic approach to active tutorial work (represented in this book by the chapters written by Leslie Button and Sue Plant), the Schools Council Moral Education Projects 8 to 13 and 13 to 16 (both of which started with a survey and analysis of the pupils' perceptions of what mattered to them) and the Humanities Curriculum Project in which areas of practical living and of controversy became the focus of reflective rather than traditional discursive reasoning. Furthermore, in one of the most influential curriculum documents to be written in the past few decades, namely *A Basis for Choice,* the Further Education Unit (1979) puts among the 12 aims of its core curriculum the following four:

(1)   To bring about an informed perspective as to the role and status of a young person in an adult society and the world of work.

(2)   To provide a basis from which a young person can make an informed and realistic decision with respect to his/her immediate future.

(3)   To bring about an ability to develop satisfactory personal relationships with others.

(4)   To provide a basis on which the young person acquires a set of moral values applicable to issues in contemporary society.

Two significant features of the ABC curriculum are, first, as has been indicated, a focus upon personal and social qualities, attitudes, experience and knowledge rather than upon the subjects – the products of intellectual inquiry – that have traditionally made up the curriculum; and secondly, the positive response from colleges and schools to these proposals. It is as though they have articulated an educational way forward that had previously been seen only dimly. Even, too, in the working papers and the proposals of the Manpower Services Commission, despite its primary concern for better training for jobs, there has been an emphasis upon the importance of developing personal and social qualities. Leaning upon the research of the Institute of Manpower Studies, it points to the crucial importance attached to these qualities by employers even though they traditionally do not loom large in the curriculum thinking of schools – a sense of responsibility for one's own actions, a capacity to listen to others' points of view, a flexibility of attitude towards new approaches, and initiative and ability to establish good working relations with other people.

The shift from the impersonal to the personal, however, needs to be accompanied by a rediscovery of 'community'. Indeed the dual theme of Hargreaves's book (1982) was that of re-establishing a sense of personal dignity in a context which recognized the inextricable links between personal growth and the wider social context – its resources, institutions, values – in which that growth takes place. Hargreaves points to the link between the perception of his or her worth by each pupil and the educational values of the school as they are embedded, but rarely made explicit, in the formal curriculum. These underlying values suggest a cult of individualism, an importance attached to academic achievement to the exclusion of personal and social values, a narrow interpretation of success, a limited view of 'worthwhile culture', a diminishing significance attached to the expressive arts. His solution in general terms lies in thinking of the school much more as a community than as an aggregate of individuals and in fostering a sense of solidarity. The battle of comprehensive education had too often been fought in terms of equality of opportunity vs individual freedom. The third element of 'fraternity' had been largely neglected since Dewey and perhaps Tawney. To quote Tawney in his corrective to the exaggerated emphasis upon individual advancement:

> in spite of their varying character and capacities, men possess in their common humanity a quality which is worth cultivating and . . . a community is most likely to make the most of that quality if it takes it into account in planning its economic organisation and social institutions – if it stresses lightly differences of wealth and birth and social position, and establishes on firm foundations institutions which meet common

needs, and are a source of common enlightenment and common enjoyment. (Tawney, 1938, pp.55–6)

Hence by way of solution Tawney suggests that, in addition to getting rid of gross inequalities of wealth, 'what a community requires, as the word itself suggests, is a common culture, because without it, it is not a community at all' (ibid.).

The sense of community within the school, however, will be of little avail unless it is linked to a wider sense of community – a re-examination of values, a focus upon the personal, a concern for individual dignity, and a sense of solidarity which is shared with different constituencies in society. We see this anticipated in the Taylor Report (1977), *A New Partnership in Our Schools*, which sought a closer identification of the aims of the school with those of the wider society but the achievement of this through co-operation and a widening of the educational debate rather than through imposition.

**Personal development**

There seems now to be enough research undertaken in develop-mental psychology to enable us to see how a shift from the impersonal to the personal might be translated into terms which make curriculum sense. By 'person' I refer to those objects (a) which have some form of conscious life, and are able to conceptualize, to order and to interpret experience; (b) where part of that conceptual scheme involves the recognition of others as persons to be related to and to be respected as such; (c) which can act intentionally; and (d) which in acting intentionally can be held responsible for what they have done (and thus be open to praise or blame). Obviously so to characterize 'person' – as a conscious, intentional, responsible being able to enter into 'person-like' relations with others – needs to be argued at much greater length. But given the acceptance of such an analysis, one can begin to see more clearly how a developmental story might be told about 'being a person', how such developments might be fostered or indeed hindered by schooling, and what it means for pupils to be respected as persons.

*Coming to see others as persons*

We know, for example, how the capacity to perceive others as persons does itself develop in different ways. First, only gradually, as any reflective parent knows, does the child become aware that the other's 'inner life' is not, in any particular situation, exactly like one's own. Even though I am feeling lively, the other person might be feeling tired, and although I need to learn how to recognize the signs of different mental states, this learning requires the prior ability to distinguish between one's own state of mind and that of other people. It is the absence of this ability which Piaget (1926) refers to as ego-centrism – and of course, as in any changing psychological capacity, the transition from ego-centrism to altruism is a gradual one. Secondly, one can have the concept of person but, through lack of imagination, fail to apply it as widely as one might. Different periods of history show how the concept of person was not applied to particular people – to blacks, to women, heathens, slaves or to children. It was as though they lacked certain attributes, such as the capacity to think or to reflect or to act responsibly, which were considered essential for being a person. Thirdly, however, connected with this developing sophistication of personal under-standing is a qualitative change in the sort of relationships that one can have with another. Such development is briefly mapped out by Peters (1974), a change from the rather instrumental to role relationships with others, and thence to those relations in which the individuality of the other is fully recognized.

*Acquiring a capacity to think morally*

We know, too, how the capacity of young people to think responsibly does itself get transformed from the rather egoistic concerns of young children, first, to the acceptance of a conventional morality that transcends their own self-interest, and then to a sense of justice that enables young persons to look critically at conventional morality and to establish a set of more universal principles which they are able to make their own. The work of Kohlberg and his colleagues over the past 30 years has charted a developmental route from an initial stage of pre-conventional morality in which 'fairness' is identified with self-interest to a post-conventional level of morality in which people are able, and have a tendency, to think through a set of principles which they, in an impartial and disinterested way, would see to be acceptable as universalizable principles of conduct. And the importance of achieving this is argued by Kohlberg, as follows:

> In terms of principles of justice Watergate and My lai both illustrate, not the decay in morality, but the failure of conventional morality to handle civil and human rights. This is not something new in national history. What is new is the situation in which the educational system is expected to develop a majority of citizens governed by principles once assumed to be the prerogative of a moral elite. Our educational system has failed to produce a majority of citizens who, like Lieutenant Calley and President Nixon, are only good at giving and taking orders. What is specifically new to education is our expectation that high school students should be unprejudiced or non-racist. Implicitly, this is the expectation that students should go beyond the moral level of concern for upholding the norms of their group, family and nation to the moral level of concern for universal principles of justice and respect for human dignity. (Kohlberg, 1979, pp.9 and 10)

There is now an impressive body of interconnected research (Kohlberg, 1981b; Kohlberg, Levine and Hewer, 1983, on the development of principled moral thinking; Selman, 1976, on the growth of social perspective taking; and Hoffman, 1975, on the development of altruism) which would suggest, first, that it makes sense to talk of personal qualities which enable young people to cope in a morally significant way with new and unpredictable circumstances, and secondly, that these qualities can become realistic aims of the curriculum.

*Acquiring respect for persons*

There are different levels at which one can talk about respect for persons as we have defined it. First, there is the simple recognition of people as having minds of their own and having distinctive points of view. Very probably, when pressed, everyone might be said to respect everyone else as a person in this sense. But one needs to be wary here. It could be the case that such recognition may not, within particular cultures, be extended to certain groups of people – to people of different ethnic background or to children. Or it may not occur in certain ordinary, everyday relationships. I may, for example, demonstrate again and again in practice my failure to see the children in my class as persons in this sense – disregarding their points of view as having any significance. At this first level, therefore, my respect for someone as a person requires the practical recognition that he or she is capable of thinking and thus has a point of view which, even if wrong, deserves serious attention.

Secondly, respect for persons refers to an attitude towards other people in which also their wants, feelings and interests matter. To ignore such wants, feelings and interests is to ignore what is essentially individual and particular about them as persons. Respect for persons therefore, at this second level, requires the development of this caring for other people in the sense that one recognizes that their intentions, feelings and aspirations matter and should be taken into account. Furthermore, the deepening of this respect would lie in the enhancement of this recognition of how others do in fact feel and of what they aspire to.

The greater focus upon 'the person' requires, therefore, some worked-out notion of personal development – the qualities that enable young people to act responsibly, autonomously and with respect for other persons in a world where new and unpredictable problems are arising, where the past is not in many cases an adequate precedent for future cases and where different perceptions of the problems and their solutions will need to be tolerated and respected. There are, too, ways in which such qualities might be enhanced. First, there are ways in which they can be the focus of curriculum planning and activity. Secondly, however, there is a need to examine what impact the curriculum as a whole, the very experience of education, and the effect that non-educational social institutions have upon the sense of self-respect and personal worth of young people.

## Condition of development

It would be wrong, therefore, to see the focus upon 'the personal' and the development of appropriate personal qualities to be simply a matter of a formal curriculum programme. Far from it. Much more significant is what the Rutter Report (1979) referred to as the ethos of the school. The Rutter Report was an interesting study of 12 different schools in the Inner London Education Authority. The main question it raised was: do schools make a difference? To answer this question it needed to identify certain outcomes which would seem to be significant indicators of the differences that schools make – examination results, pupil behaviour and pupil attendance. Furthermore, it tried to analyse those factors which were most closely correlated with these differences in outcomes. Such a report has inevitably been subjected to extensive criticism, and indeed it has been most careful not to confuse correlations with causes and effects. None the less, the results are quite startling. Schools that seemed roughly comparable in social and physical conditions produced very different results. Poor behaviour, for example, measured in terms of vandalism, graffiti, bullying, rudeness, etc., was significantly different in different schools, where these differences could not be accounted for in terms of the values or behaviours or expectations that the pupils brought with them into the schools. The report correlated these outcomes not with any single factor, but with clusters of factors. What above all seemed significant was the 'ethos' of the school. Three inter-connected elements in the conditions appropriate for personal growth would seem to be the following.

### School ethos

John Dancy (1980) analyses 'ethos' as it is used in Rutter (1979) in terms of the values, aims, attitudes and procedures of a school which interrelate and which remain a relatively permanent feature of the school. For example, one can identify certain regular procedures in the life of the school, such as displaying the work of pupils, which reflect attitudes towards pupils and towards work which, in turn, are reflected in the school's aims (even if these are not made explicit) and ultimately the dominant values of the school.

To get at the ethos of the school you need to examine the various stable procedures through which business is conducted towards individuals and their work, towards the community as a whole and towards those outside the school. And picking out these significant procedures is exactly what Rutter did. What correlated highly with pro-social behaviour were such teaching procedures as displaying children's work on the wall, recognizing achievement through praise, preparing thoroughly for lessons, entrusting pupils with responsible tasks and turning up punctually for class.

*Use of authority*

According to Piaget in his book *The Moral Judgement of the Child*:

> Young people need to find themselves in the presence not of a system of commands requiring ritualistic and external obedience, but a system of social relations such that everyone does his best to obey the same obligations, and does so out of mutual respect. (Piaget, 1932, p.134)

The developmental progress outlined by Piaget was essentially a change from the early perception of rules, as part of the necessary furniture of the world, either fashioned by or mediated through unquestioned authority, to a perception of rules as socially agreed conventions for the regulation of behaviour. These could be more or less just in so far as they arose out of an impartial concern for each person's well-being. A shift in the perception of rules required a parallel shift in attitude towards authority – from one of 'unilateral respect' to one of 'mutual respect'. It was important therefore to create the conditions in which this change could take place, in which those in authority could exercise it in a manner that encouraged this change and in which moral values did not remain dependent upon a view of authority that would be increasingly questioned as the young person matured. Indeed perhaps the most significant element in personal development is the exercise of authority by those in whose charge the young people are.

*Just community*

A criticism frequently directed against Kohlberg's work is the disconnection between thought and action – between the development of moral reasoning ability and the tendency to behave accordingly. There are many reasons why people do not act as their moral reasoning suggests – weakness of will, apparent triviality of the moral issues, the prior importance of other considerations, peer pressure, and so on. One significant element, however, that Kohlberg identified was the discrepancy between the moral level at which the school or community behaved and the moral level expected of the pupils. Schools, for instance, too often demand a unilateral respect for authority and a moral reasoning level that rarely rises above the pre-conventional level that Kohlberg (1982) talks about. For that reason Kohlberg argued for the need for what he referred to as 'just community schools':

> In summary, the current demand for moral education is a demand that our society become more of a just community. If our society is to become a more just community, it needs democratic schools. This was the demand and dream of Dewey. (ibid., p.40)

The democratic principles that Dewey had in mind concerned the opportunities for young people to address themselves to matters of justice and fairness that mattered personally to them and that they would have a real chance of influencing – not playing at democracy or moral decision-making, but 'doing it'. Furthermore, this would take place against a background of school policy and administration that was non-secretive and impartial in its formulation and application. It is difficult to get young people to think and act in a spirit of justice and respect for each individual in a context that is not characterized by such qualities. The experiment with a 'just community' approach to education is described by Wasserman and Garrod (1983, p.17); the hypothesis was: 'that by building collective norms and ideas of community at a stage higher than that of many of the members of the group, more responsible student action would be promoted.' This required participatory democracy in which staff and students shared equally in socio-moral decisions about the rules and discipline of the school. It was hoped thereby that pupils would assume greater responsibility for decisions that affected their welfare and that, in having to think through the problems democratically, they would develop into a more caring community. It was assumed, as Dewey had assumed, that a group of individuals might operate at a higher moral stage of deliberation and judgement than that of the individual members of the group. If that is the case, then, as teachers concerned with the moral development of young people we should attempt to reform the moral atmosphere in which individual decisions were made.

Much more needs to be said about the conditions in which that personal development might take place. The school cannot be insulated from values and forces that prevail outside the school walls. For fitting attention to be given to the exploration of values, and to the development of those personal qualities essential for this to be done responsibly, a framework needs to be provided within the wider professional and non-professional community for open, critical discussion.

The Schools Council had begun to provide such a forum within the educational profession before its unfortunate demise. But one can see here a central task for the newly formed governing bodies of schools which represent a range of professional, parental and community interests. However, there are many different levels at which this must occur. For example, it is exceedingly difficult for schools to make a realistic response to the demands made upon them, where the universities fail to broaden their own vision of educational success, thereby forcing many schools, often against their own educational judgement, to remain within Morrell's 'impersonal curriculum', which cannot cater for that person-centred examination of values which he (Morrell) judged to be so important. In an address to the Anglo-American Educational Alliance given just before he died in 1969, Morrell states:

You will see at once that this is very much a turncoat's perspective on curriculum. When I was at the Schools Council I should have found it difficult to perceive, as clearly as I do now, that the curriculum . . . is a structure erected on a base of reciprocal personal relationships. I should also have found it difficult to assert, as again I now do, that in curriculum we are concerned with human beings whose feelings and aspirations are far more real and immediately important to them than the cognitive development which is the educators' main stock in trade. (Morrell, Address to the Anglo-American Educational Alliance, 1969)

But this must not by any means be seen as a rejection of the cognitive development fostered by hard work within the respective academic discipline and upon which universities quite rightly put so much weight. Far from it. It was an attempt to see that development in perspective. Morrell goes on to say:

> The object of the exercise is to help children towards an integrity of two rationalities: that of feeling which is no less real than cognitive rationality but which may be largely private to the individual child, reflecting his experience of a hostile unloving world: and that of cognitive rationality, which has to be painfully built by the careful disciplined analysis of all available experience, and which then provides a means of sharing our feelings with others, maximising those which are productive of reciprocal satisfaction and minimising those which shut in a hostile private world. (ibid.)

## 14 to 18

In thinking about education for the future we will doubtless have in mind pupils at the secondary stage of education, although by no means exclusively so. We are however already witnessing radical developments in the curriculum and the nature of schooling for those within this age range. Where justification is given, these changes are seen as an attempt to prepare more effectively young people for an unpredictable future, meeting the problems I have outlined and reflecting a shift from the impersonal to the personal.

But the exact shape that such changes take is still to be determined and already we are seeing how the educational institutions and wider social forces might reshape the emerging educational response, so that it will not meet their needs. Let us briefly state what these needs are, and then what – in theory at least – is the educational response.

*Needs*

We can distinguish here between personal and social (or economic) needs. On the personal level there is the problem of little employment available at age 16, possibly only intermittent employment after 18. At one local school last year only 14 per cent of 16-year-olds found jobs whereas in the previous year it had been 33 per cent. In some urban areas where traditional industries have declined or disappeared, there is little chance for some of ever finding a permanent job. Furthermore, apprenticeships as they have traditionally been understood are fast disappearing; 40 per cent of 16-year-old school-leavers took apprenticeships in 1960, but only 20 per cent in 1980, and it is far less than that now. In the past ten years one million unskilled jobs have disappeared, and in the next ten years a further one million will go.

The effect of these changes upon young people is profound, the relevance of schooling to adult life is, for many, far from clear. School achievement is no longer clearly linked to improved employment prospects, which many see as the main point of schooling. There are no longer routes open to secure and predictable futures. Already therefore we are seeing a sense of disillusion that is reflected in attitudes to work, in social behaviour and non-acceptance of traditional values, in attendance at school and in styles of music or dress.

Society, however, sometimes sees it very differently. The need is for a better trained workforce to meet the technological and economic challenges of the future. The craft-based industries of the past have given way to technology-based industries, with a need for more highly trained technicians and less room for the unskilled or semi-skilled worker. In what has been described as a supply-led economic recovery, the need is for a highly sophisticated workforce that has acquired those 'generic' rather than specific skills which will enable employees to adapt readily to technological changes which are unpredictable. Reference is made here to personal qualities, but they are qualities of adaptability, problem-solving, flexibility of mind rather than those which prepare young people psychologically for the personal exploration of value which they must engage in.

*Response*

This might be considered on two levels: that of the providers, and that of what is provided. At the first level we have seen quite remarkable changes in the past few years in the sphere of responsibility for tackling the preparation of young people for the future, with an accompanying change in educational philosophy. The New Training Initiative came from the Department of Employment rather than the Department of Education, and aspires to guarantee training with an educational component for all young people up to age 18. Apart from those undertaking traditionally academic courses through the A-level route, it is expected that most young people will remain under some form of traineeship up to 18, acquiring those skills that will better serve the rapidly changing world of work. It is an employer-based training scheme that, at least in its mode of operation, if not in its explicit philosophy, is firmly rooted in the 'impersonal curriculum tradition', the inadequacies of which to meet personal needs Morell pointed out.

On the other hand, there has been a rapid development of 'pre-vocational courses', influenced indeed by *A Basis for Choice* (FEU, 1979), that are being increasingly incorporated into schools' thinking about the education of young people from 14 to 17 or 18. The Technical and Vocational Education Initiative (TVEI) has acted as a catalyst for quite radical educational programmes to meet the needs of young people for whom 16 is now no longer the normal termination of their formal education.

In theory, at least, such programmes represent a shift from the impersonal to the personal that Morrell spoke about. This is reflected, as we have pointed out, in the aims of the FEU's *A Basis for Choice*. Characteristics of the emerging 14–18 curriculum are: *experiential learning* (with emphasis upon systematic reflection upon the experiences of the young people), *negotiation* of the learning experiences that the young persons see themselves to be in need of, *guidance and counselling* as a central curriculum concern rather than a fringe activity, *communication skills* including the critical appraisal of the values and messages purveyed through the media, the acquisition of *basic skills* necessary for economic survival (whether in employment or not), *personal and social qualities* (establishing an acceptable and workable set of values, 'coping or survival skills', the development of self-esteem, confidence, the ability to form personal relations), *political, economic and social awareness* and *community orientation.* Certainly there is insistence upon technological and business studies, but these are seen firmly within a person-centred curriculum. All, too, is set within a framework of *assessment* and *profiling* which endeavours to do justice to the full range of achievements and personal qualities of young people, not just the narrowly defined academic achievement.

The key issue however is this. How can these general curriculum aspirations be translated into practice where there is no tradition for such educational thinking to draw upon? How can schools, colleges and indeed universities make the change from the impersonal to the personal where there are few precedents for this in detail? Despite the analysis of what is needed – the need to place firmly at the centre of the curriculum the exploration of values and the formation of an acceptable set of values where there is little social agreement on what these should be and where the future we are preparing young people for is an unpredictable one – there seem to be insuperable problems in adapting institutions, social expectations, educational philosophy or teaching styles to meet those needs. In the past there have been two sources of curricular change: first, the intellectual traditions represented by academic subjects, with their training programmes on undergraduate courses and their professional associations; and secondly, the analysis of social and employment needs from which training programmes, often of a vocationally specific nature, at operative, craft and technician levels, have been derived. Neither of these traditional sources is adequate for providing an educational response to the problems that I have been referring to.

The danger, therefore, is that either one or the other of the two traditional sources of curriculum change will take over the attempt in schools or colleges to provide an adequate educational response to the personal needs of an increasingly disillusioned group of young people and to the social needs of the wider society which are much deeper than the provision of work-related skills. The very features of the curriculum that I have outlined in general terms can be interpreted narrowly or generously – *personal and social qualities* narrowly as social and life skills, or generously as creating autonomous, self-respecting, responsible citizens; *political and social education* narrowly as knowing about existing social institutions and political procedures, or generously as equipping young people to participate effectively in those community and social institutions that affect their welfare: *communication skills* narrowly as form-filling or doing limiting and limited exercises, or generously in the spirit of the Bullock Report as providing a means to articulate their feelings and to enter into meaningful and critical dialogue with other people; and *experience-based learning* narrowly as a socialization into a limited set of work experiences, or generously as giving due weight to what the students bring with them to school or college.

## Conclusion

In educating young people for the future we cannot predict with certainty the skills and the knowledge they will need. Nor can we draw upon a shared tradition of values to meet the many problems that young people will face in their personal and social lives. Nor indeed have we the same confidence that existing social and political arrangements will sustain the allegiance of those who are currently being taught. Therefore, we cannot, in preparing them for such a future, rely upon our traditional authority in teaching with confidence how they must deal with specific problems. First, we are not clear in detail what these problems will be. Secondly, part of the present moral and social climate is a distrust of authority, especially in the realm of values. Thirdly, without an agreed tradition of values it is not easy to see how one can promote with confidence one particular set of values rather than another.

The solution, therefore, must lie in a deeper concern for the person – a respect for pupils or students as persons, enabling them to articulate and to 'refine' their feelings to achieve self-esteem and sense of personal worth, to develop the capacity to engage in principled thinking, to acquire the ability to reflect upon experience, and to accept seriously the values and attitudes that they bring to school or college.

We have the considerable knowledge – the research and development base, if you like – of how we might and should proceed in order to achieve these goals. But educational change takes place within a wider institutional and political context. And it is very likely that these desirable educational aspirations will be transformed into ways of working that have little relevance to young people's needs.

# 2 Social education for an uncertain future

*Peter Scrimshaw*

## Introduction

This chapter is an attempt at identifying some of the problems involved in seriously accepting the claim that we need to provide a social education for children that will enable them to contribute to the society in which they will live. Traditionally this has been seen as a matter of preparing the young to fit into society as it is at present. The implausibility of this is now generally evident and we are urged instead to think in terms of preparing the young for the society in which they will spend their adult lives. But what questions arise when we try to think through what this involves by way of social education? At a minimum social education involves preparing the young to live with other individuals, within small groups, communities and in society as a whole. Within each of those contexts a person would require relevant detailed factual knowledge, a commitment to desirable values and attitudes, a range of social and life skills and desirable qualities of character and personality. Some would say that a person also needs some general understanding of social theories and a commitment to desirable social, moral and political principles.

Where the controversy really begins is in the detailed content we provide within these general categories, and the relative emphasis given to each category. However, if we take seriously the idea of preparing the young for the future, then much of the debate about what to include within social education becomes at best irrelevant and at worst self-defeating. To show why this is so we need, first, to look at currently popular views on what is involved in educating for a future society, to locate their strengths and limitations.

## Alternative viewpoints

One way to approach social education is to think only of what a student will need in the first couple of years after leaving school. It is indeed possible to provide quite specific and visibly relevant social training and advice of this kind in the final year or two at school if both the student and his or her immediate future plans are well understood. Given the importance for the individual of successfully making the transition from school to outside life, such training is not to be sneered at. However, the provision of such a social first-aid kit (however desirable as a starting-point) does little to prepare the student to meet longer-term problems. Indeed even this very short-term approach to social education can be problematic for both teacher and student because it is sometimes impossible to predict whether a given person is going to obtain work at once or not. This is obviously a central issue in the crucial matter of developing appropriate attitudes to work and leisure.

An alternative strategy is to take a longer view, seeing the task as that of working out what British society will be like in the future and then preparing our students for it. However, this assumes that the future can be predicted with sufficient accuracy already to indicate what we should be teaching today's students. If we are considering educational preparation for the first ten years of a child's adult life, this requires (allowing for time to bring in any proposed changes) that we must now identify what Britain will be like in AD 2000. But as far as social education goes, what would we need to be able to predict about society in AD 2000 in order to do this? At the very least the following information would be essential:

(1)    Whether Britain had been involved in a nuclear war, and if so what parts of Britain were still habitable.

(2)    The rates of birth, death, immigration and emigration over the next 15 to 20 years, the last two being subdivided further in terms of skills, age and cultural backgrounds.

(3)    The size of the Gross National Product over the next 15 to 20 years, both in absolute terms and relative to other countries.

(4)    The total amount of work being done for pay.

(5)    How this work is distributed among the population, classified by age, gender, social class and type of work.

(6)    What political entity the children will then be part of and its political, cultural and commercial relationships with other countries and groupings.

(7)    The expectations that will be held in AD 2000 of citizens in terms of social and political skills and attitudes.

(8)    The range of social values that will be accepted as legitimate by AD 2000, and the ways in which this acceptance is distributed among the population.

To see if these predictions are ones that could be plausibly made, consider recent history. If we take 1905, 1925, 1945 and 1965 as examples, in how many of those years was a correct prediction of the answers to these questions for 15 to 20 years ahead even plausible? Do we have any reason to think that the next 15–20 years will be more predictable than the last 80? Given that the elements listed could alter independently of each other and that the results of their interactions are themselves unpredictable, I think it is clear that attempts to predict social and political change even 15–20 years ahead are futile. To say, for instance, that everyone will have several different jobs during their lifetime, or that early retirement will become near-universal by AD 2000 is to do little more than make what (in 1986) seems an intelligent guess. Furthermore, even if successful prediction were possible, how would we convince people now that the prediction was correct? How, for instance, would anyone persuade the present government to start preparing schools to meet the needs of a decentralized socialist society on the Yugoslavian model, should that be what futurologists were predicting for AD 2000? In addition, if we are preparing today's students for some predicted future society, then this will involve not only decisions now about what balance of social and vocational roles that society will require, but also decisions about which specific children will occupy them. If, for instance, we envisage a future society made up of a minority who work hard at highly skilled and interesting jobs, while the majority are pleasantly but undemandingly unemployed, it is obvious that the social skills, attitudes and aspirations of members of the two groups will have to be very different if everyone is to be happy with this situation and their own position in it. But that, in turn, involves prior educational preparation of the children at present in our schools for whichever of the two roles we predict they will hold in their early thirties. This process of allocation would have to begin quite early in schools if the appropriate social preparation were to be completed in time. (Perhaps 11 would be a good starting-point?)

Preparing children for a predicted future involves, as I have tried to convey above, a very passive stance towards what is to come. It assumes that educators must predict and then conform to the presumably inevitable tide of events, educating children so as to make them happy with what that future provides for them. There is, however, no need to discuss whether this attitude is acceptable because it is based on predictions that simply cannot be successfully made or acted upon.

A quite different strategy is to try to choose a preferred future and then create it, with schools as one of the agencies for achieving this. At first sight this general approach looks very attractive, with its appealing vision of today's educators quietly shaping the future of the nation for the better. Unfortunately it is at least as impractical as the first approach. Creating Britain's future is as hard as predicting it, given the aggravating tendency of the rest of the world to carry on as though they had as much right to influence events as we have. Try drawing up a short list of the decisions taken in the last 20 years that have most affected Britain. How many were taken in Britain, and of those how many were made largely on the basis of factors outside British control?

This is not, of course, to say that decisions about social and political preferences cannot be made; indeed they cannot be avoided. But in an increasingly economically and culturally interdependent and politically volatile world any action based on these preferences is likely to have unexpected results, and the cumulative effects of this over 15–20 years makes long-term planning unproductive.

One reaction to the problems identified above might be to consider withdrawing schools altogether from the area of social education for a future society. In one respect there is something to be said for this. Already schools get nowhere near achieving the aims set for them by teachers, parents and society at large. This is not because teachers are incompetent, but because everyone's expectations of schooling are quite unreal. This has two highly undesirable effects. One is that attempts to say what schools are about too often drift off into an educational rhetoric that is so visibly irrelevant to what can actually be done that it ceases to exercise any motivating effect on teachers or students. The second is that those students and teachers who do take the rhetoric seriously are consequently obliged to underrate the real achievements that they make. Improvements in schooling are certainly possible, in social education as elsewhere, but only if clear and realistic priorities are set, consonant with whatever level of resources is provided. One additional benefit of such an approach, incidentally, is that it makes the real effects of reductions in resourcing upon educational achievement clearly visible in terms that are generally intelligible to the public at large.

One way of responding to this proposal for reducing at least the rhetorical demands made upon schools would be to remove any expectation that they directly promote social or moral development. This would bring them into line with institutions in post-compulsory education, and is entirely practicable, should it be thought desirable. The notion that teachers are in loco parentis and have an obligation to provide social education for their students is one which can be challenged as easily as any other educational assumption. However even if schools did withdraw from formal provision of social education, they would still be concerned with the social attitudes and skills of students, in so far as these directly promoted their other learning. The gain from withdrawing from the formal provision of social education would lie in the releasing of resources and, more important, teachers' emotional energies for other tasks. However it would leave the task of social development still undone, unless other institutions took it over. Whether the gains would outweigh the costs in those circumstances is an open question.

Another response to the problem of the unpredictability of the future is to teach fairly general social skills and techniques that can be applied in a variety of situations. What we might call 'skilled amenability' involves combining such skills with the creation of an attitude of dependence upon others to define the moral and social ends to which these skills are to be directed. This strategy assumes that detailed factual knowledge about social situations can be gained in the situation, and that what is needed is an ability to 'read' people successfully and respond to them. The Watergate story provided us with several concrete examples of this sort of social training in action. It is clearly true that this is a genuinely flexible kind of training, and as the sequel to the Watergate case itself showed, the skills involved can provide an income and a happy life to their possessor in even the most quickly changing social or political circumstances. Indeed if our only concern were with increasing GNP and with the pursuit of some loosely defined kind of individual happiness, skilled amenability is probably a viable approach.

If skilled amenability requires dependence upon others to define our values for us, it is diametrically opposed to approaches that emphasize autonomy as the central aim of social development. On one interpretation the promotion of autonomy involves educating students to make independent decisions based upon moral principles. In its purest form this view suggests that what makes decisions and actions right is not their content, but the reasoning which led to them. It is a position that involves thinking at a high level of generality, and to that extent is well suited to use over a long period of time and in changing circumstances. There are, however, at least three difficulties with this position. First, most adults are apparently not able to think morally in this sense. How plausible, then, would it be to expect all students to achieve autonomy? Secondly, how do you persuade people to support such an approach, when a majority are unable to understand what it involves? Thirdly, is how people decide moral and social issues really more important than what they decide? And even if you personally believe this, is it a view that commands enough support in society at large to be the basis of a practicable general policy for social education in schools?

## A possible way forward

As they stand, all of the strategies looked at so far have problems of one sort or another. Perhaps the way forward is to ask first what are the essential requirements for a practicable future-oriented policy for social education. At a minimum it must be widely acceptable (say to 90 per cent of adults) in content so as to make its implementation practicable. It must also be relevant to any reasonably plausible future for Britain. I suspect that only a limited range of objectives for social education would meet these requirements, and that most of these would be qualities of character and attitudes. You might like to draw up your own list of the qualities and attitudes that you think would meet both these requirements. Notice, though, that it is a purely factual matter which actually will. Some form of national survey or at least a serious public debate would be required to find out what common core of attitudes and values meet the 90 per cent rule. Similarly, the range of plausible futures for Britain would need to be actually mapped out in some detail to see what attitudes were relevant to all of the realistic possibilities. Having said that, my guess (by way of concrete illustration) is that the eventual list would probably include at least the following:

(a) self-confidence;
(b) self-respect;
(c) determination;
(d) open-mindedness;
(e) courage;
(f) honesty;
(g) compassion;
(h) fairness.

In themselves these are widely relevant and therefore 'future-proof' objectives. But to realize them in action (and why value them if they are not to be so realized?) involves possessing factual knowledge and skills that are often highly situation specific. Such skills are not future-proof, and therefore require frequent updating as both society and the life experiences of the specific individual concerned alters. As far as the knowledge and skills components are concerned, then, we must think in terms of a recurrent education in which the relevance of these core attitudes to new situations is reviewed for each person as and when necessary. The beginnings of such a programme can in fact already be seen in the TV, radio and book-based programmes and short courses now becoming available for people approaching particular stages of life such as parenthood or retirement, or requiring help in dealing with some role change or new interest. This sort of provision would be an essential element of any national programme of social education for a future society, and would need to be available to all as of right throughout life. If this were accepted, what then would be the role of the schools? They would need to achieve two sets of objectives. First, they would need to ensure that every child reached a basic acceptable level of development in all of the attitudes and qualities of character that met the '90 per cent' and 'future-proof' rules, for if these qualities are not developed in childhood, then it is unlikely that they will be picked up later. Secondly, the schools would need to provide the knowledge and skills needed by children to use these qualities in the situations already facing them, or soon to face them, as children. At different stages of schooling this would require them to understand such issues as parent–child relationships, sex, friendship, race and workplace roles. They would not generally speaking include war, politics, civic or world affairs and these topics would therefore not be included in school curricula, at least until the 16+ stage was reached.

There is, incidentally, no reason to assume that all children would need precisely the same content for the factual elements of their social education. Terrorism, for instance, would be ignored in the school stage of most children's education, but would have to be directly dealt with in those areas of Northern Ireland where it is a fact of life that children have to face and come to a view about.

While this approach removes many important topics from the social education curriculum in the school, the opportunity to study all of these would be available to everyone later. For many topics this availability would continue throughout life, as part of everyone's automatic entitlement to recurrent education. For example, those topics relevant to deciding how to vote would obviously be introduced initially in time to contribute to the individual's first choice of party, and be on offer from then on. The key point is to present issues to people when they can see that they are about to face practical situations in which these issues will arise, rather than trying to cram them all into the school curriculum using the (fallacious) argument that anything worth learning must be taught and furthermore must be taught in schools.

The organizational consequences for schools of adopting such a national policy seriously would be considerable. In particular, the following general questions would have to be answered in the early stages of the implementation of such a programme, even leaving aside the post-school elements in the proposal altogether:

(i) How are different levels of these core attitudes at present distributed among the young?

(ii) What represents an acceptable basic level of development for these attitudes, and how can we check to see if it is being reached?

(iii) What is the minimum level of resourcing needed to achieve these levels?

(iv) What methods, ethos and organization does a school need to help children reach them?

(v) Is the present distribution of effort and resources between levels of schooling the best possible to promote social development?

(vi) Can some aspects of social development best be encouraged by action outside the schools altogether by, for instance, greater pre-school provision or family support?

These are not easy questions to answer, but if an approach based on the idea of fitting children for the future is to be taken seriously, addressing such issues at the outset would be an essential preliminary.

# 3 Aspects of the social and political context

*Geoff Stanton*

## Introduction

My brief is to provide some analysis of the social changes which have affected the educational and personal values we hold, and of the political developments intended to control and effect these changes. I wish to approach this topic from a particular slant, and my justification for doing so forms part of the general point I wish to make about this area of education. Throughout I shall be concentrating on the 14–18 curriculum.

At one level this chapter could be about the social changes that have taken place on a national scale, and one could analyse the effects of such things as high youth unemployment, greater (and timely) sensitivity to sexism and racism, changes in family structure and the fact that our economy is now, for the first time, based more on service occupations than productive industries. Similarly, discussion of the political developments intended to control and effect these changes would refer to the growth of the Manpower Services Commission and its influence (particularly on 14–18 education, non-advanced further education (FE) and in the context of the Youth Training Scheme), and a tendency towards more centralized decision-making about content and standards in education as a whole.

## Issues arising

All this *is* very significant, and not always in the most obvious ways. For instance, youth unemployment has not just affected the motivation and immediate destination of school and college leavers. It has also:

(1) re-opened the debate about the source and justification for the 14–18 curriculum (in so far as it was ever open);

(2) created a *de facto* raising of the school leaving age, and in order to cater for the resultant need for a more genuinely comprehensive provision, has promoted:
   (a) much curriculum development, including new materials, methods and approaches to the curriculum development process itself;
   (b) liaison between the education service and other agencies in the community which can be learning resources;

(3) stimulated a redefinition of 'vocational' to include the need for, and development of, personal qualities as well as technical skills.

As far as the first of these issues is concerned, I would argue that there have traditionally been two sources for the 14–18 curriculum – the demands of jobs and the requirements of university admissions tutors. I have personalized the latter source deliberately. The shadow cast by the idiosyncratic selection policies of individuals and departments is a long one. And yet those on whom the shadow falls, in secondary schools and colleges, have no effective means of influence on them. The major worry is that the admission tutors' judgements seem not to be made on the basis of a close examination of the quality and content of any new course. Very often they know little about this. Rather they judge by the suitability or otherwise of individuals they meet who possess the qualification. There is, of course, a self-fulfilling prophecy at work here. If doubt is expressed as to the adequacy of a course as a preparation for higher education (or simply if a positive indication of its currency cannot be obtained), then students who have a clear intention of going on to a higher course avoid taking it, but stick to the traditional courses. Some weaker students who lose out in the competition to gain a place on the more prestigious courses may take the new course for want of anything better, and if the course is then judged by their achievements on or after it, then it naturally never does attain credibility with admissions tutors, whose initial caution appears to have been justified.

The significance of all this for personal, social and moral education (PSMEd) is that whereas many new courses recognize its importance, to the extent of building in appropriate objectives and experiences, in more traditional courses it remains very much part of the 'hidden' (some would say 'phantom') curriculum. Therefore, if a student's achievements in this area are formally promoted and recognized by his or her course, that can be the sign of a (socially) second-class course. This can be held against you even if the course in question was taken at 14–16, since much selection starts before later results are known. On the other hand, some detect growing disenchantment with conventional 'academic' courses, particularly when they no longer carry any guarantee of access to higher education. They are usually condemned on the grounds that they do not develop sufficient vocational or personal effectiveness. This view has been expressed by both central government and employers' organizations. However, while both promote courses which embody new approaches, they conspicuously fail to establish clear progression routes past their own gatekeepers, let alone the semi-independent ones mentioned above. The danger remains, therefore, that the new courses will occupy a 'tertiary modern' sector of education, inhabited only by other people's children.

As far as 'vocational' courses are concerned, it might at one time have been true to say that they were educationally narrow, only finding space for the development of those talents of use in a specified job. Even then, they were not any narrower than some A-level combinations as taught in some institutions. But now it is vocationally dangerous to specialize too early. The emphasis has to be on skills and capacities which are of use in a wide range of careers, and on developing the personal qualities required if one is to transfer learning acquired in one (vocational or other) context to a different one. Going alongside this is the fact that as jobs become harder to get, the vocational relevance of a course becomes more important to prospective students. This may be ironic, but it is understandable. It does, however, generate a moral dilemma for some teachers who find themselves with vocationally motivated students on a vocationally oriented course, but with too few jobs available. Many have overcome the problem by using the vocational interest as a vehicle for the general education of the students concerned, and by building on the fact mentioned earlier that personal effectiveness may be more vocationally valuable than the acquisition of any specific technique.

The fact that the education system post-16 has, until comparatively recently, been selective, is discussed further below. One of the effects of this has been a certain lack of moral force behind some of the arguments coming from the education service, now claiming to be defending the interests of young people who we used to recommend should leave us and find a job. But that was before falling rolls. That is, of course, unfair on many dedicated and innovative staff. But the fact that the system as a whole did tend to operate in this way *has*, in my view, resulted in both a lack of expertise and a lack of influence with respect to a comprehensive 14–18 curriculum.

### Relationship between teacher and taught

For the rest of this chapter I wish to focus on something other than the national context, namely the effects of the changing educational environment (including the factors described above) on the relationship between teacher and taught, and the degree to which control of the learning process and its objectives is – or should be – passing from the teacher to the learner. If you assumed that the topic as summarized in the first paragraph could *only* refer to the tension (creative or otherwise) between central agencies and the teachers, I would ask you to pause for thought. One of the hypotheses I wish to put forward is that the traditional struggle for decentralized control and definition of the curriculum has been about making those things *teacher-centred*. Arguments may have been deployed to the effect that teachers require professional freedom in order to cope with the varying needs of their pupils or students, but there is, I would maintain, little evidence of a systematic effort on the part of teachers to give the learners the necessary power, skills and responsibility which are required if they are effectively to express their needs and determine their learning programme.

The following are illustrations of the ways in which we have, I believe, elevated the centrality of the teachers (and, therefore, of *our* courses) at the expense of the status of the learners and of their perceptions of their needs. All apply to the 14–18 curriculum in particular.

(1)   We have largely accepted that students need to be selected for pre-planned courses. Our curriculum development is done with respect ,to notional 'target groups', to one of which the learner is expected to belong. We rarely design a course around the needs of an individual.

(2)   We tend to evaluate courses by means of testing the participants. We have sophisticated machinery by which to determine whether a student has passed or failed a course. By contrast, we have few formal procedures aimed at investigating whether the course has been suitable and effective – or whether it has failed the learners.

(3)   Learning is usually group based and group paced. This may be for administrative rather than educational reasons, in that we find it difficult to resource or timetable a more individual approach, but the effect is to imply that learners need to adapt to the course rather than vice versa.

(4)   We are overconcerned with *preparation for* the future (defined by us) at the expense of more *support during* current challenges (which can only be defined by the learner).

(5)   We use experiences as illustrations of what we are teaching, as opposed to allowing and providing for current experience to *determine* what needs to be taught. Instead of coping with an experience-led curriculum we have (in the recent past, at any rate) often attempted to withhold experience (such as that of work) from certain learners until they were judged by us to be ready for it – or until their education was 'finished'. This well-meant protection was often against their wishes.

While not wishing to support uncritically current government policy, I suggest that it is because there is, to some extent, an alliance on these points between the policy-makers and the majority of non-studious (but not necessarily unintelligent) young people that the education system has been under such pressure to change. If it had been the case that our students (and their parents) had been wholeheartedly in support of the methods adopted in secondary and further education, if they had been confident of the relevance of our aims, and had felt that all students' personal talents were fully encouraged and rewarded by the examination system, then pressure to change for political or economic reasons – as opposed to educational ones – could have been more easily resisted.

It is not the case that the system as a whole lacks the ability to operate in any other way. At either end of the age spectrum, in junior schools and on post-experience management courses, we usually manage to avoid these pitfalls. It is with regard to secondary and further education – and particularly that for the 14–18 age-group – that we have adopted a relatively inflexible model. Ironically the 14–18 sector raises particularly interesting issues when it comes to a debate about the extent to which a curriculum should be teacher-centred or learner-centred, or how we might define 'relevance' in education; 14–18-year-olds span the compulsory/non-compulsory boundary, thus raising questions in any case about the nature of our 'contract' with them. They are in transition to the adult world, and therefore its nature and their relationship to it are ever-present aspects of their consciousness. Changes in, say, its economic or social state might be thought to have immediate relevance for their curriculum. At the same time, it is unlikely that the full range of experience required to satisfy or 'feed' them as learners can be acquired solely within the walls of an educational institution. Nevertheless, it has often been in this sector that we have been the slowest to change, and where we have been most concerned to protect our charges from the pressures of the real world. As it happens, there is a range of agencies available to contribute to provision for the age-group. Indeed one of the spin-offs from a somewhat unhappy and incoherent period in the provision for this group has been the discovery of what can be provided for school-leavers by an integration of the efforts of (for example) an employer, the training officer, an FE college and the youth service. There are unfortunately many bad examples of ineffective provision, but other schemes show us what can be achieved.

**Relationship with PSMEd**

There are many relationships between these general issues and personal, social and moral education. Some of the more direct links are:

(a)    the relevance of social and interpersonal skills to performance in many jobs, and to the getting of all of them;

(b)    the need to prepare young people for an uncertain future, possibly containing several changes of career direction, within a society which is also changing;

(c)    the trend towards the education and training of a much higher proportion of the age-group beyond the compulsory school leaving age.

This last point brings me back to a moral issue which I believe faces the education service. Although we have always been much concerned with the pastoral care of those within the system (indeed I have heard the need for continuity of care being used to argue against transition to a tertiary college at 16), we have to face the fact that we have, until very recently, only provided such continuous care to those of higher academic ability. Those who have failed to achieve good academic qualifications have traditionally been sent out to fend for themselves. Not only that, but the part-time learning programmes which we have provided for (some only) of them have often been conspicuously lacking in adequate personal and social education. More than in any other area of learning, it is surely important that we are here seen to practise what we preach. The ways in which we select and group students, and differences in the facilities and opportunities that we offer them; are more exact expressions of *our* values, and more potent influences on *their* values, than are exhortations in the prospectus. There is also, of course, an important link between the methods by which we attempt to deliver this area of learning and our aims and objectives. Our approaches must not simply be appropriate to our objectives, they must embody them. It is the approaches used across the institution that are at issue, not just in certain lessons. Questions are also raised about how the institution is organized. It is, by now, a cliché to say that there is no point in teaching that the only virtuous way to govern a community is the democratic one if the school or college – as a community – is run some other way. Either we must admit the value of other approaches in some circumstances – and teach how these other approaches work – or we must adapt the community to be a working example of what we wish to be learned.
But are there more subtle tensions?

Can *respect for the individual* be inculcated where only group-paced learning is practised?

Can *self-esteem* be promoted when assessment systems 'fail' a substantial minority, and also fail to report on many things which they *can* do?

Is group co-operation compatible with norm-referenced assessment, and our definition of 'cheating'?

Should we enforce attendance at a compulsory lesson on *freedom,* or expect them to make mature decisions while being denied influence on the objectives of their own learning programme?

It is easy to be glib about this. The issues involved are, of course, complex ones, involving teachers in difficult value judgements, and requiring a high level of pedagogic and administrative skill if they are to be resolved.

**A possible way forward**

Nevertheless, I believe that we may be in the process of refining the use of a range of devices which not only promote many of our aims for this area of education more effectively than does the conventional curriculum, but also embody them. The devices include:

(i)    the definition of a common-core *checklist* from which an individual learning programme can be negotiated, thus permitting individualized schemes while maintaining standards, quality and currency;

(ii)   a profile on which can be recorded the results of a variety of kinds of assessment, and a *process* of profiling which can involve the learner in developing skills of self-assessment, and which can make the teacher more accountable;

(iii)  participative and resource-based learning methods which can adapt to a variety of learning needs within the same group, and which make more use of the community as a resource.

There are many problems which remain. In particular, I believe that we need honestly to examine our own attitude to personal, social and moral education. Why is it that, despite the fact that this area of learning is accepted by all us pundits as a good thing, there is all too often a tacit conspiracy involving both teachers and learners to neglect the area as a mutual embarrassment. It may be to do with a fundamental absence of negotiation in our whole system. Most of us would feel that there is an especial need for learners to *agree* to work towards the objectives we have in mind in this area. I think we would also expect our consent to be obtained if we were to be the learners. Perhaps we fear that if really offered the choice our students would opt out (maybe because of the model of learning we give them in other areas) and therefore find ourselves caught in a dilemma.

There are also two serious dangers for teachers of personal, social and moral education: one relates to learning about values, and the other is concerned with using skills. First, it has been argued that we should be concerned with creating situations in which students can learn about values, rather than being taught them, and that this involves explorations and discovery rather than teaching. The significance of this approach is that young people can then 'own' the values they actually have, and can take authority for the implications of holding these values. Through this they can discover what it means to take an adult role in the present day pluralistic society (see report by the Grubb Institute on Developing the Tutor Role at Richmond upon Thames College, 1985). All very well and good, but this is risky for the teacher! What might come out during 'explorations and discovery', and will the community support this approach as opposed to simplistically expecting the school or college to inculcate given values? A clear view and steady nerves may be required.

A second and final point. The tenor of the argument presented here leads to an emphasis on actually learning to *do,* as opposed to qualifying to do. Others have called this 'education for capability'. There is a healthy trend in much of current personal, social and moral education towards complementing a thorough understanding of issues and concepts with and by the parallel development of skills and capacities which enable the individual to *act* effectively. Hence there is talk of 'political literacy', not just understanding others; assertiveness training accompanies an analysis of sexism. Once again, this is dangerous stuff. If such real learning *does* take place, then the power balance between teacher and taught, and between the learner and his or her institution, will inevitably change. The students may even attempt to apply their skills outside the school or college. We might then find that families, firms and the community are not used to schooling actually affecting a student's everyday behaviour.

Of course, I do exaggerate the position to help make my point more clearly. However, it is remarkable how often even if we get as far as, for example, simulating a telephone call (as opposed to describing how to do it), we stop short of allowing the students to make a real telephone call on the school or college bill. What about the cost! It is as nothing compared to an hour in the engineering workshop. No, we are inhibited for other, more complex reasons. Perhaps the students sense this reticence to engage in activities which might interest them, and we sense the inadequacy of merely discussing issues? This might explain our mutual embarrassment. Often attempting to teach for capability merely proves that we as teachers do not yet have the art to help others to act more effectively, though we can almost certainly teach them to make impressive notes on how to do so. This adds another kind of vulnerability, and is why so many of us feel so threatened in making the attempt. To succeed, however, might be even more threatening – to our authorities and institutions as well as to us as teachers. We would find out then whether all of us genuinely wanted real personal, social and moral education. To fail would be politically more comfortable, but not to try would be unethical as well as less interesting. Fortunately there are many courageous and sensitive teachers willing and able to give it a go.

# DISCUSSION

As noted earlier in the Introduction to this section, the first three chapters are intended to set the scene for later chapters in which other contributors spell out in greater detail the implications, in practice, of the basic issues raised here and suggest ways in which personal, social and moral education can be brought into the curriculum. But the authors have accepted their brief, fortunately, in very positive ways and each of them has something to say about means as well as issues; each makes proposals for educators trying to meet largely unknown – and, when knowable, highly disputable – needs of the future.

Richard Pring suggests that a possible way forward is through a shift from the impersonal to the personal and in his analysis of this shift he discusses some very important points. These include what we understand by the concept of 'person', how one might develop moral capacity – an essential aspect of a person – and a person's respect for others. One of the ways he suggests these needs might best be met is by the setting up of what Kohlberg calls 'just community schools', and it is interesting to see in later chapters the extent to which other contributors depend, implicitly, for the success of their programmes on schools moving towards 'just community schools' – whether or not they are in fact called that.

Peter Scrimshaw too makes positive points for progress; one notion is his suggestion that the reader might draw up his/her own list of personal qualities and attitudes which are most likely to meet the essential requirements for the practicable future-oriented policy for social education. His list includes self-confidence, self-respect, determination, open-mindedness, courage, honesty, compassion and fairness. Occasionally we ourselves have tried this kind of task with groups of teachers and one is struck by the fact that, like Scrimshaw's list, most teachers' lists are also highly pro-social. One always promotes useful discussion when one suggests that one looks at *practices* in particular schools or colleges and sees to what extent these practices militate against the development of these admired qualities. The dilemma of this duality is raised later.

Perhaps Stanton's chapter suggests the most sweeping curriculum and pedagogical reforms though the other two contributors hint at these. He discusses the need for the education of the 14–18-year-olds to move towards student-determined goals and towards student-initiated and controlled learning. He puts it all very clearly at the end of his chapter: 'The tenor of the argument presented here leads to an emphasis on actually learning to *do,* as opposed to qualifying to do'; later he says: 'Hence there is talk of "political literacy", not just understanding others; assertiveness training accompanies an analysis of sexism.' The danger here, as he points out, is that if such learning, resulting in action, takes place, then the power balance between teacher and taught and between the learner and his or her institution will inevitably change. It seems to us that these three chapters open up for further discussion some fundamental and related sets of issues.

The first relates to the precise nature of 'personal, social and moral education' as an entity: PSMEd has become an accepted shorthand for a set of approaches which, it might be assumed, will have some common goal or goals, even though each one of 'its' practitioners might have different goals and different ideas about how they might be achieved. But in fact 'personal' education, 'social' education and 'moral' education can be quite different things, each with its own goals or sets of goals. Perhaps especially when we move into a deeper consideration of the values underlying different approaches to PSMEd, lumping them together in this way increases the conceptual and practical complexities. In fact Scrimshaw expressly addresses himself to 'social' education and the heart of Pring's approach is the person and 'personal' education.

This particular problem is highlighted when one looks at the concept of needs which in this section, and elsewhere in the book, is perhaps rather loosely used. Presumably we are talking about 'psychological' rather than 'physiological' needs – even if the need Pring emphasizes in his chapter is that of 'getting a job'! But are we talking at any one time about *social* needs, determined for the child, with or without his agreement, by society and its agents (teachers in the present case), or *personal* needs, perhaps determined by the child? (We are not sure about the concept of *moral* needs.)

Here one can raise the traditional distinction between 'wants' – which somehow have an immediate, selfish, improvident flavour – and 'needs' – which are for the *child's* 'good' and which are likely to be approved of, even if not decided by society.

This leads naturally into perhaps the most difficult issue of all, that is the notion of student autonomy. As we have seen, Stanton begins to set out some of the implications of *allowing, encouraging –* even *obliging* (though this last might be seen to be a bit of a contradiction in terms here) children (down to what age, down to what level of ability) to determine their own goals, initiate and control their own learning.

All is easy when these goals and approaches gel with society's (schools') notions; but what about when they conflict? Or is conflict to be avoided in the cause of a contented community? Should one always try to neutralize contentious issues before they become conflicts? Surely it must be the case that conflict of values between generations (and perhaps often they are 'right', not us) will occur; and that one can only sensibly use this conflict as productively as possible. Conflict can be creative in its outcome if properly handled. Unfortunately the productive handling of conflict calls for a high degree of maturity – and one is not equating maturity with age necessarily. Another obvious problem with conflict in schools and classrooms is that, in terms of established position and status, the dice appear to be so heavily loaded in the teacher's favour – especially if the ground chosen is cognitive and verbal. So many adolescents *feel* strongly but often are inarticulate about their feelings, they *think* deeply but find it difficult to find the words. They often also find it hard to accept hypocrisy and find it sickening when they realize the gap that often exists between the professed and the practised in school. One might argue – we have heard colleagues argue – that this is 'the way it is in the world', that school is a microcosm of our wider society and that the sooner young people realize this, the more quickly will they grow up and be treated as adults. We reject this view and feel that the best hope for the uncertain future is for adolescents, as far as they are able, to carry their idealism with them into maturity and that an essential cornerstone of this idealism is that mature people should be expected to maintain a rough agreement between what they say and what they do.

Perhaps Hargreaves's notion of *dignity,* introduced by Pring into his chapter, adds a little more to this brief comment on conflict and conflict resolution. To accord people dignity is to respect the people who hold views, attitudes and values diametrically opposed to one's own, and to try to bring these disparate qualities into *fruitful* opposition.

A final issue relates to how one brings about the necessary changes in *educators* if we are to take seriously the notion of student autonomy (student-determined goals, student control of learning, etc.) as one way forward. Perhaps those engaged in or at least interested in teacher training (initial and advanced) will have a special interest in this issue. (This includes most of the contributors to this book.) How much learning in departments and colleges of education is student initiated, controlled and directed? And if the answer is 'not much', what kind of a model are we providing for the teachers-in-training whom we might be persuading to allow and encourage student autonomy in the schools in which they will teach?

It is probably the case that with increasing interference from outside bodies (CATE, HMIs) any move will be away from, not towards, such approaches. It will be interesting to see in later sections of the book the extent to which what is said *should* happen in schools can be related to practice in our own teacher training institutions. For instance, should 'Education for Peace' have a place in teacher training, and if it should, should the approaches which Alan Morrison feels are essential in peace education apply also to the teaching of teachers of peace education? If they are, the implications would be quite startling.

# Section B
# Psychological Perspectives

# INTRODUCTION

As Richard Pring pointed out in his chapter, a possible way forward in preparing children for an unpredictable future is to follow Morrell's suggestion and shift the educational emphasis from the impersonal to the personal and to focus on the feelings, concerns and self-perceptions of young people.

In a secular scientific age such concerns are largely the province of psychology and it is to a social sciences perspective that we now turn. The work of Piaget describing the stages of development from ego-centrism to autonomy is often cited as is the work of Lawrence Kohlberg in the development of principled moral thinking. Their work and that of other psychologists has been used as a basis for educational thinking in the area of personal, social and moral education. In Chapter 4 Helen Weinreich-Haste ranges widely over cognitive-developmental, psychoanalytic and social learning approaches in psychology. She examines their contributions to a moral psychology and examines the relationship between these psychological findings and what is possible within school-based moral education. Her paper works on a broad canvas, while in Chapter 5 Peter Kutnick examines the educational implications of a specific model of autonomy derived from the work of Piaget.

# 4 Is moral education possible? A discussion of the relationship between curricula and psychological theory

*Helen Weinreich-Haste*

## Introduction

Moral education has existed for many thousands of years without the benefit of formal developmental psychology. Parents have raised their children according to the practical precepts of their culture, that is precepts which contain buried but identifiable implicit models of human nature and of human development. Even more basically, children have learned to survive and thrive in the peer social group, acquiring the necessary social skills to absorb and negotiate group norms, sanction deviants and take responsibility for younger peers and siblings. In contrast, the forces of established religion and education have tended to make their models of development more explicit, and to have expressed a rather more definite idea about the fundamental goodness or otherwise of human nature – and consequently to have tailored their educational practices with some fairly well-defined goals in mind.

The common term is 'character'. It is a concept which we all understand, because we share a common cultural background. It has meaning to us, and it has meaning to the many generations of educators who tried to instil it, most explicitly perhaps in the public (and later grammar) schools. This meant the education for leadership, integrity, team spirit, honesty, and so forth, mainly through the use of competitive games and a hierarchy of responsibility. In a somewhat different form the progressive school system instilled a more co-operative version of 'character' through participatory democracy and the encouragement of self-determination. Youth movements of all colours have tried to do the same thing. All that differs are the defined goals and the desired virtues; that the school and the youth leader should have some responsibility for moral education is an ancient concept.

But 'character' is a diffuse concept. Its constituent elements are weighted differently by different political and social perspectives, and by different social classes and subcultures. It does not survive the philosopher's scalpel; the philosopher wishes to differentiate morality based on reasoning and justice from morality based on virtue or affect. It does not survive empirical psychology either; as everyone knows, Hartshorne and May failed to find much of a predictable relationship between different moral traits and behaviours, nor between moral behaviour and membership of character-building youth movements like Sunday school or scouts (Hartshorne and May, 1928–30). While Hartshorne and May can be criticized both for using essentially Mickey Mouse cheating tasks (like most psychologists who have subsequently studied cheating) and for drawing an over-pessimistic picture of the inconsistency of moral psychology, nevertheless subsequent psychological research has probably been on fairly safe ground in focusing on very specific and narrowly defined patches of the 'moral domain' (Emler, 1983).

We must remember that developmental psychologists interested in the field of morality have inherited all this cultural baggage, *and* an appreciation, however untutored, of the various philosophical positions on what constitutes the 'moral'. In an effort to do manageable and relatively rigorous research developmental psychologists have firmly delineated their terms of reference, and there have emerged several distinguishable positions. While it is probably unfortunate that these distinctions look sometimes like battle lines, and that a certain amount of bristling and rhetorical exchanges go on about what counts as 'proper' scientific method and 'good theory', nevertheless the effect has been a valuable clarification of developmental processes and different aspects of 'morality'. We can now say with a certain amount of confidence that we know something about moral development, and we can also make some statements, albeit tentative, about what is likely to be possible within the context of school-based moral education.

## Major dimensions of moral psychology

It has turned out that the distinctions and lines of delineation within 'moral psychology', as I shall call it for convenience, unsurprisingly follow the major lines of current psychological theory. But they also follow the main lines of philosophical debate about morality, which raises interesting questions for those who would like to make psychologists more aware of the close relationship between philosophy and psychology. In brief, there are four dimensions along which one might differentiate the dominant themes, or in educational terms the ideal goals, of moral development, and there are four theoretical traditions in psychology, each of which offers somewhat different explanations of the development of morality.

To understand something of the incompatibility, even of conflict, between the various dimensions and explanations let us first consider some lay definitions of the 'virtuous person' – the kinds of definitions which one might encounter in policy discussions of moral education, in fact: 'someone who is concerned for others', 'someone who acts according to what they believe', 'someone who doesn't break the rules', 'someone who is honest and trustworthy', 'someone who is concerned about rights and justice'. On reflection these are not the same animal: the rule-follower may not be capable of autonomous, principled action; the person who can analyse an injustice may be relatively unfeeling in interpersonal relations. And, of course, vice versa (Peters, 1981; Weinreich-Haste, 1979).

The four dimensions of moral psychology are autonomy vs conformity, thinking vs feeling, pro-social behaviour vs anti-social behaviour and individual vs social. For the psychologist these dimensions reflect dominant research preoccupations. But they also contain different assumptions about methodological and theoretical questions. It is a matter of emphasis; for example, the psychologist interested in moral thought does not deny the importance of developing good habits, she regards it as only a partial explanation. But these dimensions do represent in practice somewhat different implicit theories of morality, and for the educationist this may matter; can one simultaneously teach moral autonomy and moral conformity?

The main differences between *autonomy* and *conformity* approaches are as follows: the autonomy model assumes that the outcome of moral development, and therefore the 'goal' of effective moral education, will be a person who can make independent moral decisions and act upon them; this may involve countering group and normative pressures. In contrast, the conformity model assumes that development and education result in proper knowledge of social norms, good behavioural habits and a tendency to avoid sin. Clearly the developmental mechanisms are different; the autonomy model emphasizes cognition, judgement and an appreciation of responsibility for one's own actions; the conformity model emphasizes the development of appropriate guilt anxiety, the acquisition of certain kinds of social skills and habits, and a receptivity to the approval of others. To cite but one study, Hoffman and Salzstein found that young adults who showed signs of 'autonomy' had parents who were not particularly affective in interaction with them, but had stressed *induction*; the child had been encouraged to consider the consequences of her actions and to draw her own conclusions about the wrongness of them. Young adults who were equipped with strong consciences and who tended to be conscientiously law-abiding had parents who practised affective techniques, such as love-withdrawal, when they transgressed (Hoffman, 1973).

The second dimension is *thinking* vs *feeling*. Should we attempt to educate the emotions as well as, or even instead of, the intellect? Is the morally educated person someone who has a sound set of ethical principles, or someone who is sensitive, empathic and loving? The two are not necessarily incompatible; the person whose principles are affronted can also feel anger or compassion on behalf of those who suffer, and the person whose feelings well up at a particular situation can subsequently reflect and generalize from that response into a well-articulated principle – indeed many people become 'converted' to a moral cause as a consequence of an emotive response to an isolated incident. But developmental psychologists and moral educationists have tended in their research and writings to concentrate either on the cognitive or the affective mechanisms.

The development of moral thought involves cognition about rules, roles and relationships. Most of the work on moral thinking has been conducted within a cognitive developmental framework, and has (1) focused fairly heavily on the child's understanding of rules, rights and justice, and (2) much of it has looked at moral development in terms of stages of thought – the child's understanding is seen as a *structured theory* of how the world works, and development involves *transformations* of these structures into more complicated forms of reasoning. Such transformations occur within the ordinary course of events, or else they can be stimulated through cognitive conflict. The main work in this field has of course been done initially by Piaget, and subsequently in considerably greater detail by Kohlberg, who has empirically identified five stages of moral reasoning (Piaget, 1932; Kohlberg, 1976; Kohlberg, Levine and Hewer, 1983).

The development of feeling, in contrast, concerns the ways in which the person becomes sensitized to others. This involves interpretation of the emotions of others, and the ability to respond empathically to those cues and to moderate one's own behaviour so as to avoid hurting. Much of this kind of development can be seen as a form of social skills learning (Staub, 1978; Hoffman, 1984; Mussen and Eisenberg-Berg, 1977).

The third dimension is *pro-social* vs *anti-social behaviour*. Shall the psychologist and the educator be more concerned with the avoidance of sin or with the development of altruism? Both pro- and anti-social behaviour depend upon social norms and expectations; much of what is called juvenile delinquency, for example, once one has parcelled out broad variables like social deprivation, can be seen as conformity to subcultural norms and social identity. Similarly, altruism is subject to normative effects, as the studies of bystander apathy and intervention demonstrate (Emler, 1984; Staub, op.cit.).

The approaches have normative factors in common, but otherwise they diverge conceptually. The avoidance of sin is seen by lay persons and psychologists alike as being a matter of impulse control. Impulse control stems from properly learned good habits and behaviour patterns, and from a reasonable level of guilt anxiety and internalized prohibitions and controls. But it also involves a more complex set of skills, associated with dealing with one's own internal conflicts; it is not enough to know that aggression will be punished, or that one will feel guilty if one aggresses against others, it is also necessary to know how to handle one's aggression and direct it into acceptable outlets (Kurtines and Gewistz, 1984).

Pro-social behaviour has had rather less attention from the researcher. It involves empathy, the skills of co-operative behaviour and consideration for others and the capacity to take responsibility within the community – very much in fact those skills we considered under the heading of 'feeling'. But there are certain kinds of supererogatory forms of altruism which go beyond mere concern for others, and involve going against what appears to be a norm of *non-interference*. A number of researchers have concluded from looking at studies of bystander intervention, and at the Milgram studies of obedience, that going out on a limb against group or authority pressures requires the individual to take a perspective of the situation in which she sees herself as *personally* involved, and *personally* responsible for taking action. This has been termed 'moral competence', and it appears to correlate strongly with level of moral reasoning (Huston and Korte, 1976; Kohlberg and Candee, 1984).

But from this research there emerges clearly the importance of *social psychological* variables. The media and on occasion politicians tend to present a view that the purpose of moral education is to prevent anti-social behaviour; in practice the running of any organization, and in particular the running of a school, requires the establishment of a whole structure of *pro-social* expectations and norms; the actual restraint of anti-social behaviour is a relatively small part of the process of maintaining order in an institution (Rutter *et al.*, 1979).

The fourth and final dimension I will consider is the *focus on individual* vs *the focus on social processes*. Research on the development of predominantly individual processes emphasizes the individual's acquisition of good habits, guilt anxiety and the internalization of parental and social norms. Within such an approach social interaction with parents, peers and school are *catalysts* in the individual's development; they act upon the individual and mould or facilitate the acquisition of morality. In the case of moral reasoning development an individual approach emphasizes the changes which go on inside the individual's head, in the structure of moral reasoning; 'social' factors, such as stimulating or disequilibrating cognitive conflicts, are *intervening variables* in the individual developmental process.

In contrast a social approach regards the social context as *causal* rather than catalytic, and moral development and action as a matter of social relations rather than of individual values, traits or reasoning. The social approach includes a wide range of psychological theory; Skinnerian behaviourism, for example, treats the individual not as a 'moral' being, but as the product of a social process which moulds acceptable or unacceptable social behaviours through reinforcement (Skinner, 1971). From a quite different theoretical perspective comes the idea of a 'moral career'; the task of individual development is to learn to *manage* one's role, persona and reputation in order to obtain acceptability within the social group. 'Morality' in this sense is simply a matter of expressive behaviours or rhetorics which demonstrate one's worth as a group member – or, as Breakwell has argued, as a means of establishing one's own group's legitimacy *vis-à-vis* another, less 'morally worthy' group (Harré, 1979; Breakwell, 1983).

**Possible applications in schools**

This brief sketch of what I see as being the four main dimensions of moral psychology incorporates aspects of cognitive-developmental, psychoanalytic and social learning approaches to developmental psychology, and some important contributions from social psychology. The question arising from this review is: what is *possible* within school-based moral education? By differentiating four dimensions and unpacking the ragbag eclecticism of traditional notions of 'character' I have tried to indicate that not all approaches are compatible with one another.

First, let us state the obvious. School does not begin till the age of five, and although it occupies many hours of the day, powerful affective relationships with parents and peers happen outside. The school itself is a complex institution in which a wide variety of norms exist, to govern the organization of authority and co-operative relationships, the expectation of types of behaviour and standards of aspiration and the acquisition of a variety of work and social skills. So we can make the reasonable assumption that under *normal* conditions most of the groundwork of developing guilt anxiety happens in the home, and it is parental expectations that will have set up norms for a whole range of domestic and sibling responsibilities and behaviours. In addition, by the time she reaches school age the child will have established basic peer relations in the neighbourhood.

So the school's role is confined to the transmission of specific skills, the stimulation of certain kinds of cognitive conflict and the establishment of certain kinds of norms about behaviour. To illustrate these let us consider some specific findings. For example, Rutter and his colleagues found that there were differences between schools in behavioural norms and expectations; from this they concluded that the school does have an effect on the collective behaviour of its pupils in a number of areas loosely classifiable as 'moral' (Rutter *et al.*, 1979). On a somewhat different scale, studies of Israeli adolescents tend to show that kibbutz-reared adolescents are more community-oriented and less likely to show signs of 'delinquent' behaviour than city adolescents; one explanation of this is that the kibbutz presents the growing child from an early age with a powerful norm of collective responsibility; the urban child coming into a kibbutz school is exposed to this norm also (Kohlberg, Snarey and Reimer, 1984).

One set of experiments in moral education is particularly interesting because it began as an exercise in what we have described above as a 'thinking' and 'individual' approach to education, and eventually turned into a much more 'social' approach. Focusing on the education of moral reasoning in the classroom, Blatt, one of Kohlberg's students, found that if children were exposed to the moral arguments one stage in advance of their present mode of thinking, they came gradually to see the discrepancies between their own thinking and the more complex form, and they eventually showed more complex moral reasoning. It did not work if the stage of reasoning presented was much higher than their current one, or if it was lower. This in itself provided the basis for some curriculum development; it is relatively easy to provide discussion fora along those lines in the classroom (Blatt and Kohlberg, 1975). However, subsequently Kohlberg's view of this work shifted to a more 'social' perspective; he argued that institutions have a 'hidden structure', in that the form of interaction and authority relationships are an enactment of stages of moral reasoning. A prison, for example, with its absolute hierarchical authority and summary retribution for deviance, is an expression of a stage 1 view of the world; it is unsurprising if the inmates operate with a stage 1 structure of thinking – at least with regard to their prison life. In contrast, a stage 4 or 5 community would be based on principles of justice in which individual members had democratic rights and their collective decisions would determine rule-making and organization (Kohlberg, Hickey and Scharf, 1972; Kohlberg, 1980b; Power, 1980).

He initially set up 'just communities' in prisons, and then in schools. In the case of the school projects, the pupils and volunteer staff spent part of the week in the 'alternative' just community and the rest in the normal school. Most of the pupils came into the alternative school with stage 2 or 3 reasoning – which in effect means a 'we vs they' attitude to authority, and 'every person for themselves' view of responsibility. They gradually came to understand the processes of rule-making and the role of contracts in rule-keeping, and to see the function of collective responsibility in the maintenance of the group. After two or three years, most had progressed considerably further towards the next stage of reasoning, showing more accelerated moral development than controls. Participatory democracy has been used by many educators as a way of assisting moral development; Kohlberg's experiment and conceptual framework provides one way of assessing its effects.

In Britain the emphasis of what is termed 'personal, social and moral education' tends to be more on the development of social skills – on the 'feeling' dimension. McPhail's Lifeline and Startline projects explicitly are defined as 'moral education'; Button's Developmental Groupwork is not so defined, but it covers similar ground. Both approaches use role-playing and social skills training methods to improve the child's capacity for interpersonal relations and for understanding the other person. McPhail *explicitly* considers this to be the primary goal of moral education. His aim is to sensitize the individual child and equip her with greater concern for others and a capacity for empathy. Button's methods focus on changing the whole school to create a more effective interacting group at the organizational level; in such an environment children can develop social and caring skills more easily. Neither approach has as yet been systematically evaluated for effectiveness in attaining their goals, but they are both widely used in British schools and are perceived by teachers to be useful curriculum techniques (McPhail, Ungoed-Thomas and Chapman, 1972; Button, 1971, 1974).

I have not touched upon the Humanities Curriculum Project of Stenhouse, nor upon the growth of Peace Education (Schools Council/Nuffield Foundation, 1970; Verma, 1980), but both of these approaches conform broadly to the criteria of moral education that have been used in this chapter. To quote briefly from the Avon County Council's guidelines on Peace Education, for example:

An indication of the personal qualities which any programme of personal and social education supporting Peace Education might seek to develop; cooperation, trust, self-awareness, desire and ability to participate, sense of responsibility, tolerance, ability to communicate, empathy and understanding and ability to discriminate. (Crump, 1983, p. 6)

Earlier in this chapter I asked what is *possible*; I have tried to set down some criteria for answering that question by drawing on the findings of developmental and social psychology. I also asked 'should we?' The obvious response is that, like sex education, moral education goes on whether or not the school chooses to intervene formally in the process. Indeed all schools do intervene formally through the various structures by which pupils are given responsibility, by the ways in which they are rewarded for meeting the schools' expectations and norms and by the patterns of interpersonal relations between staff and pupil. The question is therefore whether there should be some formal *curriculum slot* for 'moral education', under whatever name. The milder objections to this are that it then becomes something that happens on Tuesdays between ten and eleven, and gets forgotten outside that time, and as a consequence, other lessons in which moral education could take place – and indeed does – will have less incentive to consider the implications of their curriculum. The stronger objections have been first, that it may lead to 'moral assessment', or even a 'moral development quotient', which might have pernicious implications; and secondly, that moral education means teaching one set of values rather than another.

The objection to moral assessment might have some basis; it is unfortunately the case that the more psychologists know about something, the easier it is to draw up a measure of it, and the likelier that such a measure might be misused. However, some *valid* measure of particular aspects of moral development might have value for remedial purposes, or for evaluating the broad effectiveness of a curriculum. In practice, of course, teachers are constantly asked to write comments on pupils which are quite explicitly morally evaluative. The new profiling methods of assessment build this into the assessment system (Pring, 1984).

I think the final objection, that teaching of moral education means teaching one set of values rather than another, is met by the review of the developmental research; whatever the theoretical orientation or the dominant theme of the research, all the research studies address the question of how the person grows into a 'moral being' – whether this is a matter of moral or social skills, complexity of moral thought, sensitivity of feeling, capacity to manage one's reputation or whatever. None of this is value-free, of course, but it all focuses on the *processes* of moral development rather than on its *content*. Presumably a curriculum based on principles derived from the findings of developmental psychology would aim to do the same thing.

But my final comment is that the model of one period per week of 'moral education' is likely to be ineffective; all the research tends to show that effective moral education only happens when the conventional organization of the school is fairly substantially modified, and when pupils are involved long term and explicitly consciously in reflection on their own and other people's experience.

# 5  Autonomy: The nature of relationships, development and the role of the school

*Peter Kutnick*

## Introduction

In this chapter I wish to elucidate fundamental criteria (bases) upon which a specific (derived from Piaget) conceptualization (*model*) of autonomy is derived, and explore the possibilities of its application in the schooling process. Without entering into debate of the range of definitions which can be applied to autonomy, I shall boldly state the Piagetian view: autonomy is the stage of development, arrived at only when previous stages of constraint (heteronomy) and co-operation (mutuality) have been: (1) experienced; (2) understood and reflected upon; and (3) made capable of balancing or cancelling each other out. I present autonomy not as a positive state, but as a *negative definition*.

To more fully understand this stage of autonomy I shall draw upon cognitive and social developmental theory. The theory will add focus to the necessary social relationships that promote and support autonomy (as well as inhibit and limit development). Specifically I shall analyse a model of constraint as an archetypical social relationship, and query its relevance in the study of co-operation (which has often and mistakenly been used as autonomy and the panacea for child-centred primary education). From the exposition of the social relationships of constraint and co-operation a model of development will be derived. Application of this model can then be discussed in relation to the role that schools can play in personal, social and moral education (PSMEd).

**Cognitive and social aspects of moral developmental theory**

A review of the Piagetian perspective establishes that moral development advances from autistic to stages of heteronomy and autonomy by the adaption of moralities of constraint and co-operation. Both constraint and co-operation are archetypal terms used to present a 'meeting' of an interpersonal relationship with a distribution of power (distribution of power will hereafter be referred to here as social-authority, a legitimized power relationship between people). Constraint, the initial relational/power combination, is typified by Piaget in the tie of child to parent. In constraint the child relates to an individual with greater (or unequal) power, a hierarchical authority of submissiveness to dominance. Co-operation is different in both relational and power senses. The child relates to a group (usually of peers), equally sharing power (mutual authority). Autonomy, Piaget's ultimate stage of moral development, is achieved once the individual has access to (and experience of) both moralities of constraint and co-operation.

Beyond the individual's social development (in range and quality of relationships) an ability to adapt and comprehend (logical-mathematical and social-relational) knowledge is essential for moral development. (Kohlberg, 1976, directly draws upon logical mathematical stages as necessary-but-not-sufficient underpinning for moral development.) Minimally autonomy cannot be achieved without the formal operational ability to distance oneself from the immediate social context and (hypothetically) balance between constraining and co-operative alternatives. Social relational knowledge in the form of social perspective taking (Selman, 1976) and role-taking skills (Flavell and Botkin, 1968) are another necessary-but-not-sufficient underpinning for moral development. The transition from ego-centrism to socio-centrism necessitates acknowledgement of the mutually reciprocal nature of relationships. With the transition comes a contingent knowledge of the rules and obligations of the roles within the relationship.

Inherent in Piaget's theory is a structural model of social relationships, parallel to moral development and integrating social and mental developments; the model is presented in Table 5.1. The stages will not strike the reader as startlingly new. Various approximations of the stages can be found in work by Damon (1977), Selman (1980) and others.

**Table 5.1: Development of social relationships, with logical mathematical, moral and social perspective (developmental) parallels**

| Social Relationships | Logical mathematical | Moral | Social perspective |
|---|---|---|---|
| 0 Reflex behaviour/neonatal capacities | | | |
| 1 Sensory-motor-affective schemes | Sensory motor | Autistic | |
| 2 Development of dependent relationship | Pre-operational | Heteronomous | Ego-centric |
| 3 Early rule/authority application, reflective ego-centric understanding | | | |
| 4 Concrete and rational rule/authority application; self-reflective questioning | Concrete operational | Co-operative | |
| 5 Involvement with peers, reflective mutual social development | | | Socio-centric |
| 6 Reflective ability to balance and apply constraining and/or co-operative principles | Formal operational | Autonomous | |

The existence of the stages of social relations is not a matter of debate. From the developmental sequence, most research has explored the role of the later stages in making social and moral judgement. Only a small amount of recent research has been undertaken on the early development of social relations and the adaptation process of the stage sequence. (Broad areas of conceptualization, rooted in the symbolic interactionist theory of G.H. Mead, 1964, and more recently espoused in socio-cognitive terms by researchers such as Selman, provide insight into and an interpretive frame for developmental theory and mental mechanisms.) These theories stress the active, adaptive process of the individual. They acknowledge the importance of the social context of self and significant others. Underlying the social context and the role of others is the type and quality of relationships expressed between individuals.

To gain further information on the role of relationships in development a more specific search has been made of the early social writings of Piaget (1926, 1932, 1951). From this reawakening of the importance of the early writing of Piaget, Youniss (1980) has developed a relational theory. He focuses on the qualities of the relationships characteristic of the child with adults (i.e. parents) and the child with other children (i.e. peers). Relations with parents and peers are each significant in their own right and in application to theories of moral/social development. In archetypical power terms the relations of parent and peer equate to constraint/hierarchy and co-operation/mutuality respectively. As Youniss stresses (from Hinde, 1979), the child maintains a *reciprocity* within each type of relation, complementary and mutual. Reciprocity demonstrates that both members of the relationship are each obligated to each other no matter which archetypical power distribution characterizes the relationships. (Further discussion of the qualities of each of these relations can be found in Youniss, 1980; Rubin, 1980; Sullivan, 1953; and others.)

The distribution of power and the child's reciprocal engagement in the relationships provide the building-blocks of moral development found in Table 5.1. A working example of the reciprocity is found in the initial relationship between child and care-giver, as exemplified in attachment. Attachment is based upon complementary interactions and generation of trust/dependence (Ainsworth, Bell and Stayton, 1974). The attachment relationship facilitates early cognitive development of permanence (Bell, 1970). The relationship is based upon sensitive, sensory and physical contacts (an intertwining of affective/emotional, social and cognitive development) between child and care-giver (Piaget, 1951, Schaffer, 1971); or sensory-affect units described by Stern (1977). The effect of the intertwined affective, social and cognitive schemes characteristic of this period is more than the development of person permanence, attachment, and so on. The effect is the initial stage of social authority relations; a trusting realization of an unequal power relation where basic control is effectively outside of the realm of the child (for further explanation see Hoffman, 1975b) – a complementary reciprocity or a relationship based on constraint. Constraint goes beyond the realization of the authority relationship, it is tied to the child's role responsibility of obedience (as discussed by Stayton, Hogan and Ainsworth, 1971). Upon gaining the use of verbal abilities, the young child is able to describe the authority and rule relations of their immediate environment (dominated by parents and adults) and their obligation to adhere to that authority through love, strengths and expertise. The descriptions are well characterized in Damon's (1977) early authority levels. Underlying the development of this knowledge of authority are characteristic social schemes by which the child adapts this information; from the sensory-motor repetitions with care-giving individuals which establish knowledge of the authority relationship, to pre-operative and concrete operative schemes of social authorities explored previously by myself (Kutnick, 1980, 1983a). As the reader will see, the structural basis of the constraining authority relationship parallels schemes of logical mathematical development; its base is found in the sensitive and trusting relationship (or attachment) and develops into verbal formulations of existing and then hypothetical legitimacy and obedience. An approximation of the qualities and stages of this authority relation is described in the development of social relations, stages 0 to 4 in Table 5.1. Thus the root of constraint in moral development, permanence in logical mathematical development, and dependence in social development, are initiated in the child–care-giver relationship (Kutnick, 1983a).

Introduction to the peer group, hypothetically, expands knowledge of social relationships and integrates the co-operative authority found in stages 5 and 6 (Table 5.1). As such, peer relations have variously been described by Piaget (1932), Youniss (1980) and Sullivan (1953) as an authority of equals or mutual reciprocity. The social/cognitive qualities of this base to morality has often been linked to a 'morality of co-operation'; a basic component in the theories of Piaget and Bronfenbrenner. For Piaget the power–authority relationship shared among equals (peers) is qualitatively different and advanced beyond the child–adult relationship conceptualized in the 'morality of constraint'. (It is often taken for granted that the simple process of children acting together is co-operation. Piaget's writing, as well as recent sociological and educational research, contradicts this simplistic view.) Piaget noted that co-operation was a relationship of social-authority (thereby having roots and developmental sequence which may parallel that of constraint) among peers. Further, not all peer group relations are themselves co-operative.

### Co-operation

Thus the road to autonomy is paved through the stages of constraint and co-operation. I have already illuminated the development of constraint, and it is an easy generalization to say that Western children will be exposed to this early moral development (without their own say in the matter). But what of co-operation? Are children exposed to it? If so, to what extent?

Children will be exposed to co-operation when they begin to come together and start playing with one another. Notably, due to upbringing practices, this coming together coincides with the beginning of schooling. Schools themselves often perceive their role as introducing children to co-operation (discussed by psychologists and educationists as Pepitone, 1980; Johnson and Johnson, 1975) under the auspices of games, sport and social education. But the ideal of co-operation is rarely found. Recent observational evidence from English primary schools acknowledges the practice of co-action, but little co-operation among pupils in classrooms (see Simon and Willcocks, 1982). Children mainly work under the didactic or constraining influence of teachers and leaders in school; whether this be through traditional control, individualized instruction or individual assessment. There is little evidence of co-operation taking place in schools.

Also recent studies in the sociology of schooling have shown that adolescent groups (gangs) often replicate a social-authority similar to the hierarchical authority characteristic of adult–child relations (see Willis, 1977; Hargreaves, 1967; and others). A particular example of authority structure of adolescent gangs are the 'lads' described by Willis. Within their anti-school culture is a hierarchical relationship (of dominance–submissiveness) characteristic of industrial relations; that of foremen and workers or leader and followers. The lads' threat to the school does not come from a co-operative or group alternative in the teacher's eyes. They are a competing authority representing constraint similar to the authority of teachers (and school personnel) over pupils.

I do not wish to over-generalize the point about lack of co-operation in schools. Certainly I have seen classrooms which are a joy to be in – simply for the sheer spontaneity and helpfulness of one child to another. I think that Leslie Button's tutorial programme has a similar outcome, although with much older pupils. But we do need to ask (primarily) what is co-operation, and is there a reason why it may or may not work?

Co-operation, especially applied to school and social situations, has long been used as an unproblematic term to describe the state of several individuals working on a common project in a (relatively) confined space. Co-operation is seen as unproblematic mainly in the way that evidence for co-operation has been collected (quantitatively) (see studies/reviews by Bryan, 1975; Slavin, 1984). Co-operation has been assumed if individuals work on a common project in a confined space. Additionally, behavioural outcomes have been cited as evidence of co-operation. These outcomes generally include 'working together' in a non-competitive manner (as if competition was the sole mode of human interaction); noting no further advancement in our knowledge of co-operation since Homans (1951) stated that people working alongside one another tend to become friends and Sherif's (1961) structured 'camp' situation to enforce group identity and cohesion. Other research has been undertaken in (school-based) terms of academic achievement and enhancement of self-esteem (see Slavin, 1984). Here clear-cut results due to this structured interaction among individuals are few and far between.

Avoiding the often found behaviour of co-action as the definition of co-operation, Piaget notes that co-operation is an authority of equals found among peers. This mutual reciprocity has deeper connotations than co-action. It may best be described as a relationship similar to the sensitivity, mutuality and intimacy of close friendship described by Youniss (1980). Structurally co-operation appears to be based on a mutual security equivalent to the role of attachment in establishment of constraint. Co-operation cannot form in relationships dominated by constraint and is not found in all peer relations.

In summary, the following points should be made about co-operation. Practical and relevant examples of the child's entry into the broad social world of peer relations coincide with the onset of primary (elementary) schooling (see Glidewell *et al.*, 1966; and others). Effective relations with teachers are quickly built (Kutnick, 1980). But recent studies focusing on the development of relations between children do not find spontaneous or structured development of co-operation. Rather they (Galton, Simon and Croll, 1980; Simon and Willcocks, 1982; and others) show a dominance–submissive quality within peer relations; that is peer relations are based on the authority of constraint, a replication of the major characteristic of child–adult relations. Reasons that can be attributed for adoption of dominance relations by and among peers, include: (a) early socialization practices that provide a singular child–adult orientation; confirming most early development takes place in and around the parental home and limiting early effective peer interaction (as opposed to communal Russian models described by Bronfenbrenner, 1974); and (b) once children develop verbal skills, they rarely return to tactile (sensory affective) behaviours in establishing trusting, dependent and sensitive relations with others. Given the relatively late age that most children start primary education (about five years), relations with peers rarely include a sensory affective base (even 'progressive' schools do little to overcome this lack); children will talk to one another instead. Without the sensory affective structural base to relations among peers, children have little opportunity of establishing the closeness/trust of equals which will allow co-operation to flourish. The lack of a co-operative authority among peer relationships poses that these relationships retain previously established authority relations. The authority of constraint would be seen to characterize child–child interactions. Dominance, aggression and violence found among today's children and adolescents can thus be explained as replicating and extending child–adult relations of constraint among peers in the absence of co-operative relations.

## A model for the development of close relationships: the road to autonomy

In a moral and social developmental sense various cultures give more or less precedence to parent and peer relations at a time when children can form the initial sensory affective 'bond' between themselves. By describing various qualities of parental and peer relations and their domination by cultural experience, this chapter has attempted to open various concepts in the established developmental literature. To provide greater clarity as to the social relational basis of moral development the reader must look at the potential, but separate, development of each of these relationships ascribed to child–adult and child–child experiences within the Western cultural model to which we have greatest access.

The perspective posed in this chapter asserts that adult and peer relations are more properly seen as individual surface manifestations (which may be parallel or sequential) of an underlying authority structure. Authority has structural and developmental properties which can be described in a series of stages. As ideal types associated with adult and peer relations constraint and co-operation are explained as social applications of an underlying authority stage structure whose appearance is mediated through experience. Differing socio-political orientations of society and upbringing practices are the basis for the generation of specific social relations. While development of surface manifestations of adult-oriented constraint and peer-oriented co-operation can be described separately, a singular deep structure of authority (for each) appears to underlie both surface manifestations. The deep structure of authority develops in a stage sequence starting with sensory affective schemes between the infant and a limited number of individuals (parents, siblings, etc.). (A dependent relationship between child and adult or child and peers is demonstrated in behavioural scenes of obligation (see Stayton, Hogan and Ainsworth, 1971) to care-giver or 'friend'.) Logical and experiential development extend recognition and rationalization of the authority relation, which the verbal child is now able to describe as rules (of unilateral respect or sharing). Breaking the bond that ties rules to specific (affected) individuals, the child moves to a 'logical' application of rules in specific concrete situations where they are best suited (as in legitimization and mutuality). Finally, the formal operational child will free the concept of authority from people and situations, balance alternatives and reflectively apply rules. These stages of authority relations are described in Table 5.2.

## A test of the hypothesis applied to co-operation

As previously stated, it is the constraint of cultural experience which does not allow peer experiences (in Western countries) to develop as mutual or co-operative. Hence most childhood relationships are dominated and mediated by some form of constraint. The developmental model posed in Table 5.2 suggests that the peer relationship of co-operation can only take place if it is based on an initial sensory affective stage. Following the logic of this theory, I (Kutnick and Brees, 1982) adapted physical/sensitivity exercises to promote trust for use by young children (four to five years). The outcome of these experiences showed the experimental

**Table 5.2:  Hypothetical structure of authority relations**

| *Deep structure* | Adult based | *Surface structure* Peer based | Combined |
|---|---|---|---|
| 1 Sensory-motor-affect schemes | (Sensory-affective contacts) | (Sensory-affective contacts) | |
| 2 Development of dependent relation | Obedience | Peer-oriented | |
| 3 Early rule application | Unilateral respect | Sharing | |
| 4 Concrete/rational rule application | Legitimization of expert | Mutuality | |
| 5 Reflective rule application | Collaboration | Negotiation through need/co-operation | Autonomy |

children: (a) express more concern for and offer to help their peers in distress (as opposed to withdrawing or seeking adult attention); (b) move to affiliate themselves with a group if they, themselves, are in distress (as opposed to withdrawing or seeking adult attention); and (c) were more likely to take turns, share and be less competitive in a play situation than control children. The experimental children were more mutually or co-operatively oriented than the children of the control group, at a young age not generally known for this degree of socio-centricity.

**The role of the school**

I have already noted the role of the school as the context where children come together and work with one another – and for many this is the first instance where they meet with the same group over a long period of time. You will have already noticed that my preoccupation is and must be with the primary school. The focus on the primary school is quite different from the general orientation of the previous sections. My reason for the primary focus is sixfold: (i) developmentally children 'come together' for the first time in primary schools; (ii) while children have been brought up as individuals within the home, they have not extended their individuality to the peer reference group; (iii) individuality in peer groups is most often characterized by competition and hierarchical relations among children, and not co-operative or mutual behaviours; (iv) as a generalization, children who have succeeded in advancing through to secondary education are well imbued with individualism but not necessarily with co-operation; (v) to integrate a co-operative 'ideal' at the secondary level would require a *therapeutic* exercise to counter previously existing relationships; and hence (vi) I return to the role of the primary school in naturalistically providing for the development of co-operative relations.

The 'how' of the inclusion of co-operation has been discussed in relation to the establishment of a sensory affective base to peer relations and a practical example was discussed drawing upon 'trust' exercises. The 'why' of the inclusion of co-operation hopefully will have been made clear by this chapter. In order to achieve the background for a Piagetian understanding of autonomy the child

**Figure 5.1:   Reinterpretation of Piaget's stages of moral development as a stair-like matrix; interaction of interpersonal relationships with social-authority relationship necessary in progression of stages**

Interpersonal relationships with:

| SOCIAL RELATIONS / AUTHORITY | Adults | Peers | |
|---|---|---|---|
| Autonomy | | | *Autonomy*, balance between mutual and heteronomous needs, reflective responsibility |
| Co-operation | | *Mutality*, reciprocity among equals, collective ideal | Collaboration of equals, rules changeable through common need, work together for common need |
| Constraint | *Heteronomy*, unilateral respect, rules sacred, etc. | Expertise leader–follower | Expertise in specific context, collaboration of unequals in position of respect for one another |
| | Pre-operational | Concrete operational | Formal operational |

Underlying social and logical mathematical development

must have coherent and real access to constraint and co-operation. These are both authority relationships which have a 'deep structure'. Children have access to the sensory affective antecedents of constraint (in terms of parenting, and often teaching, relationships). But this first stage is not characterized in peer relationships (for reasons mentioned before) as characterized in our society. Without the sensory affective contacts among peers, trust will not develop – and co-active/hierarchical relations will remain characteristic. The role, and I believe the duty, of the primary school is to introduce co-operative relations among peers in a comprehensive manner. Only co-operation is able to balance out the authority of constraint to free the child to make autonomous judgements, as shown in Figure 5.1.

As a final note, there are three logical outcomes to my proposal:

(i)   Assumptions made of children – teachers must be aware that children are inherently *good,* and this goodness should be allowed to develop. Curriculum orientation – there is no curriculum that would characterize co-operative develop-ment. The trust exercises would have to be structured into classroom routine. The teacher must adapt teaching style to allow co-operative experience of the curriculum.

(ii)  Teachers' reactions – children are bound to challenge hierarchical authority and knowledge, teachers will have to be willing to forgo didactic styles.

(iii) Competence – from a moral orientation we actually arrive at a view of education and development based upon the child having initiative and follow-through, not being susceptible to the whim of hierarchy.

# DISCUSSION

Chapters 4 and 5 have both examined the question of what psychological theory has to offer school-based personal, social and moral education.

Weinreich-Haste ranges widely over psychological theory in search of what might be said with some confidence about moral development and discusses what might be possible in school.

She organizes her discussion around four dimensions along which she differentiates the dominant themes of moral development and links to these what she sees as the four theoretical traditions in psychology, each offering somewhat different explanations of morality.

She points out that different theoretical and research traditions in psychology offer explanations which are sometimes incompatible or even in conflict with each other. These lines of theory follow the main lines of philosophical debate which she organizes around the dimensions of autonomy vs conformity, thinking vs feeling, pro-social vs anti-social behaviour and individual vs social.

While these dimensions describe psychological research concerns, they also contain different assumptions. In the chapter she demonstrates that each of the poles of these dimensions represents a research tradition which may be in some conflict with the other pole. This may have important implications for practice. Thus there has been considerable work on moral thinking within a cognitive developmental framework by both Piaget and Kohlberg. Should we use this as knowledge to guide our attempts to stimulate the development of ethical thinking in children or should we also attempt to educate the emotions which may have to draw on a different research perspective? In practice the demands of the situation may mean that a wider synthesis must be constructed. This is the interest of the work of Blatt and Kohlberg, mentioned in Chapter 4, where the initial principle of exposing children to the moral arguments one stage in advance of their present mode of thinking had to take account of the context in which the discussions took place. This approach to education was derived from the theoretical work of Kohlberg and was characterized by Weinreich-Haste as 'individual' and 'thinking'. It was later modified by Kohlberg in the light of experience along a more 'social' dimension in the creation of 'just communities' in which the form of interaction and relationships were consistent with the moral principles being discussed.

Whether this wider synthesis of different psychological traditions is always possible is open to debate. The previous example is such an attempt and shows how the insights from a cognitive developmental model were incorporated into a framework of interpersonal interactions and structural arrangements which were consistent with those principles. However, is such a framework to be seen in the light of Skinnerian behaviourism as part of the social process which moulds acceptable and unacceptable behaviours through reinforcement? Such a view would not see the individual as a 'moral' being and would stand in sharp contrast to the cognitive developmental position.

The use of different research traditions is also seen in different cultural contexts. Thus in contrast to the tradition characterized by 'thinking' is the pole of 'feeling' which Weinreich-Haste sees as the main tradition in Britain. The work of Leslie Button described in Chapter 8 represents this approach as does the work of McPhail (1972) in the Lifeline and Startline projects. The stress here is upon developing the capacity for interpersonal relationships and for understanding the other person. This has been chosen by McPhail as the primary goal of moral education.

Weinreich-Haste asks if moral education has a place in the curriculum and concludes that it does, provided such an approach focused on the processes of moral development rather than its content. She does, however, question the utility of 'isolated lessons' without a substantial modification of the conventional organization of the school.

In contrast to the wide-ranging approach of Weinreich-Haste, Peter Kutnick teases out the implications of one approach, that of

Piaget, for practice in the primary school. He starts with the premiss that it is the role of personal, social and moral education to work towards the facilitation of autonomy. He sees this as being achieved only when previous stages of constraint and co-operation have been experienced, understood and make capable of cancelling each other out.

This is a specifically Piagetian point of view which is fully described by Kutnick (Chapter 5). Kutnick sees the experience of the 'morality of constraint' as being contained in the parent–child relationship but questions whether the experience of co-operation is a familiar one in our culture. Children need to interact with one another in order for co-operation to be experienced, and this coming together may only happen in any large-scale way at the beginning of schooling.

Despite the ideal of co-operation often voiced by primary schools, recent observational studies indicate co-action rather than co-operation, while adolescent gangs often show a hierarchical structure characteristic of adult–child relations. Kutnick sees the dominance, violence and aggression among today's children as being explained by the extension and replicating of child–adult relations of constraint to peer groups who have no experience of co-operative relations.

What are the alternatives? How can genuine co-operation be fostered? A change in child-rearing practices with more effective peer interaction at an earlier stage would be one method as seen in communal Russian models.

This would allow children to experience the tactile contact with other children which Kutnick sees as laying a sensory affective base to relations among peers. In Western society children come together in school at a time when they already have well-developed verbal skills and rarely return to tactile behaviours.

Kutnick reports some work with four to five-year-olds where adapted physical/sensitivity exercises to promote trust were used in the classroom. The experimental children were found to be more mutually or co-operatively oriented than the control group. It is interesting to note that Leslie Button's programme contains an element of physical contact (see Chapter 8) at the secondary stage. Kutnick sees this as a therapeutic attempt to counter previously existing relationships and has focused his work on the primary school. It would seem, however, that the logic of this argument would indicate that such experiences of a sensory affective side would have a place even earlier in the playgroups and nursery schools or even in child care centres provided for working mothers. The recent trend in Britain, while paying lip service to the importance of pre-school provision, has been to limit such developments on economic grounds. However, even if the necessary political will existed to provide such funding there remains the question as to whether such arrangements are seen as desirable. Would the move to more communal arrangements exemplified by the Russian model meet with general approval in Western societies (or even the, possibly less alien, Israeli kibbutz system)? Would it be seen as an intrusion into the role of the family unit especially for those groups with strong religious links?

Such interventions would be likely to be powerful in their effects but are certainly contentious issues in our society.

# Section C
# Philosophical and Spiritual Perspectives

# INTRODUCTION

The context of the renewed interest in personal and social education lies partly in the personal difficulties young people have to face in leaving school or college for a rather unpredictable future and partly in the demands of employment-related training schemes which require certain kinds of personal qualities. Of course, as has already been explained, those working within long-standing educational traditions transform such influences. In particular they re-assert the central place of values in the process of preparing young people for the future, and point to the non-utilitarian values which assent the essential dignity of each person and the error of those who measure a person's importance by his or her economic usefulness.

This re-assertion of old values has a secular and a spiritual dimension. The secular one stresses the potential autonomy of each child, the capacity to think and to decide for herself, which is the end-product of the developmental process described by Helen Weinreich-Haste (Chapter 4). The spiritual one treats this with a certain amount of disdain, seeing it as a rather desiccated perception of human beings.

In the following two chapters Robert Hannaford, first, looks critically at the concept of autonomy. His is essentially a philosophical analysis of the moral language and of the moral aims that enter into our understanding of personal development. Jack Priestley, by contrast, provides the more positive account, reminding us of the spiritual side of man which in tales of personal development so often gets neglected.

# 6 Beliefs and values

*Robert Hannaford*

Moral education does not take place in a vacuum. Children grow up and are educated in a society which values certain things above others, and penalizes those who do not share these values. Our society is to a large extent shaped by moral traditions which come to us in some cases from as far back in history as the Hellenistic culture of the ancient world. There is certainly diversity in our system of values but there is also a surprising degree of agreement and consensus. Our society is complex and diverse but moral traditions do exist and their congruence as well as their variety help to shape the cultural and social environment in which children exist.

Mapping out the landscape of beliefs and values actually held by people in our society would be a mammoth task, beyond the scope of any book. In this chapter I would like to concentrate instead upon the way in which people talk about values, and in particular the way in which they invoke beliefs in support of their judgements. This discussion will then form the basis for our subsequent reflections upon some of the philosophical issues raised by moral education. In particular, I would like to consider two areas of concern: first, the claim that the teacher of moral education must adopt a 'neutral' approach to his discipline; and secondly, the claim that the aim of moral education should be the promotion of personal moral autonomy.

## The shape of moral language

Our concern at this stage is with the pattern of logic of moral discourse.[1] The question we are concerned with is: what is it that is common to all language about moral values? It is important to note that this does not mean that behaviour and feelings are unimportant in ethics. They are, of course, crucial to the whole ethical experience. However, in philosophy our primary concern is not behaviour or psychology, but the way in which people explain their behaviour and express their beliefs.

One of the most confusing features of moral language is the way in which it combines descriptive elements with evaluative ones. A typical moral judgement might include both a description of someone's behaviour and an evaluation. Our inquiry will centre on the relationship between these two different ways of speaking.

We can begin by considering a typical example of moral dialogue. Suppose someone asserts that 'Mr X is a good man', and when asked for a reason for this judgement, replies: 'Because he is always thinking of others.' We can tell from the original judgement that the speaker is commending Mr X, and this gives us the evaluative meaning of the judgement, but the reason given adds a descriptive component. The reason given to support the original judgement is a descriptive claim and it can be established as either true or false. If we go further and ask why the reason given should be a reason for saying that Mr X is good, the speaker would appeal, not to another description, but to a principle such as 'Goodness consists, among other things, in thinking of others'. The point to note, then, is that although there is a descriptive component in moral language, the final appeal is to statements of principle, and hence to evaluations.

However, the suspicion remains in many people's minds that a statement such as 'Mr X is a good man' must in some respects be like the statement 'Mr X is a tall man'. As we have seen, it is certainly the case that people who make such statements will, when asked for a reason, typically respond with a descriptive statement. In this case the descriptive reason given, 'Because he is always thinking of others', is similar in character to the descriptive claim about Mr X's tallness. However, the similarity between the two assertions begins to break down when we realize that in the case of the original moral judgement the hearer understands its evaluative meaning even before he knows what its descriptive meaning is. That is, even before we know why the speaker thinks that Mr X is good, we understand him to be commending Mr X. We can only account for this by concluding that the evaluative meaning of moral judgements is primary.

What begins to emerge, then, is a basic pattern common to most, if not all, moral judgements. First of all, a judgement is made, such as: 'Mr X is a good father.' Then, when a reason is called for, a fact, in the form of a descriptive claim, is appealed to such as: 'Because he provides for his children.' This is a straightforwardly descriptive sentence whose truth or falsity can be tested. But when the speaker is asked why X should be considered good for providing for his children, the response will not be a further description, but an appeal to some principle such as 'A good father ought to provide for his children', and this is an evaluative statement. Thus it appears that ultimately moral reasoning depends not upon facts, but upon certain fundamental beliefs about what is and is not good behaviour.

If, then, moral judgements have both evaluative and descriptive meaning, the question arises as to what the relationship between these two elements is. In other words, what is the logical relation between an evaluative remark such as, 'Mr X is a good father', and the descriptive reason, 'Because he provides for his children'?

It might seem self-evident that reasons such as this must be the meaning of what it is to be a good father. We would be surprised and puzzled if someone supported this judgement with a reason such as 'He always mistreats his children'. However, even if someone did give this as a reason, we would still understand that they were commending this person, albeit for an odd reason. That is, even though we found the descriptive meaning odd, we would still understand that the speaker was commending this person as a father. The reason for this is that while the descriptive meaning (i.e. the reasons given) may change, evaluative meaning remains constant. Thus while there is a contingent improbability about some descriptive statements being associated with some evaluative ones, there is no necessary connection between them. We cannot, in other words, infer a descriptive judgement from an evaluative one, or vice versa. Descriptive statements remain logically distinct from evaluative ones. Philosophers call this the 'is/ought' gap. By this they mean that it is not possible to infer an evaluation directly from a descriptive statement alone.[2] The move from 'is' (descriptive statement) to 'ought' (evaluative statement) is always preceded by reference to some underlying principle, and if the principle is not explicitly stated, then the 'is' statement usually implies it. Hence if I make a judgement such as 'You ought to take care of Mr X', and when asked for a reason, I reply 'Because Mr X is your father', I am invoking a general moral principle such as 'Children owe a duty to their parents'. It is this principle that forms the primary reason for my evaluative judgement.

It begins to emerge, then, that reasoning is involved in moral discourse and that although there is some reference to descriptions, the primary reasons given are fundamental moral principles, which are in themselves entirely evaluative in content. The next stage in our inquiry must be to consider at what point the process of reasoning in moral discourse comes to an end.

It would seem odd to us if someone refused to give a reason for a particular moral judgement. Indeed if they did so, we would wonder what they meant by their judgement. If someone were to say that Mr X was good, and when asked why replied 'Because he has goodness', we would not be sure what they were talking about. We would understand because of the evaluative content of the judgement that the speaker approved of Mr X, but we would not know why. The reason for this is that the meaning of moral terms is always dependent upon some definition of terms. It would, therefore, be unintelligible for someone to refuse to explain precisely what they meant by for example 'goodness'.

Under ordinary circumstances someone would explain what they meant by goodness by listing a number of natural descriptions (e.g. thinking of others, putting other people first, etc.). However, if people are asked to explain why they define goodness in the way that they do, then it becomes much more difficult to imagine what they would say. Suppose, for example, I make a moral judgement such as 'You ought to care for Mr Y', and when asked why I explain: 'Because Mr Y is your father.' Here my reason is a description which is only morally relevant because it enshrines a fundamental principle such as 'Children ought to care for their parents'. Now, if I am asked why this should be taken as a reason for action, I might reply with another principle such as 'We ought to care for those who brought us into the world'. It is difficult to see what difference, if any, there is between this reason and the statement that it is supposed to explain. They both amount to a general statement about a child's duty to its parents. We have not given a reason but re-stated our principle.

We could pursue this discussion through many examples and illustrations but we would find as a general rule that ultimately these general moral principles cannot be defended, but only re-stated. The business of reason-giving comes to an end at some point. When that point is reached, all that we can say is 'This is what I believe' or 'This is the will of God'.

In saying that our general moral principles cannot in the final analysis be supported by reasons, we are not saying that they are indefensible or indeed unreasonable. What we are saying is that the giving of reasons comes to an end at some point and that in the case of moral judgements this point is reached with the statement of some very general principles of what is right or wrong. These general principles cannot be finally explained or justified because they themselves form the basis of all our explaining and reasoning in moral discourse.

## Ethical neutrality

Perhaps in Moral Education, more than in any other area of the curriculum, teachers have been aware of the power of their position and, as a consequence, of the dangers of manipulating and indoctrinating children (see e.g. Hare, 1964; Wilson, 1964; White, 1967; Mitchell, 1970; Snook, 1972). Whereas in most areas of the curriculum there is information to be communicated and principles of testing and verification open to the pupils, in this sphere of education such checks and balances do not exist. There is always the danger that an over-zealous and ideologically committed teacher might misuse his position of trust. It is, therefore, hardly surprising that in order to avoid these dangers many teachers and educationists have turned to a model of the teacher as a neutral chairman in a free debate about values (see Schools Council/ Nuffield Foundation, 1970; Wringle, 1974). Here the teacher's role is to chair a discussion in which children develop and formulate their own ethical position.

In adopting the neutral-chairman approach to the teaching of ethics the teacher is attempting to tread the delicate path of free inquiry and discussion. A consequence of this is that the teacher has to attempt to teach values without appearing to over-endorse a particular set of values. There are many serious philosophical and educational difficulties raised by this particular model of teaching. On the practical level it calls for a high degree of sensitivity and discretion on the part of the teacher; while on the philosophical level serious questions arise about the compatibility of this approach with our understanding of the nature of moral language and reasoning. It is with the latter issue that I shall principally be concerned.

In what follows I shall offer three alternative accounts of teacher neutrality. It will, I hope, become clear that only one of these is philosphically justifiable, and that the idea of teacher neutrality is only compatible with the nature of the subject in hand when certain clearly defined features of moral language and belief are borne in mind. In other words, teacher neutrality will only make philosophical sense when its application assists rather than hinders children not only to shape their own values, but also to apprehend the shape of moral language.

Philosophers draw a distinction between first- and second-order discourse. We can use this distinction to illustrate our first two possible approaches to teacher neutrality.

First-order discourse is the language used by people when they are making judgements, uttering beliefs and in general engaging in the ordinary business of communication. Second-order discourse is the language used by philosophers and others when talking *about* these ways of speaking. Philosophy, at least in its contemporary Anglo-Saxon form, is concerned not with whether these ways of speaking are true or false, but with the logical analysis of the language used. From a philosophical point of view what matters primarily is not what is said, but how it is said. Now, from this second-order position, the philosopher *is* a neutral observer. He is not concerned specifically with the substantive claims made by speakers, but with the form and logical coherence of their language. In the case of moral language the philosopher's task is not to decide whether a particular moral judgement is correct or not (even if such a thing were possible), but to map out the logical terrain of the language used.

It is fairly clear that this second-order approach to moral language would be an unsatisfactory basis for teacher neutrality. While the philosopher is primarily concerned with the logical framework of particular spheres of discourse, the teacher is concerned with the claims of substantive matters of value. It would then be difficult to justify any approach to the subject which based its neutrality on the philosophical second-order distinction. What this would amount to is not education in values, but education in the philosophy of morals. This would not be talk about values, but talk about talk about values, and presumably moral education is concerned with substantive matters of value rather than with the second-order business of philosophers.

We turn, then, to a second alternative, namely that the teacher of moral education could adopt a position of first-order neutrality. Here he would be neutral not as an observer looking in from outside, but as a participant in this sphere of discourse. This would be a form of neutrality over matters of substance within the language of morality and not the neutrality of the dispassionate philosophical observer. What are we to make of this possibility?

There seem to be two ways of viewing this account of neutrality. First, it could be based upon a universal scepticism about the epistemological status of all value-related statements. Secondly, it could involve a position whereby all moral judgements and beliefs are treated as having equal value, even when they appear to differ or contradict one another. The first alternative can be dismissed quite quickly. If the teacher grounds his neutrality in a fundamental scepticism about values, then it would be difficult to see why he should teach values at all. A position of universal doubt and scepticism would make the teaching of this subject practically impossible. The second position is more persuasive. This would amount to a position where, as a first-order user of language, one was open-minded about any and all moral judgements. As a participant (i.e. a moral subject) one would accept the equal validity of all value related judgements. We must then consider what might be involved in adopting this as a basis for teaching.

We have seen from our analysis of moral language that reasoning is involved in this way of speaking. It is always legitimate to ask why someone makes a particular judgement, and it is never legitimate to refuse to give a reason. Moral language does, then, involve judgement and discernment. Disputes are raised in this sphere of discourse, as in any other, and they can often be resolved by recourse to rational argument.

The basis of all rational discussion presupposes that certain conditions of reasoning always apply. One of these conditions is that when two assertions contradict one another, they cannot both be correct. In some ways of speaking it is relatively easy to demonstrate which of two competing statements of belief is the correct one. In moral language, of course, this is not always the case. Here it is difficult, if not impossible, to resolve such contradictions. However, what is essential is that, in order for their beliefs to be rationally held, two speakers who contradict each other must see that their beliefs are indeed contradictory. If they thought that both their beliefs amounted to the same thing, or that they were both correct, then we would not be sure whether they were sincere in their beliefs or whether they were held rationally. Rational moral debate does, then, involve the acknowledgement that not all beliefs are compatible with one another, and that a speaker cannot believe sincerely in his own judgement while, at the same time, accepting the correctness of the contradictory position.

With this in mind, it would be difficult to defend a form of moral education that worked on the premiss that all moral judgements can be treated as though they are equally correct. Such a position would amount to the view that moral judgements never contradict one another, when on occasions they clearly do. It is also difficult to see how such an approach could adequately teach children the value of rational procedures of judgement and discernment in this area of belief. How could you teach the value of judgement and discernment while working on the premiss that any and all moral judgements are equally valid and acceptable?

This approach would also raise a further serious philosophical question, namely is it logically possible to hold the view that all moral judgements carry equal weight and authority and, at the same time, be a participant in moral discourse? In other words, is this approach compatible with our understanding of the first-order use of moral language?

While we normally commend people who are tolerant of others and their views, we do not feel the same sympathy for someone who treats all moral judgements as equally valid. In the first place, we would not be sure whether such a person actually held any beliefs at all, and if he did, we would not be sure whether they were held sincerely. A more fundamental concern – which will I hope become clearer as our discussion proceeds – would be whether or not such a person was actually engaging in moral language at all. We have already suggested that in the end moral language depends upon certain deeply held commitments, and that these act as the basis for all moral judgements. A person who treated all moral judgements as equally valid would presumably be someone who had no fundamental commitments, and we would wonder, therefore, whether what he was talking about counted as moral language.[3]

Our analysis of moral language has demonstrated the essentially committed character of morality. There is reasoning and discussion, but in the final analysis reasoning ends and gives way to the statement of fundamental beliefs. Moreover, these beliefs are the very foundation of reasoning in morality. It would not be an exaggeration to say that such reasoning would not be possible without these fundamental beliefs. Indeed how could one discuss and debate moral issues with someone who had no substantive beliefs? It is not simply that they would have nothing to talk about, but that they would have no logical framework for their side of the discussion.

Other philosophers have noted the essentially committed nature of morality. For example, Cohen writes:

> Where moral education is concerned, an individual's right to his own moral life can only be exercised on the basis of an early understanding of the essentially committed character of morality, and the impossibility of moral neutrality as a generalised approach to matters of moral principle. (Cohen, 1981, p.54)

It is, then, a mistake to imagine that you can discuss values from a position of suspended judgement and, at the same time, claim to be a participant in that sphere of discourse. All reasoning and discussion in morality presupposes certain fundamental beliefs which are the very foundation of such reasoning.

There are, therefore, serious grounds for questioning the adequacy of this approach as a possible model for teacher neutrality. In the end it must be ruled out as incompatible with genuine participation in the language of moral reasoning.

In our search for an adequate model of teacher-neutrality we must turn instead to an approach that takes into account both the needs of children and the nature of moral belief and language.

Our analysis so far has revealed at least two important features of moral language. First, that it is founded upon certain fundamental beliefs and commitments, and secondly, that it does involve reasoning and argument.

The Schools Council Humanities project was one of the first

important educational documents to advocate the neutral-chairman approach. In the introduction to the project it was noted that there are three possibilities open to the teaching profession in dealing with controversial issues. First, that a school might adopt a standard line to be followed by all teachers. This was rejected on the grounds that it would be virtually impossible to attain the necessary consensus. The second possibility is to allow each teacher a free rein to give his own sincerely held beliefs. It was felt that this would commit the profession to defending some very idiosyncratic views. The authors of the project opted instead for neutrality as the only defensible position.

It was argued that neutrality could be adopted as a procedural policy, and that the teacher would agree not to take sides in the children's discussion. The document recognized that complete neutrality could never be achieved, even if it were thought to be desirable, but it was argued that the teacher should 'accept neutrality as a criterion by which to criticise his performance, and explain this – and the reasons for it – to his students' (Schools Council/Nuffield Foundation, 1970, p.8). Now we need to note two features of this approach. First of all, it was explicitly accepted by the Schools Council that the teacher's position, although neutral, should not be value free. The educational procedure implies certain values and these will of necessity be involved in the teaching of moral and social issues. Secondly, this approach recommends a procedural principle and not a substantive commitment to neutrality. Both of our earlier proposals implied a substantive commitment to neutrality. In the first instance, a commitment to teach not morals, but moral philosophy, and secondly a model that implied a substantive commitment to moral relativity or scepticism. These were both rejected: the first on the ground that it is not what would be normally understood as moral or social education; the second on the ground that it is incompatible with the nature and shape of moral language.

How does this third approach to teacher neutrality match up to our analysis of moral belief and language? First, it does allow room for the fundamentally committed nature of morality. It is this feature which is implicitly acknowledged in the teacher's adoption of the procedural principle. As long as it is clear to the children that the teacher has certain views and that he is refraining from expressing them only because he wants them to fashion their own, then this view need not be a barrier to the children's understanding of the fundamentally committed nature of morality. Secondly, this method allows room for reason and argument. Indeed the procedural principle is recommended precisely because it is felt that this will encourage the pupils to develop their own powers of moral argument and discussion. Neutrality need not be ruled out of court on philosophical grounds. As long as it is clearly understood that such an approach is a procedural device alone, then it would seem to be not only compatible with the nature of moral language, but also desirable as a teaching method.

## Autonomy

Personal autonomy is a favoured ideal in many educational innovations and changes. It is seen by many as the fundamental goal of moral education (see e.g. Dearden, 1972; Baier, 1973; Peters, 1981). In this section we shall consider whether or not personal autonomy as an aim in moral education is logically compatible with our understanding of the nature of moral language.

Autonomy means literally self-government or self-legislation. When a state has complete control over its own internal affairs, it is described as autonomous. It follows that any interference from outside that results in the curtailment of a state's self-government undermines the claim on the part of that state to be autonomous.

Although it seems perfectly legitimate to describe states as autonomous, the notion of personal autonomy is more problematic. A state is autonomous whenever it is entirely self-governing, but it is difficult to see how human beings could ever be described as autonomous in this sense. It is, for example, perfectly appropriate to describe a state as autonomous, even when the decisions arrived at by the members of that state are the result of ignorance and prejudice. But when we talk of personal autonomy, it is not nearly so clear that we could regard the individual members of that state as autonomous when factors such as this appear to hinder their freedom of manoeuvre. There is the additional factor that while a state may be autonomous, the members of that state are to some extent under its control and influence, and therefore have less claim to be described as self-governing. Problems of definition like this

have led many philosophers of education to attempt a
reformulation of the concept of autonomy.[4]

There is, of course, a sense in which 'autonomy' does play an
essential role in morality. It is certainly true that an agent is not held
to be morally responsible unless his actions are freely taken. A
person who acts under threat or duress is not generally held to be
morally responsible for those acts. To this extent a moral decision,
that is an action for which one is responsible, has to be the
individual's own free and independent decision. However, many
proponents of moral education want to go beyond this limited
application of the concept of autonomy. They propose not only that
we should aim to help children to make their own free decisions, but
also that children should be free to choose or create their own sets of
values. Apart from the over-arching optimism of this aim, it has to
be said that this is extremely questionable from a philosophical
point of view.[5] While most people would agree that moral agents
can only be described as responsible for their actions when their
decisions are taken freely, this does not imply that they are free, to
the same extent, in deciding what criterion of value to adopt.

Why is this stronger sense of 'autonomy' felt to be so important?
An agent can only be held to have chosen freely to take some course
of action if he alone has decided to do so. However, this does not
preclude the possibility that he is acting on advice or on the basis of
some authoritative teaching. To act freely does not mean to act in
spite of advice and guidance; it means to decide for oneself that you
will be guided by such advice and teaching. In other words, to say
that someone has acted in a particular way because, for example, he
believed that such was the will of God does not mean that it is
inappropriate to describe such an action as freely chosen. An agent
is free when he, and no one else, has decided that he will act in such
and such a way. The fact that someone has advised such a course of
action need not necessarily impinge upon his freedom. The point to
take, then, is that the notion of autonomy, in this restricted sense,
does not carry with it the requirement that the moral principle on
which an agent is acting is his own creation or of his own choosing.
Moral responsibility only requires that the agent alone has chosen
to act in such and such a way.

This distinction between the autonomy that is a necessary
condition of moral responsibility, and the autonomy that implies a
wider freedom to choose one's own reasons for making value

judgements, is a difficult one to grasp. It is perfectly clear that according to the paradigm case of 'acting freely' one can only be said to have freely chosen to do something when the action originates in the self. This is undoubtedly a logical condition of an action being described as moral. However, this condition of autonomy does not mean that the reasons given for the action have to be chosen or devised by the agent alone. The action can still be regarded as free even though the reasons for it were, for example, taught to him by his parents. The decisive thing is not where the criterion of value comes from, but whether or not the agent chooses for himself to follow such guidance.

Autonomy in the stronger sense implies that children should be encouraged not only to act freely in relation to moral situations, but that they should be encouraged to create their own system of values; prima facie, this is a very attractive proposition. Education has to do with the development of personal creativity, and we would certainly feel it appropriate to encourage such creativity in the moral sphere. However, to what extent do we really mean that children should be encouraged to be autonomous in this stronger sense? Are we to encourage them to choose anything as a criterion of value? Do we teach that morality is entirely a personal matter, in which the individual's private judgement is the final consideration? Autonomy means just what it implies – total self-government. The question that interests us is whether or not total self-government is compatible with our understanding of the nature of moral language. The logical outcome of the claim for autonomy in the stronger sense of the term seems to be that children should be free to choose anything as a reason for a value judgement, the final criterion of judgement being not that this is a good reason, or one in keeping with our moral traditions, but that they have chosen it for themselves. Now what interests us is not whether this is practically feasible, but whether it is logically possible. Can I choose anything as a moral judgement, and still call it moral?

Moral language has to do with the valuation and treatment of human beings, and its intelligible use is dependent upon adopting certain shared ways of speaking. In other words, I will only be recognizably communicating certain values if I invoke the appropriate concepts and ways of speaking. For example, if I were to assert 'This piece of wood is courageous', people would not wonder whether I was correct in my evaluation of this piece of wood; they would question whether or not I understood the meaning of the term 'courageous'. What would emerge from this would be a discussion about the use of words and not a discussion about values. It would be pointed out that I had made a category mistake, that is I had attributed inappropriate characteristics to a given object.

It seems, then, that autonomy in this stronger sense cannot mean the freedom to use language as one pleases. However, this still leaves open the possibility that one can create one's own system of values using language in a recognizably moral way. Suppose, for example, that I chose to make a judgement such as 'All left-handed people are devious'. Here I cannot be accused of making a category mistake; I am applying a valuation of character to a category of human beings. Is it, however, legitimate for me to use language in this way? The point at issue is not whether this judgement is morally corrupt or not, but whether it can be seen as a legitimate move within moral language. To put it another way, would we recognize this as a use of language in its moral sense?

Judgements such as the one in question belong in a category of their own. They appear to be so at odds with our normal ways of speaking that it is difficult for us to make much sense of them. It is not so much that we disagree with the judgement; we wonder rather whether the person who made such a judgement is talking the same language as the rest of us. Where would you begin to debate with someone who held judgements like this? The reasons that he might give in support of his judgement would obviously be as idiosyncratic as the judgement itself. Genuine difference of opinion and belief presupposes not only disagreement, but also a common framework for the resolution of such differences. Where there is no such framework, the possibility of two people genuinely disagreeing is not itself present. In the absence of this framework we cannot say that two people are in disagreement, all we can say is that they talk different languages. My point is that when someone makes a judgement such as 'All left-handed people are devious', the framework of reasoning in this case appears to be totally different from the normal framework of moral debate. The judgement looks like a moral one, and at first appears to behave like one, but it is not entirely clear that this alone is enough to guarantee its authenticity. There do seem to be some limits to what we can legitimately express as moral reasons and beliefs. Not *anything* can count as a legitimate expression of moral belief.

Therefore, autonomy can never mean the freedom to express any opinion, however bizarre, and still be taken seriously. From a logical point of view there are limits to what can be expressed intelligibly within any given way of speaking. Language has built-in limits not only about *how* we speak, but also about *what* we say.

Earlier in our discussion we saw how moral reasoning in the end depends upon certain fundamental beliefs. Although these are many and various, one would be very surprised if they did not also exhibit certain important areas of congruence. It can be argued that it is the beliefs expressed here at the fundamental level that play the decisive role in determining the limits of moral discourse.

We will not, therefore, assist children if we encourage them to explore ideas and opinions that are totally alien to our moral traditions. Moral education, as the initiation into a language, cannot involve inquiry that goes beyond the limits of intelligibility inherent in moral discourse. The limits imposed by the possibility of language as a means of communication carries with it the implication that not anything can count as a moral opinion. Therefore, autonomy cannot (logically) be seen as the promotion of unlimited freedom of expression.

### Notes

1.  There are many excellent introductions to contemporary moral philosophy, all of which will give the reader some idea of contemporary thinking on the nature of moral language. For example, there is W.D. Hudson's *Modern Moral Philosophy* (1970). London: Macmillan. This gives a comprehensive account of the main schools of thought in contemporary Anglo-Saxon moral philosophy. The reader might also consult Mary Warnock, *Ethics Since 1900* (1971). London: Oxford University Press; or R.F. Atkinson, *Conduct: An Introduction to Moral Philosophy* (1969). London: Macmillan.

2.  Many philosophers argue that it is possible to derive an evaluation directly from a description. J.R. Searle, 'How to derive "ought" from "is"', *Philosophical Review,* LXXIII, 1964, argues that a particular kind of descriptive statement, namely one that involves an institutional fact, directly implies an evaluation, or as they are sometimes called, an 'ought' judgement. The particular example that Searle chooses is 'promising'. Against the view that the 'is' statement 'Jones promised to

pay Smith five dollars', only implies the 'ought' judgement 'Jones ought to pay Smith five dollars' when it is preceded by another evaluation such as 'One ought always to keep one's promises', Searle argues that the intervening evaluation is unnecessary because the reference to 'promising' involves an institutional fact. He argues that such facts presuppose certain institutions and hence certain rules by which they are constituted. One of the rules governing the institution of 'promising' is that one is under an obligation to keep one's promises. Searle, therefore, concludes that there is a direct relationship between 'is' and 'ought' in cases like this. This is not the place to discuss Searle's argument in any detail. It has stimulated a good deal of discussion. See, for example, J.E. McClellan and B.P. Komisar, 'On deriving "ought" from "is"', *Analysis*, 25, 1964; both of these papers are reprinted in W.D. Hudson (Ed) (1969). *The Is/Ought Question*. London: Macmillan.

3. Brenda Cohen (1975). 'Principles and situations – the liberal dilemma and moral education', *Proceedings of the Aristotelian Society*, also outlines the argument that to use moral language, rather than just to talk about it, presupposes commitment to a particular viewpoint.

4. Richard Pring (1984). *Personal and Social Education in the Curriculum*. London: Hodder and Stoughton, p.72, makes reference to the chameleon-like nature of this concept when he writes 'Autonomy will of course mean different things to different people'. The philosopher would point out that such an ambiguous concept is hardly likely to aid rational discussion.

5. Richard Pring, op. cit., p.72 ff., highlights some of the practical and psychological difficulties of what I have called the 'wider' or 'stronger' sense of 'autonomy'. I have not made any reference to these since my own concern in this chapter is limited to the philosophical problems involved. Pring also points out some of the different ways in which the term 'autonomy' is used in the literature. Two in particular stand out. In the first people are described as autonomous because of the nature of their beliefs. In the second people are so described because of the way they carry out their moral life. This second sense has to do with the quality and independence of the will. My concern in this chapter is with the first of these two alternatives, namely with whether or not it makes sense to say that we are entirely free (i.e. autonomous) to make up our minds about what does and does not count as an intelligible moral belief.

# 7   Comic role or cosmic vision? Religious education and the teaching of values

*Jack Priestley*

## Introduction

To write about the contribution of religious education to the teaching of values should be a simple, straightforward business. Historically and, I should want to argue, conceptually the one has grown out of the other. In fact it is a surprisingly difficult task, nor is it made easier by the fact that it has been attempted often enough before. There already exists a large literature on religious education and its place in the current curriculum. It remains largely unread outside of specifically religious educational circles (see Swann, 1985, Ch. 8). That is the nub of my problem.

To bring religion and religious considerations into a general educational discussion today is rather like speaking English in a French café. The most one can expect is to be ignored with politeness. In Britain the literature of religious education tends to inhabit a private world. This is not the case in other places such as, for example, in the United States. Although religious education is not permitted by law in state institutions, there is nevertheless a lively and healthy exchange of views between secular and religious educators, particularly in the realm of values education. By contrast, in Britain teachers of religious education tend to find themselves, if they are not very careful, inhabiting a separate thought world from other educationists. How can this barrier be broken down?

If a study of analytical philosophy did anything for me at all, it was to persuade me that often the solution to a problem lay in analysing the problem itself and not in looking outside it for answers. I shall begin, then, with asking what is the nature of this breakdown of communication. In the answer which I intend to offer to that question lies the further question of whether or not values can be properly communicated without reference to what I might term the religious dimension of human experience. To respond to that I do not intend to offer yet another defence of religious education. Rather than defend a religious perspective I shall attempt to demonstrate the shortcomings of a secular one. What is omitted when only secular considerations are taken into acount is what constitutes the contribution of religious education. The value of this chapter, therefore, is largely to be found in what it does not say, although at the end I shall be explicit.

**Religious education in a world of secular educational language**

In one of his most telling aphorisms the American educationist Gabriel Moran states, 'Whoever owns the words owns the world' (Moran, 1974, p.32). It is an Orwellian point and one about which there is much concern in the worlds of politics and advertising. The important question for us is: who owns the words and, therefore, the world of education?

The language of education is always a parasitical language. Education is a view of the world from the point of view of learning to live in that world. Its horizons and its limitations are close to the society of which it is a part although it necessarily conducts itself with a greater emphasis on the future. It is this which inevitably demands an idealistic, not to say a transcendent, quality to the whole enterprise.

Not long ago the language of education was predominantly philosophical and even theological. It is no accident that our educational institutions, including those of the maintained system, have religious origins. When John Henry Newman claimed 'There's not a man in Europe speaks against the Church but owes it to the Church that he can speak at all', he was stating nothing more than a mid-nineteenth-century empirical fact. In passing it is worth noting that in such a context it was hardly necessary to include a subject called 'religious education'. There was no other sort.

Today, however, the short and direct answer to the question arising from Moran's statement is that the language of education is now the language of the social sciences. Indeed Education as a subject is usually itself listed as a social science. One direct consequence of this is that whereas now, in contrast to former times, it is perfectly possible to complete a professional course of training without a study of theology or even philosophy, it has become inconceivable that one could do so without some sort of psychological or sociological training.

Let me say immediately that I am not in any sense deploring the advent of the social sciences, nor in any way attempting to diminish the outstanding benefits they have brought. Their contribution to our understanding of educational processes has been enormous. What I am pointing to is not contribution, but control – and in particular control of language. I am suggesting that to be considered to be talking about education at all today it is regarded as necessary to employ the thought forms, the grammar and the syntax of psychological and sociological forms of inquiry, together with their scope and limitations. It is on this point that I wish to concentrate, for it is in the scope and limitations of social scientific inquiry that I think we can detect a major problem which is central to all our thinking about values education in general and religious education in particular.

Put succinctly, if not simplistically, it is this: in their ideal state the social sciences claim to be value free but Education is a value-laden concept. I use the words 'in their ideal state' because I am well aware that social theory has come a very long way since Auguste Comte produced his *Positive Philosophy* in 1854 in which he argued that his new sociology would be objective to all things apart from religion and metaphysics which it consciously sought to replace (Comte, 1853). Nevertheless, something of that mood and assumption remains. A psycho-sociological view of the world still aims to be as objective as possible, to deal in facts and to attempt to be value free. Wittgenstein's *Tractatus* (1961) offers us an account of what is linguistically meaningful in such a world. It opens with the propositions, 'The world is all that is the case. The world is the totality of facts'. But Wittgenstein went on to say how little was achieved when all the problems of such a world were solved.

That world is not the world of religion or of ethics or of the arts. Their world is the world of values. And so is the world of Education.

We have, then, this central dilemma. A value-laden activity has assumed a value-free language and the corresponding profession finds itself trained in value-free assumptions while being sent out to practise a value-laden craft including, irony of ironies, the teaching of values. Small wonder that we have become confused and that we appear to be faced either with the prospect of reducing the most value-laden aspects of the curriculum to data collection and processing or, alternatively, to seeking solutions which involve the abandonment of a professional teaching role for the sake of adopting a personal one (Button, 1974). For as Wittgenstein went on to state towards the end of the *Tractatus*, 'In it [the world defined as the totality of facts] no values exist' (ibid., para.6.41). Value lies outside such a world. It is for exactly this reason that religious education and, increasingly, aesthetic and arts education (to say nothing of personal, social and moral education) must lie outside any educational dialogue which is bounded by the empirical.

Of course, they can all be talked about in empirical terms. Health education can be reduced to collecting data *about* health; moral education to statistics of moral behaviour and religious education to the compilation of facts *about* religions. But this is all reductionism. My point is that Education itself becomes reduced to something narrower. We may continue to give it the name but it no longer deals with the whole personality. Its concern becomes centred only on the measurable and losses occur. As T.S. Eliot noted back in the 1920s,

Where is the wisdom we have lost in knowledge?
Where is the knowledge we have lost in information?

(Eliot, 1963)

Such losses are imperceptible simply because they are qualitative rather than quantitive. When the language of Education becomes controlled and not just contributed to, by empiricism, then values become lost or hidden. We actually invent phrases like 'hidden curriculum' to cover up our inability to know what once we knew but for which there are no terms in the new language. Moreover, we begin to use a term like 'curriculum' as if it were a synonym for 'education' (see Priestley, 1985a). In short, the very notion of Education becomes reduced to the empirically measurable. We deal with only a part of the whole, but pretend that it is the whole.

Religious Education highlights this dilemma. That is why we find it so difficult to talk about. In its own eyes it speaks a richer, fuller, more comprehensive language. This immediately sounds arrogant but it simply cannot survive in the restricted code of the new language in which it is constantly expected to justify itself. The language of religion is the language of simile and metaphor and images as well as of facts. Along with literature and the arts religion has always been a major vehicle for the transmission of values. The question now is whether or not that task can be taken over by the newer disciplines such as social psychology and communicated in the language of such disciplines. Many claim that it can and no one more so than Lawrence Kohlberg. It is his widely acclaimed work which I now want to examine in an attempt to expose its omissions. Those omissions, I shall argue, make up the contribution of religious education to moral education. A similar case can be made out with regard to health, personal and social education (see Desausmarez and Priestley, 1980). My basic argument is that an empirically based approach to these subject areas is perfectly possible but that it must lead to trivialization, to a concern for the minutiae at the expense of the momentous.

### Lawrence Kohlberg and a secular model of moral education

Kohlberg's writing is copious. At the time of visiting his Centre for Moral Education in 1984 I was presented with a publications list which included the titles of seven books, 50 book chapters and 68 journal articles and papers. All were on the one subject of moral development and moral education. Apart from his basic work (Kohlberg, 1981a), I intend to limit myself to just three or four of these publications. They are those in which Kohlberg himself touches upon the possible relationship between his own secular-bound work and the religious dimension of human experience; they are also among his more recent writings and have given rise to a lively debate with religious educationists in the United States, which is little known outside. I shall draw on the contributions of Craig Dykstra and Gabriel Moran to that debate and also on the long-standing but quite separate contribution of Robert Coles.

From the beginning Kohlberg has held that his theory is based on two academic disciplines, moral philosophy and social psychology. He argues that the philosophical basis of all his thinking lies in Plato's argument that justice is the supreme virtue with a consequent rejection of what Kohlberg terms a 'bag of virtues' notion. Using well-established sampling techniques over a longitudinal study of 75 American males, Kohlberg claims to have shown how it is possible to plot the stages of development by which a person might move from an essentially ego-centric and selfish basis of moral reasoning towards a highly developed mature position in which he will give reasons for his behaviour in terms of abstract principles centred on a concern for justice. It must be emphasized that Kohlberg claims to be concerned with reasoning rather than with behaviour but there is ambiguity here. It is only when one looks at Kohlberg's work in the context of his native country that one realizes that the gaps between reasoning, behaviour and education are not as wide as might be imagined. This has relevance for my major argument.

## The American context of Kohlberg's non-religious framework

One of the main attractions of Kohlberg's work in Britain as much as in the United States is the fact that he works entirely within a secular framework. His basic aim was to present a model for moral education which was, in his own words, 'neither indoctrination nor totally relative'. It is common knowledge that religious teaching is not permitted within public sector education in the United States, but partly for that reason it has always been difficult to identify a specific base for moral education in schools. Kohlberg was, in fact, introducing a new and controversial subject into the curriculum (Kohlberg, 1978).

His appeal in Britain was for different reasons. Religious Education not only existed; it was compulsory and had for a long time been regarded as the major vehicle of moral education. By the early 1970s there was a widespread feeling that associating morality with religion was undesirable. The charge of indoctrination became common. But there were important differences between the debate on indoctrination in Britain and in the United States and they are significant here.

In Britain the indoctrination charge has always centred around content, that is about teaching as fact material that might be contentious. Anthony Flew summed up the case in four words, 'No doctrine, no indoctrination' (Flew, 1972). In the United States, however, the debate centred around method. The doctrine was not disputed. Children at school were to be taught the democratic American way of life. The question was whether it should be taught democratically, so that some might reject it, or whether it should be instilled (Moore, 1972). In other words, did children have the same rights as adults? It is this question which is very much at the root of Kohlberg's thinking. For a long time he argued that they had. More recently, as I shall show, he has changed his mind and has come to accept the need for indoctrination in both the American and British senses.

There is more to it than this, however. As far as I am aware the cultural milieu within which Kohlberg works has never been given sufficient attention outside the United States itself. But as several American commentators have pointed out, two events are never far from Kohlberg's thinking and they appear to become ever more prominent in his later writings. These are the Vietnam War and the Watergate scandal (see Kohlberg, 1979, 1980a). At the heart of Kohlberg's concern is a passionate desire to see American democracy working and the Constitution and the Bill of Rights functioning as the founding fathers meant them to function. To be aware of this is to understand that Kohlberg has a clear end in view – a vision that he wants to uphold – and that there is less confusion in his mind than some of his critics have suggested. By this I mean that the suggested ambiguity between moral behaviour and moral education hardly exists because in terms of the American context the two come together. To be able to reason at a certain level is a prerequisite for making American democratic government work and every child must achieve it if he or she is to participate. If the great mass of the people prove incapable of entering into the social contract represented by the Constitution and the Bill of Rights, then the whole system falters. Even worse, if those at the highest level of government cannot achieve a high level of moral reasoning, then the system is even more open to corruption than some other, less democratic systems. For it has to be remembered that it is easier for an averagely educated person to reach the highest office of state in the United States than in other countries where leadership comes from one's ability to impress parliaments and Cabinets.

The shattering discovery of Kohlberg's early inquiries was that most of his fellow Americans were incapable of operating at the required level and that most were actually opposed to the Constitution and the Bill of Rights when the contents of those statements were put to them out of context. A mammoth educational job needed to be done. But what all of this adds up to for my purposes is that Kohlberg is not, and probably never has been, just a disinterested empirical investigator plotting what is the case. He operated rather from an ideal, a vision of what might be. He is as much concerned with what ought to be as with what is; he has a doctrine as well as a method.

In fact he seems to have more than one, for beneath his whole structure there appears to lie a belief in the inherent goodness of humanity. He argued from the start that his system was not indoctrinatory for the reason that what it did was to reveal rather than advocate. Justice is not a value to be imposed. It exists naturally within us and the educator's task is to release it. Kohlberg rejects what he terms the 'social scientific popularity' of the view that a child's values come from outside. Goodness lies within, waiting to be discovered. In short, he stands more in the tradition of Rousseau than of Golding. I am not for a moment disputing his right to do so, but I would want to claim that again this is belief rather than fact, and indeed as I shall show, he now admits to this. Right from the start, therefore, we find an empirical system which is in fact straining at the empirical boundaries.

**Breaking the empirical boundaries**

Kohlberg's stages are now so well known that I do not intend to offer more than the very briefest description. In non-technical language he concluded the first part of his survey by suggesting that we passed through four successive stages up to an important major leap into a fifth and sixth stage. First, we justify our actions by reasons concerned with fear of authority (stage 1, Punishment and obedience orientation) and then proceed to giving reasons more connected with bringing pleasure to those who tell us what to do (stage 2, Instrumental relativist orientation). By the next stage we are likely to be giving reasons which will be acceptable to our peer group (stage 3, Interpersonal concordance) before moving to the stage whereby we justify our position by reference to the law or to rules (stage 4, Society-maintaining orientation).

The crucial step, and one which the majority appear not to make, is the one which follows. At stage 5 people acknowledge that laws must constantly be amended to express the deeper principles which lie behind them. It is, of course, on just this sort of recognition that constitutional democracy depends. Leaving his sample at this point, Kohlberg cites Martin Luther King as illustrative of what he has in mind and in particular the following passage of King's letter from Birmingham Jail, words which also appear on King's memorial outside Marsh Chapel at Boston University where he was a theology student:

> One may well ask, 'How can you advocate breaking some laws and obeying others?' The answer lies in the fact that one has not only a legal but a moral responsibility to obey just laws. One has also a moral responsibility to disobey unjust laws, though one must do so openly, lovingly and with a willingness to accept the penalty. An individual who breaks a law that conscience tells him is unjust, and accepts the penalty to arouse the conscience of the community is expressing in reality the highest respect for law. An unjust law is a human law not rooted in eternal law and natural law. A law that uplifts human personality is just, one which degrades human personality is unjust. (Kohlberg, 1974, p. 10)

Such a statement not only illustrates stage 5 thinking. It moves us straight into stage 6, defined by Kohlberg as representing those 'who are orientated to a universal ethical principle in which the various strands of principle, reasoning and moral action fuse together in a holistic integrated personality'.

But with such an illustration and such a statement we also begin to move into a mass of problems. For one thing, as we have noted, Kohlberg's sample begins to fail him. Few of his 75 respondents reached stage 5; even fewer reached stage 6, so that he is compelled to find what he terms 'examples from literature'. Secondly, empirical language together with empirical forms of measurement become inadequate. King uses 'conscience' as a measure and his reference point is something called 'eternal law'. He knows what distinguishes just and unjust laws by what 'uplifts' or 'degrades' and one wants to ask just how such knowledge is acquired and measured. Kohlberg, whether he realizes it or not, is faced with the problem outlined in my introduction. He cannot keep religious people out of his scheme, and religious people employ religious rather than empirical language. Martin Luther King, and Mahatma Gandhi whom he also cites, were both deeply religious people. Can they be explained in non-religious language? It is here that

Kohlberg is compelled to ask questions about a possible stage 7. This he did in a 1981 article entitled 'Moral development, religious thinking and the question of a seventh stage' (Kohlberg, 1981b). Aware of the recent work of Fowler in plotting religious development, Kohlberg notes that he had himself speculated about a seventh stage prior to coming across Fowler's research. Such a stage would involve 'the adoption of a cosmic as distinct from a natural view of the relation between moral principles of justice and the ultimate'. And he goes on to state, 'This could be a pantheistic or a theistic conception'.

Straight away we notice that psychological and positivistic language has been abandoned. We are straight back into metaphysical expressions. And metaphysics is the art of using metaphors. But the empiricist in Kohlberg does not give up so easily. He criticizes Fowler not so much because he may be wrong in fact, but on the grounds that it makes 'the empirical study of religion to morality difficult'. The method of inquiry becomes paramount over the field of inquiry. This is confirmed by one of Kohlberg's most faithful followers. Robert Carter in an article appropriately entitled 'What is Lawrence Kohlberg doing?' (Carter, 1980) makes a plea for Kohlberg to stay firmly within the empirical realm, to concentrate on those things he is good at and not to be drawn away. And what he is good at is empirical methodology: 'Kohlberg's incredible insight is that in moral deliberations there is some way in which to measure and collect data empirically' (ibid. p.94). By contrast, Kohlberg's problems come from 'his desire to place over this data an interpretive grid which would fit in such a way as to solve the key questions in the history of philosophy'.

In both of these statements we are clearly being told that if the methodology becomes inadequate to deal with a subject, then the solution lies in restricting the subject matter to the limits of the methodology. In that way the problem will disappear. It becomes hidden not because it ceases to exist, but because we consciously blinker ourselves, so that we shall not see it. There is, of course, nothing intellectually dishonest in an empiricist stating that this is as far as those particular methods can go: the inquisition only starts to operate when other methodologies are disallowed. The school curriculum introduces children to a range of methodologies. When the language of any one of them comes to dominate over the others, certain types of knowledge become unavailable.

Carter himself plots in his article the expanding ripples of human consciousness which, starting from the centre, he names as:

(1)   self;
(2)   at least one other;
(3)   one's peer group or equivalent;
(4)   one's nation;
(5)   broader group defined by Bill of Rights, Constitution;
(6)   mankind as a whole;
(7)   the cosmos as a totality?

He places a question-mark against this last. Does it exist? Can we measure it? Let us return to safer gound, he pleads. He seems unaware that he has rediscovered for himself what is probably the main reason for the ancients' attachment to the mystical number seven.

Meanwhile Kohlberg notes that thought about a stage 7 can only be speculation, and comments: 'the religious orientation required by universal moral principle I have in part called Stage 7 although the term is only a metaphor' (Kohlberg, 1981b, p.233). Strangely he does not seem to have realized that if stage 7 is a metaphor, then so are all the other stages. His system is unfinished and as Søren Kierkegaard commented of all such systems, a system which is incomplete is simply another hypothesis (see Kierkegaard, 1945).

## Secular stages or leaps of consciousness

Those familiar with the work of Kierkegaard will know that he too presented a model of moral development and one which did allow for the religious dimension. His stages, however, were not so much those of natural progression as leaps into new perceptions of the world. By an act of will one might jump from seeing the world ego-centrically to seeing it morally and thence to seeing it religiously. Kohlberg's first four stages are merely those of natural maturation. What Kierkegaard may well be able to teach him is that there is nothing surprising about that process levelling off. The move to what Kohlberg calls stage 5 is not natural maturation at all. It is a leap, a change of total consciousness. (Kierkegaard's notion of the 'leap' and of the ensuing changes of consciousness are clearly dealt with in Hannay, 1982, see especially pp.98 ff., 158 ff.) It is commitment to the moral life, to other persons, to society, to the responsibilities of being a citizen. Few take it and those who do, argued Kierkegaard, find it ultimately frustrating. The deeper stage is that which comes from a further and larger leap – the leap into religious consciousness, an acceptance not of the irrational, but of the non-rational. Faith is beyond reason. That is why intellectuals find it more difficult than many others. 'Take away passion from the thinker', asked Kierkegaard rhetorically, 'and what have you got? You have the university professor!' (Kierkegaard, 1946). Moral decisions are made in the full context of our human personalities, not with the detached intellect alone. Emotions are involved and they can change the perspective by which our intellects view the world. Or, as Kierkegaard's great admirer, Wittgenstein, was to put it more soberly, 'The world of the happy man is an altogether different world from the world of the unhappy man' (Wittgenstein, 1961, para.6.43). Wittgenstein's great admiration for Kierkegaard has only recently come to light. It is summarized in his words, 'Kierkegaard was by far the most profound thinker of the last century. Kierkegaard was a saint' (see Rhees, 1984, p.87).

This is quite beyond the scope of empirical methodologies to grasp. Deliberately catching leprosy, as with Father Damien, is a non-rational action quite inexplicable to modern health educationists. If morality becomes reduced to the rational, then sacrifice becomes an outmoded concept rather than the highest level of moral behaviour. And this appears to be exactly what has happened with Kohlberg's system. Attaining justice rather than suffering injustice is the highest point which his empirically bound eyes can see. Small wonder, then, that Marcus Aurelius (see Kohlberg, 1981b, p.234, 1974, p.15) becomes his chosen exemplar in preference to any martyr figure. Kohlberg gives two reasons for the choice of Marcus Aurelius as his moral exemplar. First, he is outside the Judaeo-Christian tradition (which presumably makes it permissible for him to be mentioned in United States schools), and secondly, because 'in the world of the Roman Empire in which absolute power corrupted, this man with absolute power was the only one who was incorruptible, absolutely principled'. And small wonder also that much of the most poignant criticism of Kohlberg's work in the United States has begun to come from religious educationists. That criticism centres not on Kohlberg's findings, but rather on his failure to take into account the real nature of the subject with which he purports to deal. What he has to say may be correct but does it amount to very much?

## Dykstra and the morality of vision

Perhaps the most telling criticism has come from Craig Dykstra, professor of religious education at Princeton, in his book *Vision and Character* (Dykstra, 1981). First, he accuses Kohlberg of misunderstanding Plato on the subject of justice, and secondly, he charges him with failing to appreciate the nature of morality. The first criticism is one now shared with some of Kohlberg's closest colleagues and I shall return to it. Dykstra's second point offers a more specialized religious contribution to the debate.

Morality, argues Dykstra, is simply another abstract noun of prime concern to the intellect for detached analysis. It does not exist outside of persons. If the world were not peopled, there would be no morality: 'Morality is something we ascribe to people and people are more than what they know.'

It follows that there is far more to morality than responding to dilemmas. What we really mean when we speak of a person's moral life refers to what Dykstra calls their 'ongoing quality of life'. It involves something very elusive indeed and something which has a holistic quality, a total 'vision of life':

> an analysis of deliberate choices is not, as Kohlberg claims, the best and only justifiable way of studying moral development. The study of people's morality and the way it changes will require a much more subtle examination of the texture of their lives. (ibid., p.23)

Dykstra notes that in practical classroom terms Kohlberg has recently begun to call this type of education not moral, but civic. It aims to make good citizens of the United States by which he means those who can endorse what lies behind the Bill of Rights and the Constitution. But to do that they need to have a vision of the 'American Dream'. This is not to denigrate Kohlberg. Dykstra, too, is proud to be an American and shares the dream. But his purpose is to point out that Kohlberg, like his stage 5 examples, is driven not by natural maturation, but by vision, and vision derived from his own community. In the final analysis morality lies in Kohlberg the person, not in Kohlberg the social psychologist. Kohlberg's self-deception lies in thinking he has somehow separated the one from the other. The origin of his vision of the world is not his academic rationality. It is the idealism of the living community of which he is a part, the story to which he belongs. That story may contain a rational element which can be translated into empirical language but it is very far from being the whole of it. That which is not accounted for may be non-rational (not ir-rational), but it is the more powerful element and the more relevant.

Dykstra's main argument, then, is that some form of vision is necessary for any proper account of morality. It is vision which initiates action, and 'to act' is a more moral verb than 'to behave'. Vision comes from that inner life of an individual which, for want of a better word, we call the human spirit. He also raises the question of Kohlberg's original assumption of some form of natural progression towards an increasing sense of justice. Morality may be drawn out rather than pushed in but it does not flow forth gently like toothpaste out of a tube. Rather there would seem to be evidence that justice and goodness emerge kicking and screaming in some sort of conflict with their opposites. St Paul's observation that 'the good that I would I do not while the evil that I would not, that I do' (Romans 7:19) seems to have as much support as any notion of a developing sense of natural justice.

But in fact there is no need to argue this case against Kohlberg. He had accepted it for himself before Dykstra's work was published. Writing in *The Humanist*, he acknowledges as a result of practical experience in school the need for some form of indoctrination in moral education. Because of his somewhat convoluted style of writing, it is unfortunately necessary to quote a long passage at length to establish what is a central point. He writes:

> Some years of active involvement with the practice of moral education at Cluster School has led me to realise that my notion that moral stages were the basis for moral education rather than a partial guide to the moral educator, was mistaken. I realise now that the psychologist's abstraction of moral cognition from moral action and the abstraction of structure in moral cognition and judgement from content are necessary abstractions for certain

psychological research purposes. It is not a sufficient guide to the moral educator who deals with the moral concrete in a school world in which value content as well as structure, behaviour as well as reasoning, must be dealt with. In this context the educator must be a socialiser teaching value content and behaviour . . . In becoming a socialiser and advocate the teacher moves into 'indoctrination', a step I originally believed to be philosophically invalid. I thought that indoctrination was philosophically invalid because the value content taught was culturally and personally relative and that teaching content was a violation of the child's rights. I thought indoctrination was psychologically invalid because it could not lead to meaningful structural change.

I no longer hold these negative views of indoctrinative moral education and I believe that the concepts guiding moral education must be partly indoctrinative. This is true, by necessity in a world in which children engage in stealing, cheating and aggression and in a context wherein one cannot wait until children reach the fifth stage to deal directly with moral behaviour. (Kohlberg, 1978, p.14 f.)

Kohlberg, it would seem, has discovered sin, but equally important, he would seem to be recognizing that his form of research employed educational data collection to serve the purposes of socio-scientific abstraction rather than to have direct benefit on educational practice.

Dykstra's other major criticism was that Kohlberg had failed to appreciate what Plato meant by justice when deciding that it marked the summit of human moral endeavour. Kohlberg's senior colleague Carol Gilligan has substantiated this by methods similar to Kohlberg's own (Gilligan, 1982). I believe there is significance here, too, for religious education and its role in moral education.

Kohlberg's sample was made up entirely of male respondents. Gilligan has redressed the balance by choosing only female ones. Perhaps even more important, they were also involved in a moral situation, so that feelings as well as intellect were inescapably bound up. All were pregnant and all were deciding whether or not to have an abortion. Gilligan's findings are, therefore, of high significance, perhaps even more so than she herself has yet recognized. Gabriel Moran has suggested that this in fact is the case (Moran, 1983). The damage of limitation relates very closely to my main argument concerning the language in which moral education is talked about and the significance of that for the relationship between moral education and religious education. There are two points I wish to concentrate on.

First, Gilligan demonstrates that her sample do not rate justice as highly as caring. For her women moral development was centred around an understanding of responsibility and relationships rather than an understanding of rules and rights. To this Kohlberg has suggested that Gilligan has failed to come up with an alternative account of a highest moral stage saying that she has only pointed to alternative attitudes in the developmental process. Moran's response is to suggest that what Kohlberg appears not to have noticed is that Gilligan's failure to offer an alternative account of a highest moral stage is because she is questioning that there is one:

> The question is whether a higher morality is necessarily a better morality. This distinction is difficult to make because in the moral notions assumed today the only way to go is up. Success is above and failure is below. A genuine alternative to Kohlberg is not 'an alternative account of a highest moral stage' but an ethic of virtue/care/character/community in which movement is not simply from lower to higher. (ibid., p.90)

What is ultimately at issue here, therefore, is not just the Kohlbergian structure, but the whole notion of psychological developmentalism. This is Moran's real target, viewed from the bunker of a religious concept of education. Gilligan's work supplies him with much ammunition. By changing the definition of maturity she has, in her own words, 'recast the understanding of development, changing the whole account'. She has, Moran argues, not so much recast as broken in pieces the very notion of development itself in the sphere of moral education. Development loses all meaning the moment there is any lack of agreement about ends.

The second aspect of Gilligan's work to which I want to draw attention is the one which brings me back to my starting-point. It is that of language. Gilligan's major thrust is that there are different languages of morality. She is concerned primarily with what she detects to be the difference between the ways in which men and women talk about this area. While they use the same words, they often encode disparate experiences and consequently there is enormous scope for mistranslation and misunderstandings.

We can, however, go much further than this. I venture to suggest that whatever Kohlberg, Gilligan and others may have to teach us about social psychology, they have nothing to say about the nature of morality which has not been known for a very long time. Far from being new the debate over justice and compassion forms the basis of Shakespeare's *The Merchant of Venice,* as Gilligan at least appreciates, but long before that it formed the basis of the first-century argument over gospel and law which resulted in the split between Judaism and Christianity, and eight centuries before that it formed the major content of the writings of the Hebrew prophets. No doubt they were not originators of the argument either. All that we have today is a translation into a new and probably very temporary language. It is, moreover, a language which appears to hide as much as it reveals. The question then arises as to what sort of language might reveal it more adequately. The answer to that question, I believe, is not at all profound. It is in fact disarmingly simple. It is the language of narrative or story.

**Moral education and the language of narrative**

Kohlberg himself, it will be recalled, acknowledged that by stage 6 he was compelled to take 'examples from literature'. Yet it has become part of our Western empirical twentieth-century conceit to think that stories are for children, a sort of sugar coating to the pill of real knowledge, while adults deal with facts. A detailed critique of Goldman's research into the use of religious story with children is given by Priestley (1981a, pp.17–24). But such a notion was far from the view, for example, of Plato, for whom Kohlberg professes such admiration. In all the Socratic dialogues, either explicitly or implicitly, the point is made that the argument has progressed as far as is possible by reason and that it has become necessary to resort to story (mythos). Plato had little doubt that mythos was at the root of all education.

This point has been taken up more recently by Ted Hughes in his essay 'Myth and education' (Hughes, 1978) in which he describes a basic religious story, such as the Christ story, as an 'Irreducible lump of the world'. This is echoed by the Indian writer R.K.

Narayan, who sees his own Hindu epics as 'a base from which all stories have come, a prototype, the mould from which all characters and patterns flow' (Narayan, 1979). There are, of course, stories and stories. At the shallowest level there are those which fill our TV screens as 'soap opera'. Then there are those which we classify as literature. Thirdly, there is the type of story to which Hughes and Narayan refer, the cosmic narrative, the religious mythos (Priestley, 1985b). Roughly they correspond to Kierkegaard's three stages of living, the natural, the moral and the religious. Traditionally, values education, if that is what we now have to call it, has been done largely through literature, by which I should also want to include all that we know as the arts. It has also been done through this third dimension – the religious.

What, then, is the moral nature of the religious mythos? (I use the Greek form 'mythos' to avoid the association with untruth which the Anglicized form of 'myth' has been allowed to acquire.) Harvey Cox (1969, p.14) gives one answer to that question when he describes the religious man (*sic*) as 'one who grasps his own life within a larger and cosmic setting. He sees himself as part of a greater whole, a longer story in which he plays a part'.

This is surely the real nature of what Kohlberg terms stages 6 and 7. There is a direct connection with what Robert Carter described as 'the Cosmos as a whole?' and every other circle of consciousness back to the basic awareness of self. Martin Luther King and Mahatma Gandhi were not just highly moral characters who happened to be religious. They were highly moral characters exactly because they saw their own lives in the largest cosmic setting. Their self-image was that of being part of something much greater, a longer story in which they were playing a part. It is that which makes sacrifice possible. It is that which was the source of their vision. It was that which constituted their religiousness. They became moral leaders because they were *not* bound by the mores of convention. Rather they lived in a secondary world of vision and imagination which they sought to make a reality in the primary world of empirical experience. Nothing happens without first a dream. King and Gandhi were in the business of making dreams come true, not in the business of being good. Far from being a luxurious extra the cosmic setting, the mythos, is the fundamental *sine qua non* of all their action. And if that is not measurable by the process of data collection and analysis, then so be it. If we cannot get to the stars with Euclidean geometry, we do not pretend the stars are hidden from us and nor, incidentally, do we say that Euclidean geometry has no uses. The failure of certain instruments to measure mythoi should not blind us to the possibility that the mythoi might be the ultimate measure of the instruments and not vice versa. The myths continue to inspire moral action in a way for which there is little psychological explanation.

### Ruby and the Rednecks, or how the South was won

One scholar who has long recognized this is Robert Coles, Professor of Psychiatry and Human Medicine at Harvard. Coles's lack of recognition may well be his refusal to fit his cases into a system because he recognizes that human beings are always more than any system by which we might seek to measure their attainment, especially their moral attainment. In the final analysis all we can do is tell each individual's story.

Coles's lifetime concern has been to put himself physically where children and young people are in situations of crisis and to tell their stories. Collectively his volumes cast severe doubt on any Kohlbergian-type system (Coles, 1968). Again and again he shows that those who triumph over adversity are invariably those who possess a vision of a better world rather than those who become socialized into their immediate world. He himself most often quotes the example of the girl he calls Ruby because it was she who determined the direction of his own career. What follows is documented briefly in Coles's book (ibid.), but this description is taken from notes made during Coles's William James Memorial Lecture, given at Harvard Divinity School on 12 April 1984.

Ruby was six; she was black and she wanted to go to school to learn to read and write. And she was going to school because the federal court judge had ruled that she could. The trouble was that no one else was going to school because this was an all-white school and her attendance led to a boycott of schools in New Orleans. While others investigated how the 'rednecks' who lined her route to school every day could scream and shout abuse and issue threats of violence and murder to one little six-year-old girl, Coles himself watched Ruby. He knew she must crack under the strain. She didn't. To his amazement she not only endured, but he found that she prayed for the rednecks the prayer 'Father forgive; they don't know what they are doing'. Because of her six months' persistence, the boycott was broken, the schools were integrated. Thirty years later Ruby has never sought psychological or psychiatric assistance. Well might Coles ask whether her behaviour was pre-conventional, conventional or post-conventional. Well might he suggest that her real problem was that she did not know the language of the social sciences and consequently remained ignorant of the fact that she was culturally and socially deprived. And well might Coles conclude that all she had was a story, a story of which she was a part.

Coles cites many other similar examples of children and young people volunteering to become the first to break conventional morality for the sake of helping to implement another worldly morality based on a mythos. One irony of this, which seems never to feature in any empirical assessment, is that those with the greatest self-esteem which enables them to stand as individuals against a hostile world are exactly those who see their own lives as of lesser significance than the overall story. Because their mental horizons are those of the cosmos as a whole rather than of self, family, peer group or even nation, because they have a sense of time which far exceeds their own lifespan, they see themselves only as a tiny part of a much greater whole. Nevertheless, it is just this loss of self within the greater whole which holds the self together and gives it meaning.

This can be just as true corporately as individually. The Jews must be among the most resilient of races and one has only to eavesdrop on a Jewish family at a Passover meal to sense the truth of Cox's words. It is the youngest child (no conceptual problems apparently) who asks the question 'Why are we doing this?' The formalized reply comes in terms of what has happened to *us*: 'When *we* were in Egypt', and ends with the futuristic: 'Next year in Jerusalem' (see e.g. Scholefield, 1982). What else has held together such a disparate group of people for over three thousand years, almost two thousand of them without a territorial base? Similarly, what holds together the diverse peoples of the sub-continent of India if not the *Ramayana* and the *Mahabarata*? It is of the nature of the religious mythos that it is not complete; it has a future which the present generation must help to build.

In other words, what we are presented with is not a rigid stage-by-stage development so much as an unbroken living organism in which the various parts interrelate and grow together. The parts create the whole and the whole gives meaning to the parts. At a very much lower level football teams for some possess the same quality. When a mythos dies or becomes hidden, new ones have to be invented. It seems to be the case that only when the self loses itself in a greater whole does it discover itself.

I come back then to the question which forms the basis of this chapter. What is the contribution of religious education to the teaching of values? It is to tell the cosmic story or, in the case of a pluralist society, the cosmic stories. My attempt at doing this for children is to be found in Priestley (1981b). Because within the cosmic story everything is accounted for right down to the individual self and his or her actions, there is always the temptation for religious education to withdraw from the cosmic and to settle for the 'relevant'. It *can* and it *does* concern itself with the minutiae because it is concerned with the whole but religion's concern for the minutiae is properly within the momentous. In practical terms, of course, teachers of religious education can participate in matters of morals, health, social studies, careers or almost anything else. But in those issues they are unlikely to have a contribution to make which is particularly different from that of other contributors. Indeed when they are put into positions where the holistic framework is forgotten or deliberately abandoned, their role becomes comic rather than cosmic.

Any secular treatment of values withdraws from the logic of the material. Towards the end of the *Tractatus* Wittgenstein reminds us that the value of a thing lies outside of the thing itself and that, therefore, the value of the world lies outside the world. Values are transcendent. They cannot lie within the world conceived as the totality of facts. (This is my attempt at summarizing para.6.41 of the *Tractatus*.)

'The purpose of religious education', says a modern Agreed Syllabus, 'is to help children understand religion' (Humberside, 1981). Religions may or may not have developed theologies but they all possess a mythos, a cosmic story. It is the overriding task of religious education to ensure that they are not forgotten, so that they can continue to fire the imaginations of future generations. 'Where there is no vision', proclaimed one of the Old Testament prophets, 'the people perish' (Proverbs 29:18). It is a salutary note on which to end.

# DISCUSSION

Autonomy of the individual is so often the key word in the promotion of personal development, with its accompanying moral education. The consequence of attaching such importance to autonomy is a fear of indoctrination, and thus of shaping how a young person is to think and feel. The full range of frightening possibilities can, however, be avoided if we embrace a theory of development, already outlined in this book, in which children are helped to become more 'mature' in their capacity to think about their actions. And the teacher, in helping them develop this maturity, should adopt particular classroom strategies, particularly that of classroom discussion of real or simulated moral problems. The 'neutral stance' with regard to substantive moral issues is a particular strategy, often advocated, which enables the teacher to promote this more mature attitude and capacity.

This, briefly, captures the essence of an understanding of values and their promotion which has dominated both the theory and the practice of personal and social development. The significance, therefore, of Hannaford's and Priestley's contribution lies in the questions they raise about this understanding. They see it to be mistaken philosophically as well as a seriously impoverished account of 'the moral' life which, in turn, is having dire effects upon our conception of educational practice.

First, the word 'autonomy' trips off the tongue much too readily, given the problems in its analysis. There are different meanings, and one needs, in advocating autonomy as an educational aim, to explore exactly what is meant and how what one says is reconcilable with our wider understanding of moral life and the moral language through which it is understood and communicated. Certainly in the sense of encouraging in children greater freedom in 'making up their own minds' over and choosing which is right and wrong, it does violence to the place of reason in moral life, to the committed nature of morality and to the important place of moral tradition.

Secondly, the accompanying proposal that teachers should, *vis-à-vis* the promotion of values, adopt a neutral stance (otherwise they would be denying the autonomy of the young person) needs to be treated with caution. The whole educational process is so inextricably mixed with the promotion of values and thus with a vision of personal fulfilment that the educator can hardly remain neutral with respect to values. The processes of educating embody particular values and commitments – for example, those of telling the truth, not distorting the evidence, openness of mind, respect for argument and the providers of argument. Hence there is a need to make distinctions between neutrality in the sense of locating *ethically* each view as of equal moral significance and neutrality in the sense of a particular strategy to encourage, on particular occasions, the kind of reflective reasoning necessary for the development of a capacity to have and to be committed to a defensible set of values.

Thirdly, this commitment requires a vision that goes beyond the rather impoverished concern for resolving problems on the basis of universalizable values. There is a need to look more critically at those who, from a useful but narrow understanding of moral development, disconnect this from that profounder and wiser grasp of human behaviour and motivation that is there to be discovered in literature and mythology, especially religious story. There has been a dangerous tendency to lose, under the impetus of the social sciences, that richer appreciation of personal development that is captured in story, in particular that leap (expressed religiously by Kierkegaard) from the conventional morality to a committed morality of principle inspired by a more universal concern for values and respect for nature in its various forms.

These two chapters, therefore, provide a most valuable critique of prevailing assumptions, as well as a detailed and well-informed criticism of those who have dominated research and scholarship in this area. But the critique is a positive one, pointing to the way in which we need to go if values education is not to be reduced to the rather drab and inadequate vision of the social psychologists and the social and life skills experts.

The critique is valuable, too, because it takes us into the heart of the difficulties that PSMEd must face, namely the nature and justification of the values (moral, personal or social) which it is trying to promote.

These difficulties have, of course, been the subject of analysis and debate from the very beginnings of philosophy. But problematic though they are, PSMEd cannot remain aloof from those arguments, nor can it fail to flag its own particular stance within those arguments.

For example, so much of PSMEd has been infused with the spirit of scepticism – with the view that questions of value, unlike questions of science, cannot be resolved by rational consideration. Rather is it the case on this view that values are but expressions of feeling and emotion – the reflections, no more, of the idiosyncratic and subjective works of particular individuals. The teacher, therefore, operating in a world where the very distinction between right and wrong has become blurred, would feel unable to promote any set of values at all. The big fear would be that of indoctrination and so schools should, in the absence of any objective basis for moral values, do no more than help children to make up their own mind.

On the other hand, there is the opposite position – one which, certainly in the past, has so often prevailed – namely that we have access to moral certainties and that there are moral facts just as there are scientific facts. These 'facts' are discovered by moral insight and reflection (can't you *see* that it is wrong to hit old ladies for the fun of it?) or they are found in some authoritative source like the Bible, the parents, or the 'clerisy' that Coleridge wrote about and that consisted in a morally superior class telling others what is right and wrong. Hence the teachers, much more confident on this view, would see it as their job to inculcate such values, and to make sure children behave correctly.

It seems somewhat tame to state that our own position lies somewhere between these extremes – between complete moral scepticism on the one hand, and the certainties of 'moral facts' on the other. But much more can be said, and such is reflected in the contributions to this book.

In our view it is necessary to distinguish between very specific values and rules (the value, say, of caring for sick animals, or the rule that one should always do exactly as one's parents request) and more general principles (the principle of pursuing the truth of an experiment or of an argument without cooking the books, the principle of openness and honesty in relation to others, the principle of respecting the dignity of others however odious they appear), which principles however have to be worked out by individuals in terms of specific rules and values. There are general principles of justice, of respect, of honesty, which are part and parcel of the moral life. These are what we need to develop. But we also need to develop the capacity to reason, the emotional security and maturity, the imagination and the courage, which are necessary for the responsible application of principles to specific, personal and often unique situations.

Personal development requires the growing capacity to enter into a social form of life that is necessarily infused with obligations and ideals. Such obligations and ideals are not arbitrary – not to be created anew at the whim of each individual. It is such a crude and mistaken concept of autonomy that Hannaford argues most strongly against. But they do none the less require the internalization of principles and they do not absolve young people from working out how these principles apply to their own situations – hence the kind of autonomy that we in this book advocate. The exercise of that autonomy, however, cannot take place in a vacuum; the principle we act upon concerns the dignity and interests of others, the appreciation of how others behave and feel and the understanding of complex interconnection within the natural world of which we are part. (Why is respect an attitude we show to people but not to trees?) Hence the personal development we have in mind requires immersion into these cultural forms through which human beings and the natural order have been explored. There is, as Priestley explains, room for story as well as principled reasoning in the exploration of the world of value.

# Section D
# Direct Approaches to Personal, Social and Moral Education

# INTRODUCTION

In this section we move to a consideration of work in schools and with young people which is directly aimed at promoting personal, social and moral education. In Chapter 8 Leslie Button outlines the way in which developmental group work grew out of a research programme inquiring into the friendship patterns of adolescence. He makes it clear how these action research origins continue to influence the work which is written up in two books (Button, 1971, 1974) and which, more recently, has been incorporated into a programme of tutorial work designed for use by form tutors in the secondary school (Button 1981, 1982). In this chapter Button outlines some of the important activities used in a developmental group work programme and shows how they relate to aims and values embodied in the work. He concludes by looking at the training implications for teachers and for the commitment necessary from the whole school if such an approach is to take root and develop.

In Chapter 9 Sue Plant writes about the development of a course of personal, social and moral education for the fourth- and fifth-year pupils at a secondary school. This was partly based on the work of Leslie Button and is a case study of these ideas in operation. The dedication involved in any curriculum development enterprise is clearly shown in this chapter which begins with the choice of elements for the curriculum package. Sue Plant next describes the way in which team teaching and group work principles were used in the teaching sessions. Throughout the chapter she discusses the problems and the successes of the enterprise and uses pupil and staff comments, drawn from her evaluation, to illustrate the impact of the course.

# 8 Developmental group work as an approach to personal, social and moral education

*Leslie Button*

Developmental group work is a way of helping people in their personal growth and development, in their social skills and in the kind of relationships they establish with other people. Its purpose is to provide individuals with opportunities to relate to others in supportive groups, to try out new social approaches and to experiment in new roles. Care, concern and the development of responsible attitudes are basic to the work.

I write from a viewpoint informed by a long-term programme of action research, which culminated in the formulation of methods of work that I have called developmental group work. It all began with an action research project studying the small group structures among adolescents, their friendships and the way in which the groups to which they belonged influenced their attitudes and behaviour.

The project was approached through panels of teachers, youth workers and social workers who served as assistant researchers. Each member of the panels studied a small group of young people with whom they were in daily contact, so it was possible to see movement taking place over a period of time. The young people, who knew that they were helping us in the study, had regular conversations about their relationships and their self-feelings.

The impact on the practitioners was quite dramatic. They were very moved by their discoveries, and frequently sought opportunities to respond to situations they were uncovering. This immediately penetrated their professional approaches as I had never known information or persuasion to do. It soon became clear that studies of this kind could form a most powerful approach to training.

Pilot training courses were then built on a carefully structured programme of action research, bringing trainees into intimate and creative contact with young people and providing the raw material upon which theoretical discussions could be conducted. This put the trainees in a strong position. Theoretical discussions were seen to be vital and relevant, and immediately led to tutorial sessions about the kinds of response that could be made to the situations that had been revealed. A long-term style of training evolved, which I described in my book *Discovery and Experience* (Button, 1971).

Something very similar was seen in the young people. A number of the practitioners involved in the action research programme reported rapid personal growth in the young people they were studying that seemed to arise directly out of the action research programme. Repeated and progressive inquiries within a group of peers seemed to be providing an opportunity for personal growth, such as we had never seen as a result of our normal work with young people. To test the validity of this assumption we simplified our research instruments and used them as work instruments with new groups of young people, and saw similar results. It was from this that developmental group work arose. The basic approach of developmental group work still represents an action research programme for young people, as described in my book *Developmental Group Work with Adolescents* (Button, 1974).

### Relevance to PSMEd

Personal, social and moral education is essentially about attitudes, social abilities, creative relationships and responsible behaviour. All these things are locked into an individual's attitude system and behaviour patterns, which are difficult to modify. One witnesses the use of so many seemingly excellent programmes of material that seem to fail to move young people in their attitudes and behaviour. The cognitive material is so often readily accepted by young people, but fails to enter their life-style.

In general there is a lot too much reliance on the efficacy of cognitive approaches. I well remember my frustration when faced by students to whom the relevant material had been passed by lecture and reading but who failed in seminar and tutorial to show a working grasp of what they had been told. As I have mentioned above, this was effectively changed by inviting students to undertake action research, which led to the gathering of relevant material upon which the theoretical discussions could be based.

There are some formidable gaps, indeed barriers, between the presentation of information and the modification of attitudes and behaviours. There is the initial gap between receiving the information and understanding it. It depends upon the leap that we are being asked to make, but most of us need to work on new material before we are fully in possession of it. We each have our own existing structure of knowing and believing, and the acceptance of new knowledge will inevitably disturb our existing pattern. There is, therefore, a gap between understanding new material and grounding it in a working framework. If new knowledge is inconvenient to us, we are quite capable of streaming it off into an intellectual conserve where it can remain without disturbing us.

Let us assume that we have absorbed some new information into a working framework of knowing and perceiving: there is still a very big step to be taken in applying that knowledge to an ongoing life-style. We must be convinced of its importance, and be prepared to accept the change in ourselves – to be sufficiently moved to make the effort. There is a need for daring in treading a new path, and if as is usually the case we are likely to meet pressure from those around us who rely on us behaving as usual, we may need to be very determined to brave the anticipated if not actual criticism of other people. In the face of all this it is quite astonishing how the almost blissful reliance on mere presentation of information persists as a major, possibly the main, approach in the educational world. In the field of PSMEd we are usually concerned with the modification of attitudes and behaviours, and face the full rigours of the points of resistance outlined above.

Consider, in this context, the force of personal discovery. I am likely to be committed to what I discover. My understanding will be increased by seeing the new material in context, and I may be sufficiently moved by my discovery to want to do something about it. At least I may have the motivation to move forward but still have to summon up daring to take action. In changing, however minutely, my style of behaviour I face the pressures of those who prefer that I did not rock the boat.

This is the reason that the training programmes mentioned above were based on discovery and *experience*. When new principles were established, steps were taken to ensure that they were applied in appropriate fieldwork. Often the experience was inherent in making the discovery as, for example, when teachers were invited to meet young people through direct and personal inquiries that both produced the information about young people and ensured the experience of making that kind of direct approach to them. And if all this is conducted through small groups, the support that the participants can offer one another can do much to relieve the pressure felt from colleagues who would prefer things not to change.

Personal, social and moral education is pre-eminently concerned with caring and with responsive behaviour, skills in a wide range of relationships, and a sense of responsibility permeating a whole life-style. These are all emotionally charged areas and often highly resistant to change. It is not enough to know, much less to be told. The force of personal discovery can play a vital part, and new approaches need to be experienced and practised. Unfortunately caring has been interpreted by the caring professions largely as casework. I mean by this that the worker will seek to serve young people in a one-to-one relationship. Many teachers see their pastoral role in this light. The appointment of counsellors to schools, excellent in so many other ways, has tended to support this view of the teacher's caring role. I have so often been asked for material that would occupy 29 pupils while the teacher counselled the thirtieth. This is neither practical nor desirable.

Similarly, the caring role in school has so often been seen to be about problems or crises. Our pastoral function in school needs to be developmental, building the personal resource of young people, so that they are progressively more capable of meeting the vicissitudes of life as they come along. Naturally problems and crises will arise, but we should be building a structure within which these moments can be absorbed as a natural part of the ongoing activities. The prevailing system of referrals from the form tutor to the year or house head, and from there to the counsellor or senior hierarchy, tends to overload these people, and often provides only transitory attention for the young people concerned.

The tendency of the teacher to regard him/herself as the sole provider is near to the centre of all this. In general teachers care greatly about the well-being of their young people, and many strain themselves in their pastoral role to offer themselves in a creative relationship with each of the members of their pastoral group. This is excellent in itself, but ignores the contribution that young people can make to one another if only this can be made legitimate and effective. There is a richness here to be tapped that is so often ignored. This means the transition from seeing the teacher as the total provider to acting as third party, enabling mutual help and support between the young people to take place.

Apart from the skills involved in doing this, the transition implies a change in the teacher's emotional position. Their self-concept as teachers may be threatened by the change. The kind of behaviour and obedience towards the teacher may be different, and the deference owed to the teacher may need to change to a greater level of partnership, with the teacher rather more accessible, putting the young people in a stronger position. And the work with the young people must change from being problem based to being developmental. There needs to be a programme of sequential experiences with steadily deeper penetration and exploration, putting the young people nearer the centre of their own development.

**Programmes**

There is a clear value position in all this work. I would hope that as a result of their experience with us, the young people would be more capable of running their own lives in a responsible manner. Creative relationships, caring and concern are at the centre of the work, which is outward-looking and moving towards a caring community.

A programme of this kind is inevitably highly participatory, and proceeds through a carefully structured series of personal experiences supported by the care and concern of the total group. There must be some understanding of some basic concepts to make this exploration possible and shared. Deepening self-knowledge and self-determination is allied to a growing sense of responsibility to a widening circle of a community.

It might be helpful if I were to ground some of these general aims through a description of a few of the experiences involved. First, meeting and greeting others, being both capable and concerned. The programme would begin with the members of the group moving around meeting one another. They would take one another's hands as a symbol of their coming together as a caring and supportive group. It will be noticed that I say 'taking hands' and not 'shaking hands'. This is not intended as a perfunctory convention, but rather as an expression of support and concern, and the beginning of the contracts that members of the group will need to make with one another in their determination to stay with one another when support is most needed.

The experience arising from this simple activity is complex and serves as a foundation for much that will follow. For example, a surprising number of people find real encounters difficult to take, and yet coping with people is one of the major issues in life. Many relationships – friendship, for example – imply an ability to reach out to other people. Some people find this difficult. At best they can respond to the advances of other people: they cannot make the running.

Within meeting and greeting there needs to be a capacity for feeling and expressing an interest in the other person. We are often so full of ourselves – our importance or our embarrassment – that being interested in the other person is something that has to be learnt. And in life we need to be able to cope with a variety of people, not just peers, but older and younger people, strangers and people in authority. These other kinds of contacts will be picked up later in the programme, and our first experience is but a gentle preparation. For example, soon the group will be receiving a stranger as a visitor – and will have the responsibility of taking all the initiative.

This first simple activity also carries the challenge of physical contact. The rationale of physical contact in school, or the lack of it, could form the basis of another paper. Suffice it to say that if we watch what goes on among young people at school, there is a good deal of physical contact. But most of it is of the push and pull variety, reducing rather than enlarging. In most circles the ragging is acceptable, but the expression of concern and kindliness can be taboo. We are seeking to provide a controlled situation where physical contact expressing concern, support and kindliness is legitimate.

Our work must be about life in the real world, which means that what we do in our rather special supportive groups must serve as a platform – a practice arena – for behaviour that is to be carried out into other areas of young people's lives. For this reason, assignments of activity to be carried through outside the group will be structured into each step of the programme.

I have dealt at some length with the simple activity of hand taking, the very beginning of the programme, in order to illustrate the many strands inherent in any of the activities, and the way in which each activity serves as a platform, which can be used as the point of departure for later activities.

## Support

A supportive atmosphere is vital to this work. But although it is not always appreciated, it is just as important for most of the other aspects of school life. We shall engage very little participation by young people in lesson time unless the classroom is a supportive situation. I do not mean only that the teacher needs to be kindly and concerned. Very few young people will risk making a contribution unless they are rewarded rather than ridiculed by their peers. Very early in the development of this work we saw how much more was achieved when the situation was supportive, and it was interesting that support seemed most to arise in situations where support was really needed. Some kind of stir or challenge usually triggered off the support: we need to distinguish between support and cosiness. Support usually had some challenge within it, and some of the most painful moments were also the most supportive.

Later we asked ourselves how we could nurture support and at the same time make concrete some of the abstract concepts like caring and concern. To this end we have introduced a number of activities that focus directly on support, and at an early stage in the programme we may well lead to a trust walk. The group divides into twos, and one of the partners is assumed to be blindfold and completely dependent upon the other. The sighted member of each group moves his or her partner around the room and takes responsibility for the care and experience of the partner. We usually try to deepen the experience in steps but by focusing on caring and trusting – both being trustworthy and allowing oneself to trust. We would also focus attention on the use of the other senses to explore shapes and textures, light and shade and temperatures. If possible, the door of the room would be opened giving access to corridors and stairs, the open air with plants and outdoor sounds. In due course the partners change over, so that each can have the experience of leading and being led.

It is easy during this exercise to focus on trust, support, caring and concern. All are necessary and strongly felt, and this consciousness feeds immediately into the ongoing programme. Most people find this a potent experience in some way or another, and there is usually a lot of discussion comparing the differing personal experiences arising from the activity. There are a number of other exercises focusing on support, and these will normally be brought into the programme to prepare for some personal exchanges where support may be of special importance.

**Communication skills**

Skills of communication, especially oral communication, are important when moving forward to personal exploration. It is difficult to explore one's personal position, let alone share it with other people, without the necessary language. It could be argued that an ability in oral communication is essential in the exchanges required throughout the educational process, but this is a much neglected side of education, as witnessed by the large number of inarticulate young people leaving our schools, even at the higher levels of academic attainment. Young people are going to talk their way through life much more than write it. Many, indeed probably most, people need to form ideas through their own mouths before they are in possession of them.

There are a number of ways of helping young people to become more articulate. We are particularly interested in conversations about personal matters, so this is where we begin. Sitting in pairs, we ask each pair to find out as much as possible about each other. Many young people run out of conversation after a very few minutes, and we try to help them build up an expertise in this kind of conversation. For example, we might use the same pairs, but this time as working parties, to consider the areas of life that we should be hearing about in order to come to know our partner as a person. After a few minutes' conversation in pairs we draw their ideas together, and establish a list of prompts that might help the conversation along. This usually changes the situation dramatically, and most young people find that they can sustain a much deeper conversation, using the prompts as an agenda. At first they tend to use the agendas mechanically, but before long the exchanges become much more fluent. In the course of time the preparation of agendas becomes spontaneous and one of their long-term skills.

The concept of agendas or frameworks assumes increasing importance as the programme proceeds. Soon they will be working out an agenda for meeting a visitor whom they must hold in sustained conversation. They will also be conducting inquiries, for example, with parents and other members of the community, for which they need frameworks. They will be learning to make outlines for public statements – even though the 'public' may at first be only their own classmates. The skill in formulating frameworks in the context of the rest of their work in school is a prize indeed: for essays, for marshalling material in preparation for examinations, and for the examinations themselves. These skills essential to social education become a vital contribution to the young people's academic prowess.

Within the practice of oral communication we shall wish to focus on the skills of listening. This can be initiated, for example, by continuing the conversation in twos, followed by coming together in fours. Each person will be charged with the responsibility of introducing his/her partner to the other pair. If this is done in the first person, we have not only an exercise in listening, but an experience in empathy with the young people being required to put themselves in their partner's shoes.

The skill in conversation is an example of a growing ability that will need to be applied to life as a whole, and it is important to take the experience out into the outside world. Young people usually respond readily to the need for outside practice, and will take on a remit to conduct a conversation with someone at home. Real assistance can be offered by encouraging them, through discussions in small groups, to decide how they will tackle this assignment, and to role-play their approach. An assignment of fieldwork in this way will form part of so many of the steps in this work.

The skills in conversation and speaking in front of a larger group can be accelerated by the use of Socratic group discussion. An attempt to promote discussion in a large group is so often desultory in the extreme, but the difference prompted by Socratic group discussion in the same large group is nothing short of dramatic.

Divide the group into threes – or not more than fours – and proceed by a series of sequential questions. Put the first question out for a few minutes' discussion in the small groups and then call for an exchange between the small groups, with the teacher at the centre of the exchanges. Summarize the responses, and use this as a platform for the next question to be put out to the small groups. It is not possible here to describe fully the methods of Socratic group discussion, but a fuller account will be found in Button (1974, pp.156, 161, 1981, pp.8–10, 1982, pp.10–12). The unfailing efficacy of this method needs some explanation. It is a way of ensuring that almost all the members of the group are working all the time and this can apply when working with groups as large as 100 or more people. It seems that committing the discussion to small groups has two major effects: first, each speaker is able to rehearse what they may later say to the whole group; and secondly, they have had the acceptance of the other members of their small group, and so have a sense of support for what they have to say in the open exchanges. It is the most economical method I know for preparing young people to work through small groups. In fact the groups formed for the purpose of Socratic group discussion can be used for a whole variety of purposes: forward planning, shared decisions and the modification of behaviour patterns.

What we have come to call the 'visitor technique' has proved to be a powerful experience for most young people. The visitor is received by a member of the group, is greeted by the group as a whole and is engaged in a sustained conversation, much of it at a personal level. The young people are responsible for taking the initiative and the visitor is largely the respondent. The occasion has to be concluded graciously by one of the group and the visitor cared for until he/she leaves the premises.

There is a good deal of preparation for the occasion. The agenda of prompts for conversation is formulated, and individual members of the group take responsibility for leading certain aspects of the conversation. Role play figures strongly in the preparation of the young person who is to receive and escort the visitor to the group, and in the meeting and greeting that must take place.

It is an event that capitalizes strongly on what has gone before, the meeting and greetings, conversations and formulations of agendas, and the listening and expressing an interest in the other person. The atmosphere is often charged with excitement and most young people take their responsibilities very seriously. Quite often the young person who has tended to be a little awkward suddenly becomes very identified with the activity. It can be an important experience for the visitor as well. For example, the young people discover that a senior member of staff whom they meet 'is a real person' and the visitor can make the kind of contact with young people that their normal role seems to preclude.

Consider the range of experience that can be introduced to young people in this way not only in the variety of people to be met, but also in the number of topics that can be dealt with. A group is preparing to meet a specialist in, say, sex education or growing up, and they have to prepare their agenda. In order to do this they must give serious attention to the subject and by the time an agenda has been prepared, the purpose of the exercise is on the way to being achieved. There will be no time wasted on warming up, no glazed eyes and inattention. The young people will all be sitting on the edge of their chairs because it is their occasion. It is not surprising that many teachers take this approach through to their normal subject teaching.

### Exploration of relationships

It is when dealing with relationships that active experience needs to be at its height. We can be locked into our existing style of relationships, partly by the level of our own abilities, but also by the role positions we occupy and the expectations of those around us. There is so much loneliness associated with an inability to reach out to other people. There is a difference between being able to respond to other people's approaches and being able to make the running.

It is not that we want everyone to conform to a mould of extraversion and gregariousness. But it is important that people should have the choice and not be held to an uncomfortable style of life by a lack of social abilities. It is here that a developmental build-up is so important: having words to explore and share, and having support and encouragement to dare to consider personal movement. We would encourage young people to see clearly their own position, to consider whether they wish to move, and having declared their objectives, plan manageable strategies that they can take on with the support of their peers.

Friendship is a good illustration of all this. Through our own research into friendship we have been impressed by the central position friendship occupies in life – not only among young people. We have been struck by the amount of malaise about friendship that has been revealed in our studies. It needs a lot of daring for young people to admit that they feel inadequate in this field, and this will only come when trust and support has been built to a high level. A peer support group can help tremendously. In fact the very first admission may reveal to the person concerned how warmly they are regarded by the other members of the group, and this can bring immediate joy and relaxation. Some may need to learn how they are turning other people away through their own behaviour, and be helped to try out new approaches and behaviours.

Ultimately we shall need to reach a discussion of personal roles and self-feelings because these underlie so much else in life. Individuals are sometimes caught in repetitive and unhelpful roles. They may have done much to create these roles, but once established, they will be held to them by the people around them. They must be given room for manoeuvre by their peers, but they will also need to see and practise alternative forms of behaviour.

Family relationships are bound to enter discussions at this level, and we shall hope to help young people make a creative contribution to their own family relationships. It is most important that parents should be brought into contact with this work which can be done in a variety of ways, ranging from action research by young people, involving the parents in their own discussions, to staging evenings when the parents can share the kind of activities and discussions involved.

**Teachers and the school**

It is our experience that most teachers need considerable help in working in this way. Training in new approaches needs to be highly practical, and once again this is accomplished through discovery and experience, with carefully structured and sequential programmes through which the approaches can be experienced and evaluated step by step.

The training group represents a supportive and developmental group, so that the teachers have the kind of experience that they are hoping to bring to young people. It is often said that the experience is of as much value to the teachers as to the young people. The actual work with young people is at the core of the training: the activities in the meetings of the training group inspire, inform, process and evaluate the concurrent work with young people. Persuasion to take a different stance is unnecessary. By trying out new approaches and witnessing their impact on young people the trainees are in the position to evaluate the effectiveness of the work themselves. Working in and through supportive groups, and openly with colleagues, is a new experience for most teachers. As they become committed the concept of support groups among staff enters the school vocabulary quite naturally.

It will be seen that the methods of training and work are of one piece, and it is not difficult to train teachers in these approaches given time and facilities. But it is a different matter to ensure that the methods are actually practised in the school after the training programme is finished.

There is conservatism built into any institution of standing, and this is certainly true of schools. There is usually an accepted way of doing things – accepted norms of group behaviour – and any departure from these norms brings disturbance and discomfort. There is usually an unconscious but powerful tendency to neutralize any disturbance of the accepted pattern. This means that for any innovation to survive, the institution as a whole must be engaged. This is particularly true of pastoral work in school, since most of the staff are involved in it, which brings both a challenge and an opportunity.

We have learnt that we need to structure the methods of institution development into the initial training of teachers, so that they can take the school along with them as they proceed. This requires a programme of consultation at various levels, seminars, workshops, reports and, above all, by working openly and visibly.

### Acceptance by teachers

A large proportion of teachers have been uncertain about their pastoral function, and many have very willingly accepted help in the approaches to this work. Because it is an area of uncertainty, many have been open to new ideas as they may not have been in their subject teaching, where they feel more secure. It is sometimes suggested that we have chosen the soft option in going for pastoral work, that we have abdicated the real task of changing approaches to education in general. Against this it can be argued that by focusing on the pastoral function of the form teacher:

(1)    we have reached teachers in an area where they are willing learners;

(2)    a very large proportion of teachers are caught up in this work;

(3)    something is bound to rub off, both in the spirit of the school and in the outlook of individual teachers.

A number of teachers do take some of the techniques that they have learnt in this work across into their subject teaching. Socratic group discussion, and the visitor technique, are two examples of this, but it is commonplace to find that teachers who subscribe to the philosophy that young people must be at the centre of their own development, and practise this in the pastoral area, continue to treat the same young people as passive recipients in their subject teaching.

So the charge remains valid. There is need of deliberate action and programmes to help teachers to transfer the methods across to much of the school activities. Just as we would hope that young people will come nearer to the centre of their own development, so they should be brought into a much more supportive situation and greater partnership in their scholarship.

# 9 Education for personal responsibility: A course of personal, social and moral education for Years 4 and 5

*Sue Plant*

## Introduction

With my arrival as deputy head at a new school, there came the opportunity to develop personal, social and moral education (PSMEd). It was clear that at that time the school had no major commitment to this area of the curriculum, though there was good work being done in Religious Education (RE) and traditional topics were being dealt with in such departments as Home Economics, Biology and Citizenship. It was the opportunity I needed to be able to develop my ideas and put them into practice. I began with Years 4 and 5, as it was provision for this age-group which schools were being asked to examine.

In this chapter I should like to share the process of innovation which was a joint venture for myself and my colleagues, and to highlight some of the problems we met and are still confronting in the difficult area of 'values'. The quotations of teachers and pupils are taken from the research that I have undertaken in evaluating the course.

Before dealing with specific 'value' areas, I shall try to give a general picture of the very early stages of the course, so that the reader can understand the context within which we were working.

I have to admit to a certain amount of naïvety at that stage in my own development. I had come from a background of counselling and had some experience of developing a course of personal and social development in my previous post, although there I was working more on intuition than informed decisions. However, I began by formulating some basic principles which I felt were important in this kind of work, gleaned from my previous experience. These were:

(1)  Group work seemed an ideal vehicle for an exploration of personal and social development.

(2)  As this way of working would be new to most teachers and pupils, it seemed important to build maximum support into the system. Thus a team teaching approach seemed to satisfy these needs.

(3)  In order to remove the traditional competitive approach engendered by examinations with 'success' also providing 'failure' I wanted the course to be non-examinable in the traditional sense.

It can be seen that at this very early stage certain values which I held were incorporated into the philosophy of the course. These were open to discussion but would have needed very good reasons if I were to change these principles.

These then formed the basis of an introductory document which was presented to the staff, parents and governors.

I also felt it to be important that I should be clear about the scope of PSMEd before preparing a list of aims. Several documents had been produced nationally, all aiming to develop the inner resources of the pupils – both emotional and intellectual. The ideas and advice offered by these documents, together with the extensive choice of approaches, only served to promote anxiety and confusion as each had a different viewpoint. However, the following quotations helped me to make a personal statement about PSMEd. In *A View of the Curriculum* PSMEd is described:

> the study of personal relationships, moral education, health education, community studies and community service, all provide one range of context in which such development may be furthered. Careers education and guidance, preparation for working life, work experience, an introduction to the environmental, economic and political concerns likely to face any adult citizen, all provide another source of great importance. (DES, 1980, p.2)

This helped me with the scope and possible content areas with which PSMEd curricula could be concerned.

With regard to the way of teaching, the Schools Council's *Developing Health Education* described the method of working in groups:

> Group work methods are particularly appropriate for those subjects forming part of the Personal and Social curriculum. Within those subjects is a need for the students to acquire knowledge and understand its relevance to them, to consider their feelings and values, and to apply their enlarged knowledge and understanding to the choices and decisions they have to make. (Schools Council, 1980, p.152)

Thus I was able to define both the context and the methodology in my approach to developing a PSMEd course.

At this point I felt able to formulate a list of aims which could be open to discussion. These were similar to those of Button (1974), whose philosophy was one with which I could identify, and which would encourage the development of self-awareness and identity out of the chaos of adolescent feelings experienced by many young people. My stated aims were:

(a)   To develop and encourage self-awareness.

(b)   To encourage a sense of social and moral responsibility, in both a willingness and a capacity to understand and help other people.

(c)   To help the development of opinions and values in preparation for a full caring life in the community as young adults.

(d)   To offer information that may be useful in future lives at home and at work.

Together with an interested group of staff, who were in sympathy with both my basic philosophy and aims, I drew up a diagram (Figure 9.1) which showed organizational considerations in the initial stages; it is adapted from Shipman *et al.* (1974). I intend to look at some of these factors in more detail later.

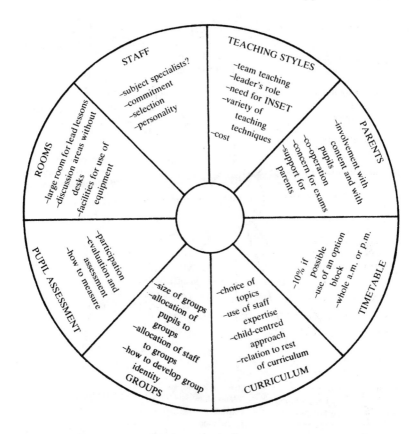

**Figure 9.1:** **Issues for staff discussion at the outset of the innovation**

We also looked at areas of content that might be considered. While taking into account the findings of such research as John Balding's at Exeter University (Balding, 1978), I decided to ask the staff (i) what topics they thought would be relevant and (ii) what they could offer personally. This decision was based on the thought that if they felt confident with the materials, the exposition of it might be more adventurous. Figure 9.2 shows the outcome of that particular meeting. The topics suggested were rationalized into eight units, each lasting about half-term – the exception being comparative religions which nobody felt capable of tackling at that point.

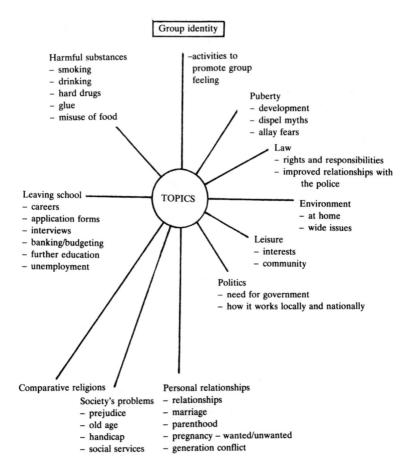

**Figure 9.2:   Outcome of a staff meeting to formulate a curriculum**

Armed with these introductory papers, meetings took place with staff, parents and governors, all of whom gave their approval to start in-depth planning. Staff committed to the work met regularly and began to make decisions about content and organization. Consultations took place with academic faculties to ensure that there was no duplication. We hoped to take a child-centred approach, which we felt would generally reinforce an examination approach.

Having set the scene for the innovation, I should like to expand on those areas of Figure 9.1 which tended to promote 'values' questions. These are team teaching, group work and evaluation.

## Team teaching

For the reason previously stated, I chose this way of working and rejected the cross-curricular or modular approaches described in Devon LEA's document 'Personal, Social and Moral Education' (1982). As well as being unable to provide maximum support, these other methods seemed also to make slower the whole process of climate-setting, which I felt to be of paramount importance if young people were to feel comfortable with their tutor and their peers.

In team teaching, as I envisaged it, the tutors would work as part of a team, remaining with the same group of pupils for the whole course, and would be responsible for teaching all the material. The concept of team teaching originated, in the 1950s, in the United States. I shall comment on some of the characteristics which were found by Freeman (1969) to be common to many team teaching courses.

(i) *Responsibility is given to two or more staff, and there is a consequent co-operative approach to teaching*
Eight or nine tutors formed the Education for Personal Responsibility (EPR) team, and different people accepted responsibility for different units, having autonomy in planning, though the materials and methods were subject to the scrutiny of the rest of the team. This would prove to be quite an ordeal as the following tutors' comments showed:

It was quite hair-raising at first – once the standard is set, you can't fall below – I'd feel that I was letting myself and others down.

Although still a super team, we still judge and evaluate each other – I don't like leaving room for criticism.

It gives support, but you become aware of your limitations.

Thus this approach put teachers under a lot of pressure to fulfil expectations. However, we agreed as a team that support should be built into the programme through weekly meetings. These were used for feedback, discussion and preparation. I do not think any of us realized just how valuable these would be when we began. The support engendered is obvious from the following comments:

Super, we discuss problems and successes.

There is too much isolated teaching elsewhere.

Teachers should stand up and be counted – it's easier in a team.

Particularly good for new teachers – being able to learn, gain confidence, hear from others.

My own personal feelings are that the support helped the tutors when they felt threatened, and encouraged their own personal and professional development.

(ii)   *There arise opportunities for devising new methods of teaching and learning*
I felt that the tutor's role in EPR was that of facilitator, and as such that they should not take up much of the talking time – a very different perception of teaching from the traditional didactic one, as stated in this 'revealing' comment:

It's the reversal of normal teaching – teachers listen to pupils!

The work of small groups will be discussed in the next section of this chapter but we learned that in order to maintain motivation and concentration within large group presentations, stimuli must be varied, interesting, comprehensible and constantly changing. This we gathered from pupils in our 'review' sessions where they are allowed to comment on the course, both in content and method:

Whan we're in the hall, you talk at us – and we get bored and switch off.

We also learned that the average concentration span is about ten minutes listening to one person. Thus our large group presentations are becoming more varied with the minimum amount of talk.

In the same way, we no longer have outside speakers as there are few people who can hold the concentration of a large group of adolescents. Instead we use the 'visitor technique', which can be referred to in Leslie Button's *Developmental Group Work with Adolescents* (1974). Here the small group has the corporate responsibility for preparing for the visitor, and its members may have to research into the topic. This has an added bonus that as well as learning cognitively, the group also has the opportunity to practise social skills.

Thus, for example, when dealing with local government, instead of inviting a town councillor to 'talk', we invite eight councillors, one to each group, to answer the groups' questions. In this way children learn what is important to them. However, in order not to miss vital information and concepts the tutor helps with the preparatory work.

(iii)   *The use develops of ancillary staff of various types*
During the early days of EPR the schools' police liaison officer joined the team. Devon's policy of liaison officers is an attempt to break down the traditional authority barriers between the police and some young people. The officer moves from group to group, meeting the pupils. He also contributes to the units covering law and its related topics.

The concept of having a policeman in the course might seem to provide a conflict in values and an inhibiting factor. He is in fact a local person who is very much involved with youth work and who relates very well to young people. He tries to de-mystify the apparent restrictiveness of the law and attempts to promote a positive attitude in young people. From the pupils' point of view our liaison officer is certainly seen as an ally, but I am not sure that the traditional authoritative image is dispelled if the following pupil's comment is considered:

Oh yeah, but he's different isn't he?

The local youth leader and two school nurses are at present also involved – their knowledge and expertise is invaluable and their relationships with the pupils have subsequently improved.

As this course is very much about personal development, it possibly has more links with parents than many other curriculum subjects. Parents are invited to a meeting in the term prior to their child entering the fourth year and are told of what the course involves, both in content and ways of working. Several parents have offered expertise and advice in the careers unit – e.g. parents who are local employers come in to 'mock' interview pupils in their small groups.

We have also had parents asking if they can take part in some of the sessions. This has proved a delicate area as one particular, very caring, religiously based group asked to be allowed into the small groups to put the 'parental' point of view about adolescent sexual behaviour. This posed a 'value' question for the team. The 'parental' view was acceptable, but the 'religiously biased parental' view might have presented an unbalanced picture. As a group we talked out all the issues and finally agreed that parents could be invited to take part in the lead lessons, but not in small group discussions – which were the private province of the pupils.

Any question of a similar nature is always difficult and there are no clear answers to give to the learner. However, team teaching allows discussion of all possible alternatives. We are by no means a group who share the same set of values and thus there is constant dialogue and every 'value position' is challenged by one of us.

## Group work

One of the most important factors to emerge from the EPR programme is that of group work. During the past few years the value of group work and participatory teaching methods has been increasingly recognized.

Groups allow an enriched reservoir of knowledge and experience. They can be a forum for ideas and opinions to be aired, providing a creative atmosphere for the development and exploration of options. A safe and secure environment is essential, however, if these aims are to be effected.

Before discussion of the work we do in groups and its

implications, I should like to describe a theoretical model of experiential learning which has helped me to understand the 'process' of learning.

## The experiential learning cycle

This is taken from Pfeiffer and Jones (1983), who describes this type of learning as 'when a person engages in some activity and critically abstracts some useful insight from the analysis and puts the result to work' (p.4). It can be diagrammatically represented as in Figure 9.3.

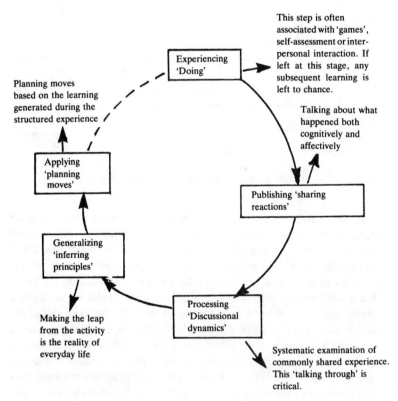

**Figure 9.3:** **Experiential learning cycle**

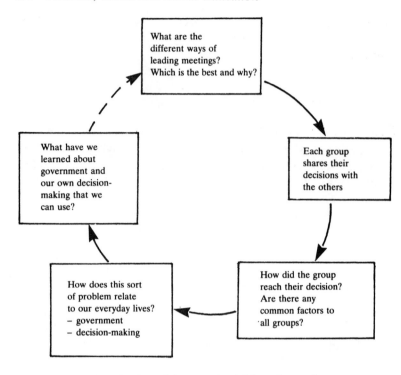

**Figure 9.4:    An application of the experiential learning cycle**

In order to demonstrate this at a practical level I should like to describe an activity which we use in the 'Politics Unit'. The aim of this is to introduce the idea of a need for government. We use a simulation which we have devised called Constitution Island, which consists of a map of an island with its landscape clearly defined. Each small group of four to five pupils represents the survivors of a plane crash. They have to form a new society and take decisions which will make it work effectively. They are confronted with a series of questions – e.g. 'When you have meetings as a group, how are they going to be conducted – through an elected leader or through a committee?'; 'A member of the group is found stealing fish from other people – what are you going to do with him?'; 'Do you need any other rules?' I will now repeat the 'experiential learning cycle', showing the way learning takes place, from the first question cited (Figure 9.4). This model has helped in understanding the need for 'debriefing' in order to ensure that learning has taken place. It also helps answer the many criticisms that are often levelled at similar teaching techniques as being simply 'games' or 'fun activities'.

*Group composition*

We did not initially realize that this factor would be important in the bonding of the group. In the first year of the course the tutors determined the groups but an end-of-year evaluation session with the pupils suggested that bonding would have been easier and quicker if the groups had been friendship based.

In the second year a sociogram was used but was still not altogether successful as we produced 'good' and 'difficult' groups (where 'good' was defined as 'forthcoming, talkative, interested' and 'difficult' as 'disruptive or very quiet, where discussion was not easy to achieve').

We finally came to a compromise of 'friendship' groups which were carefully discussed with tutors, and this had the advantage of 'diluting' the would-be disruptives and ensuring that the more quiet pupils were not all in one group, but were with at least one friend.

The fact that we had split the 'disruptives' added to their sense of failure and 'always being picked on', and we have had to work hard at giving them lots of support. What has happened in my own group is that they are often the most vociferous, able to discuss and, therefore, are valuable contributors to the group.

*Group work methods*

Within small groups the role of the tutor is that of facilitator and organizer, enabling interactions between pupils, rather than between pupils and teacher. In order to develop an atmosphere where opinions and ideas of a personal nature were to be expressed openly, the methods we used could not be the traditional didactic ways, but must include a variety of approaches aimed at stimulating the pupil at both a cognitive and effective level. Some of these participatory activities include brainstorming, role play, action research, games and simulations, self-awareness checklists and discussion.

*Discussion*

This is a very important aspect of our work and, through it, we attempt to help young people explore new concepts and opinions. The tutor's role is crucial and we regularly face dilemmas of a moral, value-laden nature. Again the weekly support group and regular INSET sessions have provided a focus for developing strategies and policies on certain issues.

The 'neutral-chairperson' approach adopted by the Humanities Curriculum Project (see Gajendra, 1980), and which we felt was important, seems not to be as value free as perhaps was intended. The fact that no teacher comment is made may lead pupils to feel that all is acceptable. At the other extreme, 'telling' them what to think or how to behave has also been found not to work either.

My thinking about this issue has changed since the start of the course, and I feel that Pring in *Personal and Social Education in the Curriculum* (1984) has a point in what he describes as 'universal values' (p.6). I feel that we have a duty to offer some guidelines, though I would hope that it is not as prescribed as previously seems to have been the case. Therefore, in my introductory 'talk' about EPR I state to pupils my basic way of life:

If my actions or words are going to hurt another person or myself, then I think again.

This seems to work well for me and is what I would call a 'universal value'. I have been challenged by the pupils, however – e.g. 'What about swearing – that doesn't hurt anybody?' I then have to point out that some people are offended or hurt by bad language. As a team we have frequently discussed our response to pupils' questions – 'What do you think?' – and perhaps the following statements from tutors will show some of our thinking:

I avoid saying anything at all which could be taken as my opinion, unless I make it quite clear that it *is* my opinion.

The standards [of behaviour] I display are *my* standards. They are challengeable, but I'm not prepared to lower them.

A specific difficulty is highlighted, thus:

On abortion, I almost went to the other extreme to overcompensate.

In answer to the criticism that there are some children who want to be told how to behave, our feelings are that the only 'real' behaviour is that which the children have internalized for themselves having been given the chance to explore their attitudes, and that if this has not happened, questioning will take place at some later stage. Thus we try to present a wide range of alternatives, allowing discussion of the merits and demerits of each, without setting ourselves the aim of 'changing' attitudes.

A measure of whether we achieve this can be seen from the following pupil comments:

It didn't frighten you, but made you think more.

They give you both sides of things, so that you can make your mind up.

You know most of it anyway, but it makes it clearer.

*Group work effects*

As a conclusion to this part of the chapter I should like to stress that group work is not an easy way of teaching, as it can be a fundamental challenge to the whole approach of some teachers towards young people, and a challenge to the ethos of the school itself. For instance, the team found the new way of working quite difficult at first:

To be successful, you have to change the traditional image of the teacher.

Traditional teaching means keeping a distance – EPR shows sympathy/empathy.

The need to build *mutual* trust and respect between tutor and group became apparent very early in the development of the course:

> We endeavour to get close to the children – build up a relationship of trust.

> On some occasions, I still have to stand back and deal with difficult children – I feel upset if it happens in EPR.

The process of learning is helped through changing the balance of control – from the traditionally teacher-controlled lesson, it becomes:

> Much less of me up-front – more of a co-operative venture

where there is a sharing of responsibility.

As positive as these points are, I have felt disappointed that the way of working has not extended with other areas of the curriculum:

> I try to make other lessons as much like this as possible, but it's quite difficult, e.g. chairs and tables.

From the pupils' point of view group work is welcomed especially with a change in the pupil–teacher relationship:

> They try to understand our feelings.

> They treat us as equal, responsible, mature, intelligent people.

> Old (non EPR) teachers have seen it all, done it all, are not interested in us.

This poses another question of 'conflicting' treatment in other areas of the curriculum. What happened was that some of those teachers who were not involved in EPR began to criticize the new ways that we were using. We seemed to be promoting a threatening position. We tried to counter this by inviting staff to take part in some sessions in order to get to know about the course. Some took up the offer and my colleagues assured me that the scepticism gradually disappeared.

A greater source of conflict came with the experience of shared control by the pupils. They were allowed to 'question' in this area of the curriculum, and wanted to do this elsewhere. At an anecdotal level an example of this was a girl asking:

Why do we have to learn Pythagoras' theorem, Miss?

Not knowing the reason, I went to the staffroom where I received the following responses:

Maths teacher 1 – Because it's in the exam syllabus.
Maths teacher 2 – Because the head of department says so.
Head of department – Everyone who is going to construct a wall with a corner needs Pythagoras.

I think that Pythagoras has 'failed' hands down, but it does raise the question of why and what we are teaching in our schools, and also how much negotiation should take place between teacher and taught.

After the 'Politics Unit', which largely consisted of simulation activities, the fifth year confronted the head teacher, who led the unit, saying that it was pointless giving them the tools to make decisions, if they were never allowed to use them.

This accelerated the establishment of a School Committee, which we had been considering for some time. The head had certain doubts, which appeared justified when the first topic was 'school uniform'. However, the suggestion was that it should *not* be abolished, but that the royal blue sweater be changed to navy – a most welcome change on the part of both parents and pupils. Thus anxiety about the 'shared' control was dispelled and the School Committee has become a viable and important body within the school, making comments about policy and offering suggestions about the school's organization to the extent that they talk with candidates for new teaching posts when they come for interview. Thus work in small groups, which at first seemed to offer an appropriate way of working, has provoked thought and problems for pupils, tutors and the school community as a whole.

Much of the conflict for the staff has been dealt with through weekly support groups and regular INSET sessions which are open to all members of staff, and to which all but five members of staff came on the last occasion. Thus the work and methods undertaken in EPR (and more recently in tutorial periods in the lower school) are shared and understood by the majority of the staff. This aspect of INSET is part of staff development and its value is admirably stated by Anita Higham:

> Staff development work is not for the faint-hearted or the autocratic; it leads to questioning, stimulating, demanding staff with increased calls for consultation and involvement. If properly understood, it leads to strengthened leadership and greater professionalism. (Higham, 1982, p.118)

*Assessment*

I was determined at the outset that EPR would be non-examinable, in that my aims could not be achieved in pass–fail terms. What made me more adamant was the fact that, as a secondary school, we were accepting 75 per cent of the catchment area who at 11+ felt failures. To condemn them to failure in personal, social and moral education seemed unpardonable.

Also in this changed way of working Ian Cunningham more than adequately stated our problem:

> Experiential learning . . . assumes that students can learn for themselves without the necessity for didactic teaching. Once the role of the teacher has changed in this context, it has implications for assessment. If learners take control of their own learning, to then expose them to traditional modes of assessment may be inappropriate. (Cunningham, 1983, p.62)

Through regular feedback sessions with the pupils we found that they felt the course had intrinsic value which seemed immeasurable. They were certain that it should not be traditionally examined:

> It's not fair that we should have an exam on or about ourselves and our responsibilities.

> If you failed, it would be like failing at life.

However, there was a feeling that it should have some form of assessment that would give it credibility 'like Maths and English'.
From the team's point of view we were by no means all in

agreement that it should be non-examined. We ranged from

> You could argue that to put in so much deserves a qualification.

and

> It would be totally inappropriate to EPR, but I am convinced that the more able could sit an exam based on its strength.

to

> It would change the nature of EPR radically.

and

> It would inhibit the children and cause anxiety in the children and possibly the staff.

However, despite continuing debate, we still have not resorted to an examination. I, personally, am sceptical about available examination courses, e.g. AEB's 'Lifeskills' and more recently the Scottish Certificate of Education's 'Social and Vocational Skills', as they tend to place emphasis on skills which is only one aim of PSMEd courses.

After long discussions, we agreed on an assessment at the end of every unit, and it involved a large element of self-assessment. This form and method of assessment proved unwieldy, and has been modified to a twice-yearly assessment which provides for discussion and negotiation between tutor and pupil, after which a report is written to be included in their school report. No grades are given and all comments are positively expressed.

This method of assessment is not yet perfect – it is still in a crude form. With the introduction of the new 14–19 initiatives (TVEI, CPVE) and profiling, more sophisticated techniques are becoming available, and I hope that EPR assessment will evolve into an even more meaningful form.

**Conclusion**

From this chapter it can be seen that the whole area of PSMEd is full of 'value' questions and these will change as society changes. Therefore, dialogue between those teachers involved in such work should be continuous, and approaches should be adapted to the changing needs of our young people. My colleagues are working at developing their skills, and while acknowledging that it is hard work, they are appreciative of the benefits to the pupils and to their own professional development. Their trust in me and unfailing support have helped this innovation which has proved so stimulating. Two comments from pupils have made it all worthwhile for me:

> I've begun to learn what sort of person I am, and to know how to approach adults so that they see the best in me.

> You don't learn in this subject – you just don't forget.

# DISCUSSION

Leslie Button's work is clearly on the 'feeling' and development of social skills pole of Weinreich-Haste's dimensions outlined in Chapter 4. Button finds the 'thinking' approach often to be found wanting, in that it fails to affect the behaviour of young people, to enter their life-style. For him the promotion of a caring, supportive climate within which people can explore their social abilities, attitudes, behaviour and relationships is at the heart of peronal, social and moral education. The focus is very much on the personal qualities and reactions of the young people involved rather than a more abstract consideration of material drawn from other lives and experience.

Button was obviously much impressed by the way in which personal growth took place in the participants of his research study into friendship. It seemed that having an adult provide an opportunity for the young people to reflect on their experiences, and yet without the adult being in some teaching or authority relationship, enabled the participants to help themselves and each other. The lessons drawn from this experience have consciously affected the group work approach. There is still an emphasis on people carrying out inquiries for themselves. Button liked to say that we can protect ourselves against everything but our own discoveries, and he saw first-hand inquiry as a potent means of people making knowledge their own and having it affect their lives. This alters the role of the teacher which he saw as moving to a greater level of partnership or as facilitator rather than a didactic position. He recognized that this shift could be an uncomfortable one for some teachers and placed great emphasis on teacher preparation with the teachers experiencing the sort of activities and undertaking the same inquiries that their pupils might be encouraged to use. He hoped that the force of their own discoveries would help them change their own attitudes and teaching behaviour.

All of this personal exploration and reflection is rooted in Button's work in a social context. He saw the first-hand exploration of social relationships as impossible without a context. However, his emphasis on the use of groups was far more than that. In a school context he saw that pupils could make a contribution to each other in this work. He recognized that simply to put children together in one place does not create a group and saw the creation of a supportive atmosphere among the pupils as being vital. This supportive atmosphere is achieved by providing exercises which attempt to 'make concrete some of the abstract concepts like caring and concern'. It is interesting to note that these activities involve a degree of physical contact which seems very like Peter Kutnick's use of physical/sensitivity exercises to provide a basis for the development of co-operative relationships. It is often precisely the same exercises which create a sense of unease in those people who see this as inappropriate behaviour in a school context. This can result in sharp polarizations about this approach in members of the same school staff.

Despite these reactions, the physical exercises remain as part of a process designed to engender a supportive climate between pupils. Within this climate Button hopes that pupils can provide feedback for each other about social skills and also provide encouragement and space for an individual to change his/her behaviour. Again there is an emphasis on the concrete social situation of the classroom to provide the experiences which Button sees as necessary for personal, social and moral development. He is interested in the personal growth of young people in a direct and sharply focused way.

Sue Plant in Chapter 9 describes the way some of these ideas have been incorporated into a course entitled 'Education for Personal Responsibility'. This is a wide-ranging course covering law and politics as well as more personal development, and it is mainly at a process level that she has drawn on Button's ideas.

This is most clearly seen in the use of small groups and the relationship of the tutor to these groups. The emphasis in the small groups was upon actively involving each member as much as possible. The small size of the groups obviously helped but the teaching approaches also stressed participation and included self-awareness checklists, role play and action research. The 'visitor technique' described by Button was used as a way of introducing information from a knowledgeable person in a way which left the responsibility firmly in the pupils' hands. The teaching style described is similar to that outlined by Button and involves a shift to a more facilitative role. Sue Plant describes the problems in knowing what stance she and the other teachers should adopt. This has obviously been a question which has had to be constantly re-examined. The great strength of the situation which she describes, however, is the team teaching approach with the opportunity for debriefing at the end of each unit of work. This has enabled the teachers to examine and question their stances in relationship to the different topics in concert with other colleagues similarly engaged. This is a rare occurrence in schools and the honest and supportive atmosphere which was clearly promoted by these meetings must be helpful in providing checks and balances on any particular individual approach. The quotations from the children taken from the evaluation document suggest that they appreciate the opportunity to consider an issue in depth and then to be able to form their own opinions. It would seem that this course was having other effects on the school, not least in providing a contrast to some of the more didactic styles prevalent, and resulting in pupils questioning the curriculum in other areas of the school.

A particularly interesting outcome was the pressure which was initiated by the pupils and which resulted in, or perhaps speeded, the formation of a School Committee.

Button sees his work as having a clear value position in aiming to foster caring concern with students by encouraging them to be a resource for each other in personal exploration and change with the overall goal of creating a caring community in the classroom and school. Questions which arise about this attempt include whether the teacher can maintain a genuine openness to the results of students' exploration and inquiry and sensitively incorporate these into the programme while maintaining the planned developmental programme which Button stresses. Is the next step guided by the teacher's preconceived directions or responsive to what is concerning the children in the here and now? Are peer groups able to achieve a supportive atmosphere for individuals to perhaps explore new roles or can peer pressure operate against the best interests of the individual in a press for conformity to group norms? It should be noted that the questions of teacher direction or not and the power of the peer group arise in any educational endeavour but seem particularly important when the main focus is the personal development of the child. Here again questions arise as to the values exemplified in the programmes and those, say, in the family. Are they similar and who decides which should prevail? For example, what if a family values obedience to clear-cut religious or cultural traditions for an individual student who is working within a peer group of students from family traditions which favour allowing young people to form their own values in an area, following a responsible consideration of the issues? Many of the contributors to this book stress the desirability of encouraging children to examine issues in a way which stresses autonomy and freedom of choice. But these values may not be shared by people who place emphasis on obedience and conformity to certain traditions. Even if such an open exploration is valued on educational grounds, there are still sensitive areas to be considered. What of the child who, because of family turbulence or other reasons, comes to the school with difficult personal and interpersonal worries? These programmes are likely to raise issues which may be distressing or painful for the individual. There is a stress in the teaching style advocated on the child being 'invited' rather than coerced into such exploration. While this principle of voluntariness is crucial if the dignity of the person is to be respected, there needs to be a close scrutiny of how this is to be achieved in a situation in which children are compelled by law to attend and where the teacher is seen in a powerful authority role. This raises the question of whether schools are the appropriate places to raise such issues. Some might argue that only within a clearly voluntary situation is this possible.

Also even if pupils genuinely choose to share to explore their real concerns, is it appropriate for a teacher to provide such an opportunity? Button would see this as an appropriate role for the school and argues that it is part of the pastoral concern of teachers. Children who are in any kind of distress come to school bearing that distress whether teachers choose to recognize it or not. Such burdens may be exacerbated by chance remarks, unwittingly made, and will almost certainly interfere with learning across the board. Are teachers willing and able to cope with these consequences which are part of the everyday reality of schools? For Button the involvement of teachers in a vigorous in-service programme before undertaking this work is very necessary if they are to be properly equipped to deal with these areas. This need for training and continuing professional support is shown in both Button's and Plant's chapters.

A different concern might be that by concentrating on the individual and his/her concerns this might distract attention from a consideration of wide social and moral issues. Button sees the supportive groups which he aims for to have a Janus-like quality. They provide an arena for personal exploration and support but also provide a platform for the children to move out from and into the wide social world to conduct the 'action research' which is an integral part of the process. It is likely that such a cycle of research and reflection will reveal inconsistencies, say, between the stated aims of the schools and their practice, but such tension or even conflict can be seen as helpful for a dynamic institution. The posing of questions can be seen as crucial to a view of education as dialogue.

Such a view of education makes evaluation of these programmes very difficult. Since the explorations are open-ended, there is no straightforward appraisal of the achievement of pre-ordinated and carefully specified skill areas such as might be possible in other programmes based in different educational traditions. However, difficult or not, evaluation of these programmes is vital. Such research will need to pay attention to the impact of the training programme and the teachers' attitudes, knowledge and skills since these factors are vital in ensuring that the necessary climate of support is realized and the individual needs of the students are properly taken into account. This is particularly important since much conventional teacher preparation does not address itself to the principles of student-centred and experientially based learning represented in this work.

A further area for research is the impact of these programmes on the students themselves. This will need to be sensitive to the personal issues involved. In Chapter 9 Sue Plant discusses the role of conventional examinations in her work and reports the view of one of her students who said, 'If you failed, it would be like failing at life'. It could be that a way forward here would be to use a profile approach which could form a part of the learning process for each student and also a means of assessing the impact of the programme for the teacher/researcher. Although it is important to monitor the affects of these programmes on a wide range of children since they are proposed as general curriculum approaches, it is necessary to pay particular attention to their impact on children who are experiencing unhappiness or difficulty in their lives.

Such evaluations, if sensitively and imaginatively handled, should illuminate and refine the teaching process as well as providing evidence of effectiveness for all those considering the value of these approaches with PSMEd.

# Section E
# Other Approaches

# INTRODUCTION
# TO CHAPTER 10

Health Education has a unique place within the overall task of promotion values. At one level it is a curriculum subject – very specific in the ground to be covered. At another level, it is all-embracing, embodying whatever counts as contributing to 'the good and the happy life'. The vacillation between the specific and the general meanings is partly a political matter – there is a ring of empirical respectability about the ways in which we might promote health, particularly physical health. That seems relatively non-controversial, and therefore the Health Education Council is a large and significant provider of funds for curriculum development. On the other hand, it soon becomes apparent that, beneath this apparent 'value neutrality', matters of considerable moral importance lurk – values masquerading as non-controversial facts.

John Balding has in the past few years been directing a project at Exeter University School of Education, financed by the Health Education Council, that reflects this controversial and open-ended nature of the area and that, at the same time, has to translate the issues raised into curriculum practice. Chapter 10 introduces us to the problems.

# 10  Health education

*John Balding*

## Introduction: Health as a contested concept

Within the area of personal, social and moral education, Health
Education appears to be the most distinct and definable
component; the results of such education may even be measurable,
since health-related behaviours are measurable (Balding, 1985a).
However, this tangible appearance may be an illusion. Philosophers
would describe health as 'an essentially contested concept', which
means that for however long a group of people might debate its
meaning, they would not arrive at a common interpretation because
of the nature of the values which it incorporates.

My experience over several years as a teacher and researcher
working with pupils/students, teachers, parents, administrators and
health care professionals has made it abundantly clear that people
can have widely different views of what is meant by Health
Education in schools. A selection of interpretations is as follows:

*Health Education* – teeth and nits and all the dirty bits, i.e.
matters of physical health and of hygiene.

– the Big Five: drugs, smoking, alcohol,
unwanted pregnancy and sexually
transmitted diseases, i.e. an exploration
of those areas of behaviour which can
lead, without proper care, to
consequences that are personally or
socially unwanted.

– sex education, i.e. a more positive

emphasis upon one aspect of personal relationships that include emotional and moral considerations as well as physical.

- normal growth and development, and personal relationships, i.e. a more embracing view of what it means to be and to grow as a person that provides a background to more specific prescriptions for health-related education.

One can see here, therefore, how health education can refer to many things from the relatively uncontroversial matters of physical health to wider, more controversial matters that go beyond physical to mental and moral well-being.

Hence the World Health Organization (WHO) continues to draw attention to three components to health: *social, physical* and *mental,* although an early definition of health by the WHO, which indicated that 'good health' was a state of total social, physical and mental well-being and not merely the absence of disease, did not survive for very long. This was not surprising as it defined everybody as 'unhealthy' for almost all of their lives. For many the concept of health or 'wholeness' also demands a spiritual component, and the triangular model (Figure 10.1) often used to help a debate on health gains thereby a central element. It should be noted that many, including myself, who engage in the 'essential contest' of the concept of health, struggle even more with the concept of the spirit, although they may be ready to accept its presence in the interpretation of others.

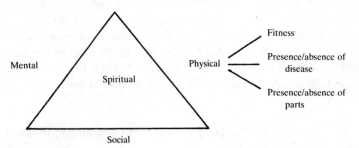

**Figure 10.1: Components of health education**

## Health education or health promotion?

The values embodied in health education are reflected in the way in which the practice of health education can, and does, benefit from the support of health authority personnel. In particular many health authorities include a health promotion service for the community and part of this concentrates on supporting school work. The title of Health Promotion Officer is relatively new and is replacing that of Health Education Officer.

Many teachers would be ill at ease with the subject title Health Promotion rather than Health Education because, for many, health education presents a moral dilemma, namely whether it should provide a balanced and unbiased view of health issues from which the individuals can make up their own minds or whether instead particular approval should be attached to certain behaviours over others. In health promotion the direction of the messages is understood and the advantages of 'good' health behaviour can be emphasized along with the disadvantages of the 'bad' health behaviour; any information in favour of the 'bad' direction receives little or no emphasis, or is totally undermined by powerful argument.

## The practitioner's view of health education

One way of clarifying what is meant by health education is to identify the main areas of interest which fall under that label. The several curriculum development projects have, over the past decade, focused on specific areas to be addressed within the school's curriculum. Trefor Williams, now based at Southampton University, has been a major force in promoting the movement in health education at the levels of infant school, primary school, secondary school, further education and in initial teacher education through a series of projects funded by the Schools Council and the Health Education Council. The areas identified by his projects include:

(1)    personal health, body management and human biology;
(2)    food selection;
(3)    growth and development from childhood through adolescence to adulthood;

(4)  relationships;
(5)  education for parenthood;
(6)  community health;
(7)  the environment in which we live;
(8)  safety and first aid.

Williams's most recent thinking within the current Health Education Council Primary Schools Project, in an attempt to provide a simplified focus, has been to identify three components for health education practice. These are a *physical* health component, a *social* component (which focuses on a young person's capacity to form and sustain satisfactory relationships with others) and, thirdly, an *environmental* component. Williams's views have been shaped by continuous contact and debate with colleagues and others from grassroots level to cross-cultural researchers.

### Formal vs informal curriculum influence

As the time spent in schools is a major environmental experience in the development of young people it is clearly praiseworthy for a school to examine critically its total effect on the healthy development of its pupils/students. Not only is the declared curriculum content an issue for review, but probably an even more significant issue is the way the institution is organized and the effects this has on the pupils on shaping attitudes and behaviours. The individual may be more permanently affected by regularly repeated experiences of the organization of the school than by what is explicitly taught – for example, the school meals service, the school bus, break-time and lunchtime supervision, the cloakroom provision, assemblies, school records, school administration and school caretaking behaviour may well have a lasting effect on the individual. (One exercise within the current Initial Teacher Education project (1984–6) addresses this aspect of the school under the title of 'The school as a health-promoting institution'.)

As schoolteachers we are more likely to consider declared curriculum content in course work and individual lessons as the legitimate route through to 'teaching' young people about aspects of health rather than the power of the 'hidden curriculum' to be found within a school's organization and environment. However, there is one salutary experience for teachers reluctant to entertain this alternative route, contained as an exercise in the Health Education project 13–18 materials (1980). A large group of teachers participating at an in-service training meeting is divided into smaller groups of about four. Each small group of teachers builds a model of origins of a different health-related behaviour or group of behaviours, for example, addressing the question, 'As a result of what background experience and current constraints and pressures do one's own (or, for example, a fourth-year pupil's) personal hygiene practices depend?' When the findings of the small groups are examined, the same powerful sources of influence are discovered for all behaviours, and the model presented in Figure 10.2 is commonly derived from the exercise.

The powerful components include:

(1)    The home background, and the wider family and socio-economic status.

(2)    The type of locality in which one lives, and its level of resource and amenities.

(3)    The organization of the school and provision of facilities (for example, the presence or lack of hot water, soap, towels, hot-air dryers and the attitude and practices of PE and Home Economics teachers in particular).

(4)    The attitudes and practices of the peer group – what is in fashion?

(5)    The personal income of the individual.

(6)    The pressure of the many messages from the media – in the case of hygiene and grooming practices this is colossal, where individual companies compete with one another for a share in the very large market that they are all promoting.

(7)    The self-concept, self-image and self-esteem of the individual – how do they want to appear to the world? Who do they want to please or displease, and whom do they want to be like?

The foregoing list of powerful influences did not include the planned curriculum, the planned course or the individual lesson as a major source of influence. In the midst of so many powerful and continuous influences how can one hour in the classroom on a particular topic have an impact? Furthermore, to what extent does the health message actually conflict with the values and practices in the pupil's home? (A good example of this can be dietary information, which must often be discordant to pupils' home experience.)

**Consequent health education practice**

This leads us to the conclusion that good health education practice involves the following steps:

(1) The discovery of the levels of health-related knowledge, and the current health practices, of the pupils (Balding, 1985a).

(2) The clarification of priorities for inclusion of different topics in the time available in the planned curriculum of the school (Balding, 1978; Open University, 1981).

(3) The co-ordination of work in different disciplines within the school.

(4) The selection of activities of classes which promote the provision of sound information and clarification of existing knowledge in the pupils. (The quality many individuals value most in a teacher is the capacity to impart knowledge and understanding.)

(5) The selection of further activities which promote feelings about the consequences of actions taken in the light of this knowledge in the present and future life of the pupils (Health Education, 1986; Balding, 1985b; Bloom, 1956).

In points 4 and 5 I draw attention to two levels of learning; cognitive and affective (see Baldwin and Wells, 1979). In reality they can

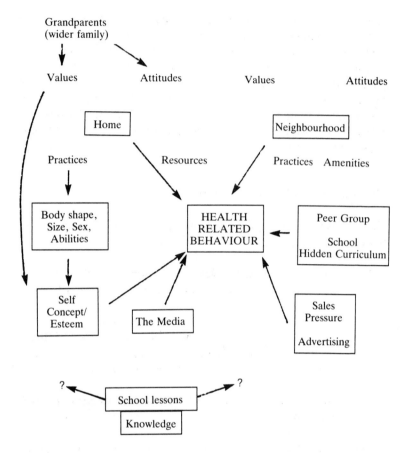

**Figure 10.2:** Schep Model – origins and influence on health behaviour (© John Balding)

never be separated, but different class teaching styles can appear to address one more than the other: the more traditional, didactic styles the cognitive domain; the more modern, consultative styles, the affective domain.

Methods and materials for all the above steps are available and really quite abundant. The key to good practice involves 'listening' to students: what are they doing? (Evans, Rice and Gray, 1981). What do they believe in? What is important to them? (Balding, 1978). What do they know? The listening exercises can involve data collection before a course starts, or be a component of the course through a class activity (Scally and Hopson, 1980; Rice and Gray, 1984) or, better still, both of these; the result should lead to clarification of needs and priorities both for the teacher and for the pupils. The next ingredient is to fit the health message into the perspective of the powerful influences depicted in Figure 10.2: where is it consonant or disconsonant? How will it relate to values at home? What does it do for self-image? How does it fit into the media message? What are the gains and losses for the individual in behaving in the way which the health knowledge would promote?

**Conclusion**

At the core of Health Education is informed decision-making. Linked to this is the extent to which the individual understands who he/she is and how much he values himself, his self-concept and self-esteem. The clarification of values, the building of self-esteem and the fostering of a capacity to recognize pressures, and when appropriate to resist them, are basic features to Health Education in schools. These same features are also bases of all dimensions of personal, social and moral education.

This chapter began with the observation that in PSMEd health education is the most tangible component. It is possible to list identifiable health issues, and then to decide to what extent schools already do, or should, address them. A coherent curriculum can be designed to fit within the existing structure to enhance it and not to undermine it.

In the past decade many good initiatives have been developed to promote and support good practice in schools. Almost all of these have had some financial backing from the Health Education Council.

# DISCUSSION OF CHAPTER 10

John Balding draws attention to one important area for promoting personal, social and moral education, namely health education, which is growing in popularity. Furthermore, in referring to his own work at Exeter University he is able to indicate very practical ways, well tested in schools, of how health education might be translated into curriculum terms.

However, there are in the context of this book very important questions of value, underpinning this and other developments, which are rarely made explicit and which, if unexamined, should give us cause for concern.

First, there is an interesting shift in the meaning of health education from its relatively uncontroversial connections with physical health (ensuring proper nourishment and exercise, and dealing with physical disorders) to mental health, and thence to 'worthwhile living' and finally to moral health. The values implied in physical health are relatively uncontroversial, in that most people would agree on minimal conditions for physical well-being – although even here it is questionable how far a teacher should press for certain kinds of diets without encroaching upon the private world of individuals or families. And even in the area of mental health, there are cases of neuroses and anxieties which people would generally accept as undesirable and thus to be overcome through greater self-understanding and insight. But here, of course, we are entering into difficult territory. There is a distinction to be made between 'mentally healthy' and 'educated' but it is a blurred one – and in blurring this distinction, as often happens, health education tends to extend its territorial claims from health issues to the whole of education. Secondly, and most dangerously, there is a tendency to treat as unhealthy (and thus to be cured) views that educationally are not popular or acceptable.

These difficulties are exacerbated when health education moves from the mental to the moral and to the 'life enhancing' spheres. Health education, often trading on the rather uncontroversial and scientifically based notions of physical health, proceeds with an unwarranted confidence into the area of moral values and ideals for living – areas which traditionally have been explored by teachers from the background of literature, of religious education or of the humanities. Parents may be ready to entrust their children to health education on matters of diet or of cleanliness. But on what grounds should they do so on matters of sexual behaviour or of civic duties? Health educators take on board surreptitiously responsibilities for guiding young people's behaviour and aspirations that many would claim are the responsibility of the family.

The problems to be faced, therefore, by health educationists are:

(1) Ethical: justifying the promotion of what are declared to be healthy forms of life (gregariousness, for instance).

(2) Moral: deciding upon particular approaches to such issues as family planning, contraception, abortion, drug-taking (including alcohol) and bereavement, none of which can be dealt with without the engagement in moral problems.

(3) Political: recognizing the wider social and institutional implications of what is taught, for example, the effects of preparing young people for parenthood upon the institution of the family and indeed upon relationships at home where quite different values might be implicitly promoted. Health education is often apolitical in manner and method, inheriting that view of health education which focused upon the non-political issues of physical health.

There are, of course, good political reasons for remaining thus disingenuous, for 'health education' does as far as politicians and fund providers are concerned still have the ring of political neutrality – concerned with getting rid of nits or of making people more hygienic. If it were realized exactly what goes on under the title of Health Education, it would not be so easy perhaps to get the subject on the curriculum or to obtain research money from the Health Education Council.

# INTRODUCTION TO CHAPTERS 11 AND 12

In an earlier section Leslie Button and Sue Plant described educational programmes *directly* aimed at promoting personal, social and moral education. In Chapters 11 and 12 Alan Morrison and Bryan Stephenson consider two newly evolving and controversial curriculum areas, 'Peace Studies' and 'World Studies', both of which, in the way they are approached by these two authors, *clearly* involve children's personal, social and moral education.

Alan Morrison's chapter 'Educating for peace' first clarifies some of the issues around this most controversial 'subject', then identifies five different 'levels' on which peacemaking is 'a relevant dynamic', i.e. the use of exterminatory weapons, solving of conflict, structural violence, understanding ourselves, transforming relationships. An important section is devoted to the personal development of young people within the school environment – and the kind of school environment (including the kind of classroom, assessment procedures and discipline control) most likely to bring about such development.

Bryan Stephenson starts his account of 'World Studies' by showing how a study of new developments in the life of a child's own village might be made the basis for a detailed, intensive and extensive study of a whole range of moral, social and political issues. The approach to learning would be 'experiential' – with children learning to discuss, to listen, to reflect, to question and to tolerate ambiguities. Another topic, i.e. African famine, is cleverly used to show how these strategies might be learned through working on particular topics; the importance of inter-disciplinary working is also brought out. The author shows clearly how moral questions arise naturally from World Study concerns and also acknowledges that politically controversial issues have to be dealt with in World Studies; ways of sensitively dealing with such issues are discussed at length. He also acknowledges the inevitable risks of such programmes: one is the real danger of eliciting from some pupils, in some classrooms, the very attitudes of 'intolerance, of bigotry or antipathy' that one might be trying to combat; another is the danger that if one obliges children to see that many of the big problems society faces have no easy, straightforward solutions, then attitudes of cynicism, despair or apathy might be engendered – if the powerful, the able, the energetic can't solve them, what's the point of discussing them?

# 11 Educating for peace

*Alan Morrison*

## Introduction: The meaning of peace

One of the key aims of educating for peace should be the expansion of our awareness of what peace actually means. The conventional interpretation is the absence of war or alternatively the condition of an armed truce such as we have between the superpowers at present. We might also refer to certain pockets of circumstance as being peaceful: for example, a secluded pondside on a balmy summer's day, that moment when your children have fallen asleep after a long and demanding day or the bliss of post-coital afterglow. Generally speaking though, these represent brief intermezzi in what is essentially a frenetic and potentially catastrophic world.

So when we speak of educating *for* peace, what kind of peace are we referring to? I would like to propose five separate levels on which peacemaking is a relevant dynamic – although they are also irrevocably intertwined. Starting with the most superficial peacemaking level and moving to the most profound, they are: exterminatory weapons; war and armed conflict; structural violence; understanding ourselves; and transformation of relationships.

## Exterminatory weapons

The abolition of exterminatory weapons represents peacemaking at its most superficial level. These weapons are not a *cause* of strife in the world, they are a symptom of a wider cultural sickness; but because of their massive cataclysmic significance, they are seen as a priority. In terms of the hidden curriculum of the planet just being alive in a world under constant threat of annihilation creates a poignant desperation in young people which is not understood by more hardened adults with logical rationales about national defence systems. For many young people the avoidance tactic is either despair, *laissez-faire* or an ostrich-like nihilism. We fail as educators if we do not encourage an awareness of the huge responsibility which we all share for the future. Instead of regarding the discussion of this subject as a taboo political hot potato, we should be creating an environment in which young people can speak openly about their fears and hopes for the future – not merely in the usual mechanistic consideration for 'employment' and technical and social skills, but seriously to look at whether or not there will be a future at all and the part we can all play in creating it rather than perpetuating the notion that we leave it to others.

An epigram that I always hold close to me is that we do not inherit the world from our forefathers – we borrow it from our children.

**War and armed conflict**

The rejection of war as a means of solving conflict must go hand in hand with the abolition of exterminatory weapons. Even if the latter were a possible current reality, we would still have to cope with the massive cultural norm of warring with an ideological opponent. Even in 'peacetime' nation-states greet visiting heads of state with a show of artillery and military personnel – surely more than a mere show of ceremony.

There have been well over 100 armed conflicts around the world since 1945 with a senseless loss of life and destruction of beauty, usually for a mere flag or ideology. Perhaps we should be questioning nationalistic and patriotic concepts rather than perpetuating them as many schools do. There seems little point in rooting out racism in educational practices when underlying it all is the taken-for-granted notion that Britain is best.

We seem to be unaware of the myriad creative forms of conflict resolution whose roots lie in justice and love rather than in jingoism and conformity. This is not to suggest that the alternative to war is appeasement or passivity which renders us as doormats to be trampled on by any old bully. Those drunk with the power of weaponry fail to recognize that cowardice hides behind a gun rather than standing naked and refusing to be suppressed.

Of course, many factors rise to the surface in this discussion and at the end of the list must surely be the question of whether or not Homo sapiens has an inherited innate violence. This chapter is obviously an inadequate setting for a satisfactory discussion of this vastly important and fascinating subject. However, I would say here that it is impossible to truly educate for peace and humanity if your belief system involves a pessimistic innate-aggressionist view of the species. Yet many teachers hold this view. Surely education under these conditions must become reduced to a system of control and regulation rather than an encouragement to self-development and personal growth.

The last word in this section comes from Ashley Montagu:

> We talk a great deal about love in the Western world, but we do very little about it. We treat the Golden Rule as if it were the exception rather than the rule. We pretend to a creed in which most of us do not believe, reserving its ritual celebration for those occasions when collectively we ostentatiously burn our particular brand of incense before our empty shrines. This is nihilism, it is hypocrisy; it represents the abdication from humanity which leads to dehumanisation.
>
> It is not sports or circuses that will provide the solution to the problems of human aggressiveness, but the restoration to that humanity which all humans possess as a potentiality, through love. The only way one learns to love is by being loved. This is neither a fantasy nor a theory. It is a fact – a verifiable fact . . . Let us always remember that humanity is not so much an inheritance as an achievement. Our true inheritance lies in our ability to make and shape ourselves, not the creatures but the creators of our destiny. (Montagu, 1968, p.16)

### Structural violence

The removal of all forms of structural violence is paramount to the creation of a peaceful world. Structural violence refers to the institutionalized forms of violence that are built into our cultural life. In fact an examination of our culture can lead one into the notion that it is actually founded on violence. Many people may dispute this, so perhaps I should define what I mean by the term 'violence'.

In the same way that a key aim of 'Educating for Peace' should be the expansion of our understanding of the word 'peace', we should also expand our understanding of the word 'violence'. I would like to offer here a threefold definition:

(1) Any action, structure or condition which creates or increases division between people at an individual or group level.

(2) Any action, structure or condition which diminishes the self-worth or violates the personal space of any living creature.

(3) Any action, structure or condition which negatively interferes with the natural environment of the earth and its marine, plant or animal life-systems and habitats.

The traditional coin-in-the-slot view of violence usually concerns physical assault; we rarely open out that invasion of a person's dignity on a physical level to take in the same behaviour on other levels.

One of the main problems is that we are conditioned to accept many situations which involve violence as defined above – we see them as being 'normal', 'part of the human condition' or 'inevitable'. For instance, our whole way of life is dependent on a major portion of the world living in beggary and starvation or without dignified and fruitful working conditions. If we were genuinely serious about creating a peaceful and harmonious planet, we would not find these things merely 'unfortunate', we would proclaim them intolerable and change them!

Other forms of violence which are structured into our cultural heritage are influences such as racism and sexism. The advent of complex legislation in these areas may have made bigotry and prejudice less overt, but these qualities lie at the very heart of our culture and are influencing our young people through many different media. Small boys are still directed towards those culturally acceptable activities and games which will enhance their masculinity and render sensitivity and vulnerability worthless and even humiliating, while their female counterparts are prepared for motherhood and nurturing and discouraged from developing certain traits which are disparagingly referred to as 'tomboyish'. Many of these structural violences are built into our system of education also.

## Understanding ourselves

This fourth level of potential peacemaking involves the process of coming to an understanding of ourselves. Everything which happens 'out there' in human terms is the result of our individual behaviour. We need to understand clearly how our conditioning, education, socio-economic status and ethnicity have shaped the way we view the world and our place in it. Most of us spend very little time on self-assessment – small wonder when we have grown up being constantly defined in other people's terms.

Understanding my limitations, abilities, self-worth, my capacity or incapacity to love and really respect others has a far greater significance for peace than a thousand years of arms reduction talks. This, of course, also has a profound significance for our assessment of school students. How much do we encourage their participation in this?

## Transformation of relationships

This final level is both an area of potential peacemaking in its own right as well as the ultimate goal of the previous four levels. If the right groundwork has been laid, there should be a spontaneous transformation of the ways we relate to one another.

War in microcosm seems to be the order of the day in many of our interactions. I recall vividly an epiphanic moment in Edward Albee's play *Who's Afraid of Virginia Woolfe?* when George and Martha declare 'Total War!' on each other. Another key aim of Educating for Peace is to foster the understanding that what happens at an individual level in our lives is a microcosm of the macrocosm of our global interaction.

On an individual level many of our relationships – with spouses, lovers, children, friends, workmates, emloyees/employers, and so on – seem so often to be based on possession and subjugation. In a truly peaceful society there would be no need for 'battles' of the sexes or so-called 'generation gaps'.

The media have an enormous responsibility here. The newspapers, cinema and TV all serve to reinforce the notion that human existence is a continuous trap of jealousy, covetousness, spite, greed, hatred and deviousness. Admittedly that is the way many people live but we do young people an immeasurable injustice by rendering such a view of life as being somehow representative of normality rather than insanity. But if the greedy person thinks only of money and possessions, the ambitious one only of fame, one does not think of them as being insane, but only as annoying; generally one has contempt for them. But factually greediness, ambition, and so forth, are forms of insanity, although one usually does not think of them as 'illness'.

This has a tremendous significance for those involved with educating young people. What purpose our emphasis on being a 'success', 'getting on', 'making a name for oneself', 'becoming somebody', when all that is at the expense of our ability to respect and care for one another. Only when our educational centres place respect and caring as a priority over academic attainment, physical prowess and rulership abilities will we have the potential for a world free from oppression and exploitation.

## The relationship between peace and education

Schools are communities which cannot be defined in isolation from the wider society and culture which they reflect in terms of values and ethos. So having posited that cultures tend to create the educational centres they need to propagate themselves in conservative terms, and having suggested that our own culture is one which is founded on violence, much of which is unrecognized, how does this manifest itself in our schools with all their significance for a vulnerable and developing young person? To return to a question posed earlier – do our schools promote peace and can they in fact do so when they are a reflection of a violent culture?

To give us a clear dimension on the relationship between the foundation of peace and the educative process in terms of school culture and the transmission of knowledge I would like to examine three areas of school life: the formal curriculum; the personal development of the young person; and the school environment.

## The formal curriculum

During recent years some work has been carried out in the examination of teaching materials for racist and sexist influences. Very often our teaching materials can transmit messages which far outweigh their purported educational content. Many history books portray war in terms of its glorification and are still being published in such a way that they define militarism and the use of force as a means of conflict resolution in terms of heroism and patriotic zeal.

In all subject areas resources can be chosen deliberately, so that they will enhance young people's understanding of the interdependence of peoples and to lead them into issues relevant to the creation of a peaceful society. Many of these issues are, of course, controversial and at this point the spectre of 'indoctrination' raises its head. These issues often can be explored under the heading of what the United Nations calls Disarmament Education or Peace Studies. They are a bona-fide part of education in the formal curriculum but because of the indoctrination connotations many schools are afraid to take them onboard.

Indoctrination is an emotive word. In dictionary definitions it means 'to instruct in any doctrine' or 'to imbue with any opinion'. Naturally there is a strong tradition in education which attempts to guard against the exposing of young people to any kind of overt indoctrination and school subjects such as Religious Education have had to do some soul-searching on this in recent years leading to curriculum changes.

Yet this is a more complex issue than it at first appears. For instance, many schools in a misplaced bid to avoid tainting their students with what our culture would regard as 'undesirable' ideas or beliefs discourage controversial topics of political or social significance from being explored in anything other than a most superficial manner in the school. Now if this stance is coupled with (and it generally is) an emphasis on conformity and obedience in other areas of school life, then there is an implied acceptance of the status quo which in itself is a powerful form of indoctrination, although because it is essentially a conservative (in the broadest sense) action, it is not perceived as such.

Those schools which do make an attempt at an examination of controversial issues will often approach them within the context of a debate. This too can be a counterproductive approach. First, it suggests strongly that there can only ever be two diametrically opposed views on a subject, and secondly, that an issue is judged by its factual presentation only. There are additional factors involved, such as making an issue seem the domain of experts which we judge as mere spectators rather than looking for ways in which we all can assume responsibility for it.

With regard to the peace issue – or more specifically the nuclear issue – the standard approach by many schools is to invite two opposing groups to speak, often involving the Armed Forces or British Atlantic Committee and the Campaign for Nuclear Disarmament or other Peace group. In view of the fact that these issues are so complex and involve many levels of consideration – not least of which is the emotional or psychological level – such an approach is hopelessly superficial.

For instance, when examining the problem of racial bigotry or discrimination, a school would be unlikely to invite speakers from the Anti-Apartheid group and the National Front. Such a format would be considered at best absurd, at worst offensive. We perceive that racial tolerance is something to be truly valued and do not consider there is a need for debate as such. Perhaps schools should extend the same breadth of vision to the issue of peace and not reduce it to a mere academic exercise.

I may seem to be straying from the intended subject of this section, but I view the formal curriculum as more than simply the subject areas of school work. The formal curriculum involves all the *overt* ways that a school transmits knowledge and values in the official school timetable. The important question to ask is: are the issues which threaten peace on personal, social and global levels being brought to school students' attention and fully discussed during subject lessons and tutorial time? However, perhaps an important point to raise here is the question of *who* actually does the deciding of the issues which are important to young people. The issues of consultation, participation and democracy will be looked at in a later section, but having spent the last two years visiting schools on a peripatetic basis and having talked to many young people there can be no doubt that the question of the 'Future' and whether or not there will be one comes near the top of the list. We do our students a profound disservice if we push it to one side for fear of its implications.

**The personal development of young people**

Again in this section I am concerned with the formal curriculum and the overt ways in which schools transmit knowledge and values, although I am here centring on personal development rather than social issues. In fact the way that individuals perceive the world is affected very much by their level of personal development. However, I am not referring to theoretical developmental considerations, but to the question of whether or not young people are being helped explicitly to acquire skills which can help them to become more self-aware and live more harmoniously with other people.

There are a number of such skills and abilities which any educator should be seeking to encourage and develop in the students he/she is involved with (as well as in him/herself). A preliminary list might include:

(i)    *Communication.* This would involve developing listening skills, being able to listen to the 'music behind the words' as well as the language and understanding non-verbal forms of communication given and received.

(ii)   *Co-operation.* This would involve the development of skills in working with other people successfully, not in the often misused sense of co-operation where one team works together but pitted against another team. Educators have a duty to ensure that every individual truly senses his or her interdependence with every other individual on this planet, regardless of colour, nationality, and so on.

(iii)  *Affirmation.* This involves encouraging people to be positive with each other in terms of feedback. So often our interactions (especially in school) tend to revolve around negative criticism rather than as a reinforcement of affirmative values. We should be creating ways of maximizing self-worth rather than devising systems of assessment which generate a lasting sense of failure.

(iv)   *Trust.* One of the primary requirements for an educative environment conducive to healthy development is a condition of trust. However, in order to achieve this there must be a basic matrix which allows for and encourages the expression of vulnerability. So often in our culture there is a pressure to appear 'strong' and 'coping', regardless of whether or not it is a mere façade, which most often it is. This is just as applicable to the educators as to the students. Teachers have to keep up a face in the staffroom to avoid humiliation and ridicule just as much as a student will have to do the same on the sportsfield or in the classroom. Until schools communicate that the expression of vulnerability, 'weakness' and helplessness are not a source of pain and humiliation, trust will be unable to flourish therein, giving rise to a constant source of conflict.

(v) *Conflict resolution.* In view of the fact that conflict on a variety of levels is existent in schools to such a large extent, it is surprising that we do not seriously address ourselves to solving it. Often the solution to conflict in a school is found through authoritarian means which only serves to suppress the problem. Can there ever be a solution to conflict which arises out of assertion of authority and power through the use of inculcation, force and obedience, other than through its dissolution?

The ability to successfully resolve conflicts is a quality that can be both caught and taught in school. Indeed it is vital: people who possess that ability at an individual and community level will have an immeasurable effect on world affairs.

Now many schools and individual teachers may claim that these skills are already being encouraged by them, and on a purely theoretical level that is probably true. However, a closer examination of school culture may show that any *explicit* attempt at the development of these skills can be undermined by values and messages being transmitted *implicitly* in other areas of the life of the school – that so-called 'hidden' curriculum again! This brings us to the kernel of what educating for peace is all about – the environment of learning.

**The school environment**

In this section we are looking at that 'hidden' curriculum, or what I prefer to call 'school culture'. What I am primarily concerned with here is whether or not there is a contradiction between the education which takes place on a didactic level in terms of moral values and that which occurs on an heuristic level. Because we may be most diligent in creating a curriculum which genuinely tries to educate for peace, but if the values explicit in that curriculum are not reinforced by those implicit in the culture of the school, then our hard work will come to nothing.

We must obviously acknowledge that schools are not merely institutions of formal learning, clearing-houses for necessary knowledge or a training-ground for vocational aspirations. Schools have a basic ethos, a set of values to which they aspire and which are supposedly applied to the life of the school.

These would usually include such principles as honesty, respect, the condemnation of bullying, 'love thy neighbour as thyself', care for animals, having a 'Christian' attitude, the importance of freedom, selflessness, equality and the worthiness of democracy. Schools students are *taught* that these principles are paramount. There is almost a piety and sermonesque quality to the way in which their value is imparted as if they were genuinely representative of our way of life. Does this match up with the reality? Are they practised as vigorously as they are preached?

After all, young people have already been presented with a range of contradictions in the wider world, as I have shown concerning society's purported antipathy to violence. For them there is already a discrepancy between the 'caught' and the 'taught'. They understand adult hypocrisy only too well with its condemnation of minor assault and condonation of warfare and weaponry. Honesty as a value has a hollow ring to it before they put a foot inside the school gates. 'Do as I say – don't do as I do' has been their main experience of adult 'morality'.

Turning our attention to the school, there are three main areas of the school environment which can be examined to check out whether or not the values mentioned previously are reinforced by the students' school experience.

## The classroom

Although there has been some reform in this area, the teacher is still often seen as the fount of all knowledge and the source of all authority. When one person solely on the basis of age and an acquired knowledge and professional status can inveigle one-third of a room for him/herself and a large table while the remaining two-thirds of the room is divided between 40 plus other people and their desks, how can young people fully understand the meaning of equality? Is equality a contagion in such a classroom?

The method of working is also important. Young people need to develop the ability to participate fully in the things that affect their lives, surely one of the essentials of true democracy. If they remain as passive recipients of knowledge, the main lesson they will learn is that their ability to contribute is not valued as highly as their obedience. Many teachers are trying to include the use of groups in lesson-time but this will have little value in terms of shared responsibility and the devolution of power if the students have had no involvement in deciding what they will learn about and how they will learn it. This seems to me to be a very basic exercise in freedom and democracy, yet it is also just about the most challenging and threatening thing that could be suggested to any school staff team. Why should this be so? Shouldn't the seeds of freedom and democracy be sown early?

In order to create a truly democratic society we need people who are fully able to participate and make decisions capably and compassionately. How can people be expected to show initiative, independence, creativity, a capacity for decision-making, an understanding of freedom and an ability to participate in the societal process when the first third of their lives – a time when our capacity to learn is at premium – has been spent on the receiving end of information, knowledge and values which have been organized, processed and assessed by others?

## Assessment procedure

The question to ask in the first place is what are we assessing students *for*? As I stated in the last paragraph, above, if assessment is simply a procedure carried out by other people and in which the person being assessed does not participate, it is an alienating process and ultimately one which can lead to failure. True and human assessment should never involve a straight pass–fail model. The more so when we know that the system we use at present produces more failures in societal terms than successes.

As I have said many times already, schools reflect the wider culture, and that culture is always ready to classify, pigeon-hole, label, stratify and earmark. People cannot, it seems, be seen simply as *who* they are, but rather as *what* they are. With young people we see them in terms of what they are going to become rather than who they are.

There seems to be an unspoken blueprint of how students should 'turn out' when they have concluded their journey on the school conveyor belt. We have a vision of the future finished product. In this there is a reflection of the wider culture's aspirations. A 'normal' and 'healthy' adult is projected as being a person who is patriotic, law-abiding, supports the monarchy, gets married, has children, votes for one of three political parties, holds down a job regardless of its usefulness, morality or potential for fulfilment and has a religion (preferably Christian). Anyone eschewing all these qualities is regarded at best as deviant, at worst as seditious or subversive.

Much of the thrust of school life is devoted, of course, to the process known as 'getting a job'. There is rarely a primary consideration of whether or not the work will be rewarding, altruistic, morally justifiable or socially responsible and useful. If, for instance, a student proclaimed that he or she intended leaving school to become a wandering minstrel, living in beggary and moving from town to town, he or she would be regarded as an educational failure. He or she would not be the subject of boastful talk at a parents' evening. There would be little regard for whether or not he or she would bring joy to himself/herself and others. Whereas if another student announced that he or she had found a job in the packing department of a computer firm which manufactured guidance systems for missiles, he or she would be seen as one of the school's success stories, lucky to have a job at all in these times of recession.

Assessment as such should be seen as a process of *self*-evaluation and we should be providing young people with the tools to carry it through. If a person's formative years are spent constantly being assessed and classified by others, what chance will he/she have to be an autonomous person later in life, free from reliance on an external authority for realistic feedback. Perhaps the question should be raised here: what would happen to our culture as it is presently constructed if it was made up of autonomous individuals who were responsible enough to have little regard for external authority?

## Discipline and control

All schools have a set of rules and regulations which are enforceable. The enforcement of these is a one-way process in the sense that any compulsion will be directed towards the students by the teaching staff, the assumption being that it is principally the former who will transgress. It would, for instance, be unusual if not unthinkable for a school to have a set of regulations worked out between staff and students on the basis of mutuality. Yet surely this would be the obvious melting-pot for the development of true democracy?

Young people are consistently seen as needing to be controlled, and the more their responsibility for their behaviour is removed from them by a controlling authority, the more controls will be needed. Ultimately you finish up with a culture which needs more than a quarter of a million laws on the statute-book to keep people in line, so diminished is their self-regulation and responsibility.

Subordination and subjugation can never be a part of the creative process which should form the core of education. What can be the justification in a school, for instance, in the enforcement of young people to use such titles as 'Sir', 'Miss', 'Mr' or 'Mrs' whenever they address an educator? Admittedly there are areas of our culture where the use of titles constitutes a respect for someone's need for distance and fear of familiarity; but it is usually expected that continued contact will result in such a need being dissolved or, alternatively, there will be a negotiation of the level of contact to be established. Surely, though, this should not apply to the young and developing person who needs real contact and an encouragement to feel part of a community rather than each member being encased in a force-field of separateness? Formality and division, especially on an extended basis, should be seen as symptoms of a diseased and alienating culture which need to be overcome rather than as misplaced symbols of 'respect'. It seems to me that the relationship between student and educator in our schools rarely moves outside the spectrum whose extremes are either rigidly authoritarian or liberally standoffish.

Other ways in which a code of discipline is used as a form of power exertion (rather than to create harmony) involve rulings on many personal habits, clothing, hairstyles and jewellery. If the attention to detail which these rulings often have were being observed in another culture, say, a country behind the Iron Curtain, they would be referred to as totalitarian and unreasonable; but so entrenched is our view of young people from an adultist standpoint that we feel fully justified.

If conduct in school is constantly seen in punitive terms as far as student behaviour is concerned, then the created conditions will be mistrust, fear, disrespect, servility, dishonesty, and so on; but if people in a school community can work together on this problem of how to build a loving and caring community, then the created conditions will be far more conducive to a peaceful and harmonious society.

The uncomfortable truth is that schools, as they are presently structured in terms of discipline and control, cannot truly educate for peace. To educate for peace we have to educate with love. We should not be ashamed of using the notion of loving as the basis of educational process. Love is simply what happens when there is no longer any violence. Having blueprints for how we expect our young to become, the exertion of power, subjugation, submission and the enforcement of false respect are all forms of violence.

Again much of this has arisen out of the widely held belief that human beings are innately violent; but if we are to educate for peace, we have to step outside that trap and think anew, to see human behaviour from a creatively different standpoint.

### Epilogue

There is an enormous fear of the challenge of youth, their frank openness and their doubting of the divine right of authority. Those schools which respond adversely to the challenge of youth are in this respect a mere microcosm of the wider society. Governments also cannot tolerate a questioning, challenging and doubting populace.

Passivity is actually in our culture's interests. How else could vast numbers of people go willingly to work each day in a meaningless and repetitive occupation? How else could millions of working people contribute to an arms industry with its resulting international arms trade which spends as much in a fortnight as the world needs to give every human being a healthy and nourishing life-style? How else could governments and multi-national corporations continue to pollute the oceans and defile the landscape without our acquiescence?

Freedom is in fact an idealized notion in our culture rather than an actuality. The whole of our historical perspective involves the glorification of the struggle to preserve freedom – indeed it is the main justification for the development of exterminatory weapons. It seems paradoxical that we should teach young people that tyranny is wrong and that freedom is something worth fighting for when a powerful message in any school is that those who defy authority will be punished and ultimately will have their freedom taken away from them.

There seems to be quite a gap between the caught and the taught. Uncomfortable as it may seem, we are indoctrinating young people into a lifetime of appeasement and acquiescence to authority – the very qualities for which we criticize totalitarian regimes. The resentment and alienation engendered in young people through this – far from bringing about peace and harmony, an unlikely result of the enforcement of obedience under any circumstances – probably increases the level of tension, separateness and potential for violence in the school and therefore the wider community.

Currently there are many innovations happening in schools: Community Education, Environmental Education, Peace Education, World Studies, schemes for tutorial groupwork, and so on; but exciting and challenging though they may be, they will only be a mere redecoration of the prison walls unless we reverse many of the pathways and re-lay the foundation stones of our education system. Without this change, people will continue to feel powerless to change the destructiveness of our troubled planet.

We should welcome the challenge and energy of our young and allow ourselves to establish a true democracy from the moment a child is born rather than adhering to the idealized notion of a utopia in the future.

# 12   World Studies

*Bryan Stephenson*

A class of ten-year-olds in a primary school are studying changes in their village, particularly those which have occurred during the lifetimes of the older inhabitants. Information has been collected by means of questionnaires and interviews, from maps and other official records. The data is then organized and collated in preparation for a display of the results of the inquiry. From their interviews with the villagers the pupils have become aware that not all the changes which have taken place are judged to be improvements. Reductions in public transport, retail services and local employment opportunities pose problems for some members of the community and the pupils' increased awareness leads to a discussion on the reasons for such changes. They want to know if such developments are inevitable, whether the effects can be predicted and who makes decisions about rural services. Because they recognize that some people are more affected than others, the children are able to identify sectional interests within the community and they consider the extent to which their own needs are met in such things as play-areas and cycling-tracks.

It is at this stage that the pupils are encouraged by the teacher to speculate about further changes which may affect the social and economic life of the village. These projections are set against the pupils' hopes and preferences. The teacher, responding to the interest in the question of who makes the decisions, has arranged a meeting with an officer from the county planning department. This gives the class an insight into policies and regulations, in return for which the planner listens to the results of the survey and to the children's expectations about the development of the village over the next generation. What emerges from this exchange is that there are great uncertainties about the future, but that there are also choices.

A project such as this is not uncommon in many primary and secondary schools and is a good example of the World Studies approach to learning. A significant feature is the active involvement of the pupils at all stages, during which they take decisions and practise many skills of inquiry and communication. Moreover, one crucial element is the importance of their own views, their ideas and feelings, about the environment in which they will grow up. This anticipation of developments in the future, within a geographical context with which they are familiar, arises from a study of the recent past. Through the meeting with the county planner their political understanding will have been improved and the gap between the individual citizen and the decision-making process narrowed.

The role of the World Studies teacher is well exemplified in the account of this village study though it is largely implicit and the commitment to a particular educational philosophy can be inferred only tentatively. In relation to a body of knowledge about the subject being studied the teacher's authority, as an expert, is necessarily circumscribed. Rather is the function that of the facilitator and prompter, encouraging ideas and giving guidance on the means by which information can be obtained. In organizing the time, advising on the division of labour and in making various other arrangements the teacher creates situations in which the pupils will have scope and motivation to exercise important skills, thereby developing confidence in themselves in their capacity as learners. If this does happen, then one of the teacher's main objectives will have been satisfied, that of enabling the class to exploit some of the learning potential within the area of study. There are many specific and practical skills which they must utilize, such as the interpretation of large-scale maps, the design of questionnaires and structured interviews and the analysis of data files. The pupils may be introduced to some of these methods as the need arises, others will have been met before. It is, however, their general motivation and their capacity for working together effectively which the World Studies teacher consistently seeks to establish and reinforce. In this approach learning is perceived as the process of making meaning out of experience. The individual learner is encouraged to explore and reflect upon experiences, to regard them as the raw material from which understanding about our world is to be derived. Here the fundamental implications are that the teacher explicitly attributes value to this process and that the pupil is encouraged to share these reflections. The practical considerations are that the teaching methods enable it to happen and that the social environment of the classroom is conducive of the sharing of half-formulated ideas and tentative interpretations.

The programme of work in the World Studies classroom will normally include a range of strategies designed to promote this climate of support and confidence. At an early stage in the development of relationships within the group the objectives of such strategies will be the encouragement of affirmation, trust and careful listening. Such practice can communicate the importance given to the attitudes which they reflect such as an interest in and responsiveness towards others. There is also a utilitarian purpose in the acquisition of those social skills, for many of the learning situations are dependent upon them (Whitaker, 1984).

Taking one example, that of listening, to illustrate these ramifications, it is obvious that practising this skill in the classroom among their peers would help the pupils in the village survey to be better interviewers. It is the intention that the speaker is prompted and reassured by the interest and the empathetic attitude shown by the listener. As an expression of a basic value it has a broader significance for the personal and social development of the individual and the group since it constitutes a predisposition to hear accurately what others are trying to communicate. The listener tries to avoid any assumptions which anticipate, pre-judge or devalue the words of the speaker, thereby demonstrating an initial readiness to elicit information and to demonstrate a tolerance and acceptance of another person's ideas. Such behaviour is consistent with the broader aim of promoting a positive attitude towards others, a willingness to hear and to try to understand opinions and beliefs which are unfamiliar. This may help to inhibit a tendency to apply pre-determined stereotypes, to generalize and misrepresent or misunderstand through over-simplification.

The ability to listen effectively may be seen to have utility in many contexts, but always with the purpose of providing accurate information and understanding. This accords with the belief that it is an essential prerequisite of the capacity to appreciate and evaluate the opinions and attitudes of others; that it will bring to the surface a range of perceptions, attitudes and arguments in an antidote against stereotyping and a reflection of the complexity and diversity of the world outside the school. Once exposed at the surface, those attitudes which are prejudiced or based on factual inaccuracy can be subject to critical scrutiny and perhaps to subsequent modification. This is exemplified in the programme of study on development undertaken by fourth-year secondary pupils. It included an exercise on images in which they recorded their perceptions of less developed countries and then compiled a descriptive profile of the 'Third World'. The teacher then provided photographs depicting features of modern affluence in India, and juxtaposed one such picture with a scene representing rural poverty. The students were required to compose decriptions of the two situations and to write another profile which accommodated both of them. This obliged some pupils to revise their earlier views. Later it emerged that there was a persistent conviction that the physical environment and over-population were the dominant reasons for the development problems of the Third World. These theories were tested against a variety of data and found to be inadequate as comprehensive explanations, given the diversity of conditions within the developing world. This exercise was followed by the simulation 'The Trading Game', in which groups of students represented six countries. The great differences in technological and material resources gives advantage to some and confines others to relative impotence and frustration. At the end of the exercise the students, first, discussed these feelings and the strategies adopted within the game, and then watched a film on the world trading system. The usefulness of the game as a learning device was considered, and modifications suggested by the class.

This account of some activities in a fourth-year unit indicates ways in which the students are given the opportunity to improve their understanding of the complex reality of the global economic system. Any readiness to apply simplistic images or explanations is discouraged by the evidence offered, but there are occasions when the pupils are encouraged to air their own views and express their own feelings. For the teacher these are as much a resource for learning as the maps, statistics or film which were used. When a student observed that he did not believe that the machinery shown in a photograph could be properly serviced by the people who used it, he was asked to give his reasons. When another argued that tariff barriers are a sensible means by which more developed countries can protect their industries the class was given a 'brainstorming' exercise on the advantages and disadvantages of protectionist policies. And when during the simulation on world trade several of the participants insisted that the conditions were unfair, the teacher responded later by asking the students in pairs to compose a definition of 'fairness'. The adequacy of the definitions was examined not only within the context of the game, but also against the pupils' own daily experiences of commercial transactions. The teacher brings to the classroom no rigidly defined body of knowledge to be imparted regardless of the pre-existing attitudes of the pupils. Rather is the start made from them. Nor are there ready-made answers to be provided because of the complexity of world problems which are often defined as problems because there are conflicting theories as to their causes. The teacher is not therefore in a position of knowledgeable authority, but is prepared to engage with the students in a collaborative endeavour to tease out some of the complexity and confusion. The teacher's expertise resides in the ability to act opportunely, recognizing the critical points at which key ideas and skills can be developed and elaborated or when fundamental values can be examined.

The ideas which underpin a World Studies curriculum are integral to a view of the world which emphasizes its physical unity, the finite nature of many resources and the delicate relationship between people and the earth's ecosystems. This perspective emphasizes the interdependent relationships within and between the physical environment and human society and, in particular, the common interests shared by the people of the world. To lay the foundations for such a view, which encompasses the widely acknowledged aims of international understanding, a respect for other cultures and for the environment would draw upon all the resources within the school curriculum. That breadth would provide the interdisciplinary approach, through the contributions of individual disciplines, which is necessary if a balanced and informed view is eventually to be developed of world society and its problems. The intellectual demands on the individual teacher and learner are considerable, and the debates and uncertainties within any one issue are such that any depth of understanding is acquired only through a coherent framework of study. Such a co-ordinated approach can ensure that contributions to the required body of knowledge and the exemplification and application of important concepts are made within many school subjects.

One issue which illustrates the inter-disciplinary and controversial nature of global problems is the famine in North Africa. Although compassionate response to media reports is understandable, the causes of the problem and the means of alleviating it are matters of debate. While it is recognized that the factors underlying the ecological disaster are to do with human occupance of marginal areas, cultural practices and population changes, it is also relevant to consider recent political and economic developments. Knowledge of simple ecosystems derived from geography and biology lessons would help to provide some understanding at the much larger scale of environmental relationships within the Sahel. Similarly, a knowledge of economic and political relationships and development strategies is relevant, as is an understanding of demographic trends. If these provide a necessary basis for an appreciation of the nature of the problem, they do not serve to provide a single solution. That difficulty is compounded by political mistrust and the reluctance of rich countries to engage in uncertain commitments. The discrepancy between official national policies on aid and the moral attitudes of individuals cannot be ignored in any discussion of the efforts needed to repair the crises which exist not only in Africa, but in many parts of the Third World. This implies a willingness to examine these moral issues in the classroom, and to accept that often they constitute dilemmas to which clear-cut criteria and judgements are not easily applied.

Because one of the main elements of the World Studies approach will be the consideration of issues of development, of the environment, of human rights and of the conditions of peace and conflict, it is inevitable that moral questions will feature prominently in the classroom. This obliges the teacher to employ methods which allow of rigorous and intellectually disciplined examination while acknowledging and accommodating the significant influence which feelings can have upon attitudes and reactions. The matter is further compounded by the difficulty of reconciling the expressed need to inculcate a certain set of values, such as respect for freedom and justice, with the avoidance of political indoctrination. Positions to the left and right of the ideological spectrum offer opposing strategies by which social justice, equity and freedom might be achieved. Explanations of the problems of hunger and under-development, if they are to progress beyond the simplistic and deterministic, necessarily involve discussion of political factors. This is one argument made for dealing with controversial issues in the World Studies classroom.

A definition offered by Dearden (1981) is that 'a matter is controversial if contrary views can be held on it without those views being contrary to reason'. The validity of any argument is to be determined with reference to 'the body of public knowledge, criteria of truth, critical standards and verification procedures' available at the time. Often that validation cannot be effected in a summary fashion, but is a cumulative one spread over a range of experiences. It is comparable in some ways with the subtle processes by which opinions are formulated. It is with an awareness of the nature of this development that the teacher is responsible for managing the programme of study and the ways of working in a manner which ensures that the full range of views and opinions is represented. Drawing further upon Dearden in his comment that 'one cannot teach without framing intentions about what is to be learnt', the purpose is to provide the pupils with an awareness that there are alternative views about important matters and to give them the skills by which to evaluate those views. Since this means that any opinion or theory is open to question and validation, it implies that the teacher's own position is not protected from scrutiny. The expectation that the teacher will adopt a neutral stance in dealing with the many issues which involve political controversy is seen as being compatible with the aim of promoting an open, questioning attitude by the pupils. Indoctrination implies, even necessitates, the opposite condition. The essential element of the teaching approach derives from the teacher's self-awareness, which implies an acknowledgement of a predisposition towards certain values and perspectives. So if the principles of honesty and justice are to be inculcated in the students, there is a continuing obligation to treat the nature of evidence, its relevance and reliability as matters of major concern within the classroom. This requires a disciplined methodology to ensure that an appropriate range of information is available to the pupils and to determine what parts of it can be used as evidence. It is similarly important to see that there is sufficient debate about possible interpretations of data, so that inferences are not automatically influenced by previous attitudes or the appeal of particular kinds of evidence. In reality the classroom situation can apparently fail to satisfy the requirement of neutrality. Not only has a value judgement been made in deciding what should be the content of the programme of study; there is the obligation to encourage the pupils to question attitudes, values and opinions which they, their families and friends may hold or which may be characteristic of a large number of people. To be successful in this objective the teacher often finds it necessary to provide information or a perspective which disturbs a widely held assumption. In doing so it is possible that a lack of balance is apparent in the management of that particular discussion in so far as the purpose is to challenge a prevailing and perhaps facilely held view. At the same time, there may be an equally demanding task for the teacher, that of persuading the pupils that the issue is one that should be of concern to them and that it merits careful consideration. This has strong implications in terms of student motivation and the relationships that have been developed over time within the classroom. In the more limited context of a particular lesson it may mean that the teacher uses a strategy which is capable of opening up a new perception or affording a new insight. This is one justification for the use of experiential approaches in World Studies, and while they do not provide a complete safeguard against the possibility of manipulation, such methods do allow the pupils to make direct comparisons and associations between their immediate reactions and some wider issue. Thus over a period of time a class might move from an exploration of the idea of trust to the question of loyalty amongst individuals and groups and thence to the notions of patriotism and nationalism. In another example the stimulus is provided by a simulation exercise in which the well-being of the group as a whole is dependent upon the willingness of individuals and sub-groups to eschew opportunities for personal advantage. In such an exercise there are many permutations on the actions which participants could take and the outcome may be judged more or less satisfactory depending on the criteria applied. Reflections upon their experiences are likely to bring forward arguments from pupils about fairness and justice, competitiveness and co-operation, responsibility and selfishness. At such a time the teacher's skills will be exercised to clarify the issues and to ensure that no simplistic connections are made between the artificially induced classroom situation and the more complex problems of the real world. The purpose of the simulation is to involve the pupils, to raise levels of interest and motivation and to provide some raw material for subsequent refinement.

The temptation is to criticize teaching methods such as these by isolating a particular unit of work rather than following through that process of refinement which may subsequently discard much evidence as irrelevant or inadequate. There is the further criticism that some teaching strategies can be used to effect a straight equation with the world outside the classroom, offering models, explanations and moral parallels. While such methods can serve to illuminate some basic issues, it does not promote a better understanding to reduce the problem to a straightforward moral question which will determine what the right course of action should be in order to resolve it. That is not to suggest, however, that the ethical principles invoked by many of the graver issues, such as the enormous disparities between and within rich and poor nations, should be blurred or ignored. The purpose of the teacher is to help students to appreciate that many problems are a complex of interests and interpretations, that often the very definition of the problem is a matter for debate and that any proposed political solutions must be uncertain. It is also an aim in World Studies to expose something of the intricate system of linkages which exists within and between those problems. For example, at one level there are connections between environmental damage in tropical regions, demographic changes, the need for foreign currency and the demand for food and raw materials in the industrialized temperate zone. That same chain can be extended to the individual's behaviour as a consumer and the relationship with commercial developments in the local shopping-centre. At both levels there is a need to consider the economic forces which sustain or change such relationships.

Such an understanding would remain inadequate if it did not include a knowledge of the political structure which, in turn, sustains the major economic systems. The tensions and hostilities which can be generated by the suspicion which exists between competing ideologies forms a part of the subject matter of a World Studies course. One aim is to encourage a resistance to the crude and superficial stereotypes and to develop some insight into the means by which such images are acquired and the functions they serve. There are many ways in which the teacher can go about this. A start can be made at the personal level, investigating attitudes towards those whose behaviour is seen as different and strange, or by looking at the use of propaganda in time of war. Often it is approached through the study of newspapers and broadcasts, analysing the content for biased statements and stereotyped views, and attempting to determine what constitutes a news-worthy item. Another inquiry can be directed towards the texts used in humanities classrooms, and the manner in which they too can serve to promote distorted images, for example, through the selection of illustrations.

The broad purpose of such studies is to examine the bases for our views of the world, other cultures and countries. Where the focus is upon political systems, the student can acquire a better appreciation of the basic values which are fundamental to the truly democratic society, using these values as criteria by which political systems can be measured. Here then, in Dearden's (1981) view, is another example of the framing of intentions, and a clear commitment on the part of the teacher to a particular and publically approved set of values. We can suppose that these will be explicit when a teacher is discussing the subject of apartheid or any other examples of the flagrant denial of human rights.

But just as the main pedagogical task is to interest the pupils in the subject, in many cases it may be that the subject elicits from them such attitudes of intolerance, of bigotry or antipathy that the difficulty of the task is magnified. Most obviously this can be so in the classroom where there is a strong sense of deprivation, disadvantage or alienation and where the pronouncement of liberal values and a demand for intellectually rigorous tests of truth can be provocatively inappropriate. It is in an attempt to avoid the confrontation within such situations that the World Studies approach is conceived as the steady development of classroom relationships and procedures over the whole of the period of compulsory schooling, and particularly in those earlier years when the attitudes of pupils may not have hardened into prejudices (Carnie, 1972).

Perhaps the main challenge to the teacher is to be found in the need to enable the pupil consciously to tolerate so many uncertainties about the world. The intellectual effort involved in accommodating alternative and competing arguments is greater than that required in the acceptance of a single authoritative statement. It is that extra investment which has to be justified, for it implies something beyond an academic evaluation of different theories. It is at this point that the neutrality of the teacher can be compromised, when personal judgements and values influence choice. Yet it is precisely that capacity to exercise choice in an informed manner which would constitute an intended outcome of the educational process for the pupil. The professional and academic integrity of the teacher resides in the honest intention, within the limits imposed by classroom and curriculum circumstances, to ensure that the range of views upon a controversial issue is presented. It is possible that this will be effected spontaneously through classroom discussion, perhaps by studying newspapers or by listening to visiting speakers. It can be achieved also through drama and the use of role play. Such strategies are widely used and commonly believed to be a sufficient means to bring an awareness that there is a diversity of attitudes and that often there is no means by which all interests can be satisfied. And just as often it should be apparent that there are no straightforward solutions to the hitherto intractable problems of society. A frank admission of that fact can, however, induce precisely those attitudes of cynicism or apathy which education should seek to discourage. If the best efforts of the able, the energetic and the powerful have failed to bring guarantees of world security, harmony and well-being, then the conclusion for the young person might well be that the individual is better advised to look after self-interest and personal gain.

Through the World Studies approach the aim is to encourage positive and optimistic attitudes. There are many reasons for this. There is a need to avoid imposing upon children in a relatively affluent society any sense of guilt or responsibility for the misfortunes of others. There is a further danger where the curriculum content is concerned primarily with issues in which the inhabitants of poorer regions are depicted as the hostages of misfortune, disaster-prone and incapable of self-help. The means by which this image is inhibited include studies which are sensitive to the enterprise and ingenuity of people in coping with hardship and in sustaining hope in conditions of extreme disadvantage. It is equally desirable to investigate the bias which is implicit in the application of Western criteria of development and in Western perspectives on other cultures and their achievements. It is therefore seen as important in World Studies teaching to bring out the needs and aspirations, at social, economic and political levels, which are common to most, if not all, societies.

The notion of an educational process which sustains democratic values carries the expectation that the individual pupil will mature into a citizen able and willing to make choices. And that many of those choices will not be determined for selfish or material ends without regard to the interests of others. It is a major aim of World Studies teaching to set such choices not only within the immediate social context, but also – by revealing the links which exist within global systems – within that of the world community. Such an ideal further assumes those personal qualities and circumstances which allow of a degree of autonomy, an assumption which has long been embedded within the British educational canon. The ideal is seemingly reduced to the trivial, but not to absurdity, if the choice-making is set at the domestic level. The decision to become a vegetarian or to use a bottle bank may not seem to have significance as an educational outcome or a political act. But the effectiveness of consumer boycotts has been proved and no one doubts that the strength of campaigning organizations is dependent upon the commitment of the individual member. It is such a longer-term outcome to which the World Studies curriculum is directed and it is therefore seen as a necessary condition that the student is not passively or despondently acquiescent to overwhelming social, economic and political forces, but entertains the belief that the world can be a better place. For the teacher and the school there are considerable difficulties. The message which is implicit is that despite their best efforts at reassurance those who exercise political power have yet to agree or implement international policies which would secure human dignity and health for a majority of the world's people. A second obstacle is that the motivations which are harnessed to sustain national economic development and success are dependent upon a value system which does not appear to give priority to those whose basic human needs are far from being satisfied. These discrepancies and contradictions confront any school which makes a serious attempt to translate such aims into curriculum practice. But at a time when that value system is necessarily being discarded as the justification of the individual's utility in a post-industrial or a high-technology society, whichever is the appropriate scenario, the obligation to provide alternative philosophies is greatly increased.

At one level it is agreed that there should be a consistency between the processes and relationships within the classroom and the aim that pupils should develop as questioning, choice-making individuals. The belief is that there is a positive association between the growth of such individuals and the opportunities in the classroom to express opinions, to question, to argue and to exercise some choice. The correlation is thought to exist whenever students are enabled to apply such values as tolerance, respect for the reasoned opinions of others and fairness. It is seen as desirable that they should be active practitioners and that those values are the dominant currency only so long as the majority believe in and support them. Within an institution and certainly within the context of most schools the enabling compromise is in the balance between individual freedom and individual responsibility. But there are obvious tensions when there is a rigid imposition of an authoritarian version of what behaviour is tolerable or of what cultural values and kinds of knowledge are acceptable. Similar conflicts with the aims of World Studies teaching are evident when there is a strongly hierarchical structure, which dispenses privilege in the cultivation of elitism or which patently relies upon the power of competition as the motivation to achievement. While the tensions are often not so crudely obvious as such a caricature suggests, they may be so powerful in more subtle ways that the pupils can be confused by the contradictory signals. They can also be a severely inhibiting influence upon a teacher who would otherwise be prepared to introduce subjects which some colleagues would regard as threatening or provocative within the social context of the school.

The success with which pupils engage in serious discussion in the classroom, even at an early age, or feel able to express feelings and opinions, is dependent upon the development of appropriate skills and upon the degree to which their experiences generally encourage the belief that such activity is an important part of the learning process. Clearly it is also necessary for the teacher to inform, facilitate and guide the direction of group work. But it is also appropriate for the pupils to share in the evaluation of the work rather than to be solely dependent upon the teacher in an examiner role.

Considerable reinforcement of such behaviour would obviously occur where the values and procedures are seen to be appropriate in other classrooms. This breadth and consistency seem necessary if the majority of pupils are to gain that degree of confidence and assertiveness through which they will be able to exercise their responsibilities as democratic citizens. The business of extending their understanding and concern beyond the limits of the parochial or national is equally to be undertaken across the curriculum.

There are many indications of a school's stance towards the wider world such as those of international links and exchanges, the observance of United Nations Day and One World Week, exhibitions and other celebrations of elements of different cultures, talks by foreign visitors and conferences on international themes (Richardson *et al.*, n.d.). There are occasions when pupils are encouraged or enabled to engage in fund-raising and campaigning activities. Such activities can be a significant and integral part of the school ethos. The infrastructure which would make this so is a curriculum which has a clear orientation towards the promotion of international understanding. World Studies should not be an isolated bridgehead on the timetable to which more traditional subjects may give adventitious support. Sometimes it is set alongside a programme of personal, social and moral education, but its aims are dependent upon such a range of knowledge, concept acquisition, skills and attitudes that they may be attained only if both content and process are established across the curriculum. Arguing from the basic premiss that the school has a major part of the responsibility for preparing children for a future which is uncertain in a rapidly changing society, it is pointless to set that future and those changes in an inappropriate context. Whatever the technological and economic developments and their effects upon employment, leisure and material welfare in our own national society, none of them can be understood without reference to the international context. A World Studies approach would make possible these global considerations and perspectives, in all the subjects of the curriculum.

Another critical assumption is that there will be opportunities to exercise sufficient personal choice to enable the individual to adjust to future changes; that no less than at present a person will have the freedom to make decisions about personal life-style which reflect his/her values and preferences. More significantly, at a political level, that choices can be made which influence policies on a larger scale. The positive and optimistic purpose of World Studies is to increase the individual student's awareness of that potential. To deny such a possibility would appear to subscribe to a bleakly pessimistic view of the lives of the next generation in which passivity, apathy or cynicism would be more appropriate than those qualities associated with the finer human aspirations and endeavours. It seems to be a denial also of the power of ideas, and a negation of an educational philosophy which recognizes the right of children to be concerned about the world they will inherit.

# DISCUSSION OF CHAPTERS 11 AND 12

It is fascinating to compare the contributions in Chapters 11 and 12. As we all know, 'Peace Education', despite the fact that most citizens of the world would acknowledge peace as a desirable goal, is regarded with suspicion by many educators and in some LEAs, for instance, has been proscribed in schools. 'World Studies' is not seen as such a villain. And yet, according to the views espoused here, the effects hoped for in personal terms, in terms of children's development, would have much in common. Through Stephenson's World Studies approach, one would hope that children would become more thoughtful, less prejudiced, more tolerant, better listeners, more positive and more accepting of ambiguities. Morrison would expect a Peace Studies approach to help children to communicate better (especially to listen), to co-operate, to be positive, to be trusting and to be able to resolve conflicts. (It is also interesting to compare this list of qualities with other authors' lists, notably that of Scrimshaw.)

One reason why 'World Studies' is more or less acceptable, and 'Peace Studies' more or less regarded with suspicion, in schools is that the former appears to take a more neutral, more objective stance and appears to be less threatening to existing structures in our educational system. Also if Stephenson's approach is typical, it starts from the familiar, the concrete, and indirectly, in teasing out solutions, helps to bring about the kinds of personal quality listed above. 'Peace Studies' on the other hand, appears to be more threatening; for instance, Morrison states that 'The uncomfortable truth is that schools, as they are presently structured in terms of discipline and control, cannot truly educate for peace'. I think it is the case that he is talking here about most schools as we know them;

most schools with a clear authority structure, where teachers are in charge and where children learn what has been decided they should learn; where violence, even if it is only the verbal violence of command and criticism, abounds. So Peace Education, in Morrison's terms, must be seen as threatening and to be rejected. (It is an interesting and unanswered question how many of the other approaches advocated in this book would also be seen as threatening if they were truly effective in bringing about the kinds of changes they claim they hope to achieve.)

In the earlier comments on Stanton's chapter it was suggested that it would be interesting and provocative to look at our own activities as teacher-trainers, in the light of his comments about the need for dramatic changes in teacher attitude and teaching styles. How about the teaching of 'World Studies' and 'Peace Studies' to all students in teacher training? It would certainly be easier to 'get away with it' in respect of World Studies as compared with Peace Studies. And students trained in World Studies would certainly find a market for their skills more easily than would the Peace Studies experts. And perhaps we could teach World Studies within the existing authority structures of departments and colleges of education. Would there have to be some very dramatic (traumatic) changes before we tried to teach Peace Studies?

The final comment which might be made relates not only to these two particular chapters, but also to many other contributions in this book. This relates to the 'simple' fact that there is a psychology of individual differences; that children, as well as adults, do differ, sometimes quite profoundly, in terms of mental ability, emotional development, social maturity, linguistic skill, etc. These differences are related to age differences, genetic endowment, social background, educational opportunity, etc.

This 'simple' fact is of particular relevance in personal, social and moral education approaches which, to quote Peter Kutnick, aim 'to work towards the facilitation of autonomy'.

One of us has tried elsewhere (Evans, 1983) to set out some of the problems related to individual differences and the achievement of autonomy. Perhaps here one can just ask the reader of any of these pieces, to re-read them with a particular child, a particular group of children, in mind. How do the suggestions deployed in them apply to, for instance, a 12-year-old at the bottom end of the remedial group, from a particularly limited, even deprived, home background as compared with, say, a very intelligent 17-year-old from a very stimulating home background. Would the aims and the goals of the World Studies programme and the Peace Studies approach be different as well as the actual approaches used; a particular problem exists where, as here, it is not a particular body of knowledge that waits to be taught in a particular way, but where it is ways of thinking and ways of behaving that aren't so much being taught as being learned. How far would we have to change our way of working for the two examples above? This issue, which we think is far more complex than might appear at first sight, is discussed in the Epilogue.

# Epilogue

## David Evans, Richard Pring and John Thacker

### Introduction

This collection of essays springs, essentially, from the editors' strong conviction that there was a need for a cool, sustained look at some of the basic issues underlying personal, social and moral education (PSMEd) initiatives in schools, in particular those issues revolving around questions of values.

At the end of all our discussions, having assembled the differing offerings of our contributors, we are left with the question that one often obliges one's graduate students to confront at the end of their research endeavours – so what?

We are trying to answer this deceptively simple question in this final section. First, we want to acknowledge, explain and perhaps justify the omission of certain important topics in our presentation. Then we want to try to summarize the presentations and to suggest some of the directions – in terms of teaching and research – in which PSMEd might move in the rest of this century.

Probably the most important gap in our coverage of significant issues relates to the influence on children's personal, social and moral development of the media and, in particular, of TV; and it seems likely that this will increase, not diminish. One continuing theme in the chapters in this book is the desirability of enabling/ obliging children to become autonomous in their thinking, in their selecting of values and beliefs, and it is probably the case that more and more the important purveyors of morality to children, i.e. parents and teachers, will step back and into the gap the media (especially TV) will step. The absence of explicit reference in the presentations to the powerful influence of TV – and to a lesser degree the press – in moulding children's value systems does *not* mean this was absent from the contributors' thinking; rather that it was taken as said. But perhaps here one needs to recognize, more explicitly, the importance of TV particularly. Any parent, any teacher, must be aware of the amount of time spent by many or most children in front of the TV set; if one sits and watches TV programmes for long stretches of time (as one does occasionally in the course of research!), one is struck forcibly, for example, by the acceptance of violence as a means of achieving even good ends; or again by the dominance of materialistic values and short-term goals, which seem to have at their core the de-valuing of the pro-social values espoused in so many of this book's contributions. (There has been of course in recent years research into the effect of TV-viewing on children's moral development – see, for example, recent issues of the *Journal of Moral Education*; how much concern is felt by influential figures in children's development, especially parents and teachers, is a different matter as is the kind of action that should spring from this concern.)

It is also interesting to speculate how far children who, in educational settings, might be encouraged to think for themselves, to work out their own values, are at the mercy of the most powerful standardized influences emanating from TV screens. It is at least possible that TV is contentedly filling in the gap created by parents (including progressive ones!) withdrawing their parental influences. There may be special problems around when we consider how much time young pre-school children might be spending watching the visual images of the TV (in all the above we include of course the new phenomenon of video tapes).

Perhaps all this leads on conveniently to the second obvious omission from our presentation; perhaps we have not considered enough, though clearly Kutnick's work is very relevant here, the importance of the first five or six years of life in determining basic attitudes, life-values, and so on. This must be recognized, though in defence of the contributors, our briefs to them emphasized the importance of PSMEd in the *school-age* child's development.

A third significant gap in our treatment might be thought to be an adequate treatment, as a separate issue, of the nature of individual differences. To take one obvious strand here: if the goal, perhaps the overriding goal, of a PSMEd programme is to help children to think and feel *for themselves,* then one has to recognize the wide range in the ability, innate and learned, of children to think and feel for themselves. Clearly one of the most difficult tasks for any

PSMEd educator is to tailor his/her programme, approach or even aims to the needs and limitations of the different children he/she teaches.

There are of course many sources of 'difference' – genetic and cultural, sub-cultural and social class, family educational levels, family values and beliefs, and so on. For instance, some readers may be puzzled to see that nowhere do we tackle the massive value problems that arise in a multi-cultural, multi-faith society like ours. At the time we felt, sitting smugly in the south-west, that we did not have the first-hand experiences in this part of Britain from which we could speak with authority and confidence and decided not to take up the themes of multi-cultural and multi-faith education. In retrospect, this was wrong and a number of people heavily involved in working with children from different cultures and of different faiths, some from our larger cities but also from the south-west, have pointed out the grave mistake of assuming that children and their teachers and parents in *other* areas should not be bothered about problems and issues which have as yet no seemingly pressing personal immediacy for them.

Finally, listing what we see as our larger omissions, we were all the time aware in our discussions and writing-up, that we were the older generation talking about the younger generation; and that though most of us have the intimate experience, sometimes joyful, sometimes painful, of living and working with young people, it is not easy for us to empathize clearly with them in their struggle to become persons in our chaotic world. It is in fact incredibly difficult for most of us to identify with their passions and their apathies and to build our partial understandings into our academic analyses. Perhaps what we need are more very careful and sensitive explorations with children and adolescents of how they think and feel in and about the world we have bequeathed them.

**The main themes of the book and possible ways forward**

Personal, social and moral education must begin with an analysis of the social environment in which pupils and students have to learn how to grow up. They cannot isolate themselves from the pressures and from the values that permeate the very relationships and institutions that govern their lives. Once, and possibly not long ago, that social context was relatively stable. There were dominant values that people shared and felt confident in. And that confidence enabled them to pass on such values to the next generation; PSMEd would consist quite explicitly in socializing young people into models of 'personhood' and into a set of values that society at large both understood and accepted. Certainly the spirit of criticism and of moral inquiry was not encouraged in many schools. And certainly questioning of sexual morality, political commitment or religious affiliation were not part of the curriculum experience of most pupils.

Several things have happened in recent years that have changed all that. First, there are social changes that deliver powerful but (interestingly) quite contradictory messages. Secondly, there are developments in educational research that lead to a questioning of the rather passive form of socialization that previous kinds of social inquiry had encouraged us to espouse. Thirdly, there are political and social developments that bring to the forefront issues which previously had been ignored. Each of these – the social context, the research findings and the new issues – has influenced the content and the argument of this book, and has promoted a particular view of what PSMEd must be about and of what the way forward must be.

### Social changes

The social changes are, in a nutshell, these. The industrial and the economic base of our society has changed more rapidly than the institutions and the social relations that would normally reflect that base. Communities are rarely stable entities; routes into employment are no longer clear-cut; the symbols of success and of status are not what our parents would have recognized. To such a situation two quite contradictory responses are discernible.

On the one hand, there are the attempts to differentiate and to classify students, to sort out different roles and to determine different life chances. Schooling is the process through which employment-related skills are acquired. The educational system is the means through which the economy is served with trained manpower and enabled to meet particular goals. There is little room, therefore, for the more broadly conceived mental powers of criticism and of reflection that the tradition of liberal education has fostered.

On the other hand, there is the stress upon personal preparation for a rapidly changing, complex, unpredictable future. The curriculum, far from socializing young people into economically defined roles, should lead them towards greater independence and capacity for reflection and decision-making – even in such matters as those that raise fundamental questions about values. This is all summed up in the frequent reference to 'autonomy'.

Here therefore we have a conflict of considerable proportion between on the one hand helping young people to think for themselves and to develop a moral independence in thought and action, and on the other hand influencing young people to adopt a set of values and a way of living that fits in with others' conceptions of what is good for society as a whole.

To be specific, one can see this conflict in the stress upon personal development in youth training schemes, in technical and vocational initiatives and in pre-vocational education, which also look to the needs of the economy. One can see it, too, in the pastoral care system of schools that both care for individual needs and direction and yet worry about deviance from the norms that govern the institutions as a whole.

These are not straightforward problems, easily dismissed as of only theoretical importance. As the contributions to this book demonstrate, they affect the practice of many teachers in schools and in colleges attempting to meet the requirements of community and of individual pupils or students.

**Educational research**

This conflict is reflected in different traditions of educational research. On the one hand, there has been the emphasis upon socializing young people into the values and norms, generally accepted, of society. On the other hand, we have seen a stress upon the gradual development of capacities to reflect and to engage critically with those very values. The capacity for such personal reflection does itself need to be developed. And the strength of both Weinreich-Haste's and Kutnick's contributions lies in the evidence they provide for a developmental approach to personal and moral maturity. Clearly they draw upon the developmental psychology of Piaget and Kohlberg. And these are indeed open to criticism. But there is a powerful argument in their writing which indicates a stage-by-stage attempt to develop, through the content and processes of the curriculum, a capacity to think in a principled and rational way about the responsibilities. Roughly speaking, there is a transition to be made from dependence on adults in the regulation of behaviour, through the influence of peer groups to the principled morality that helps each person, however young or old, to sustain an integrity through all the vicissitudes of social changes and social pressures.

Therefore, the book is influenced very much by a particular kind of research and (underpinning this) a particular view of morality, namely that which emphasizes autonomy as an ideal and the developmental steps towards that ideal. But we recognize too, bearing in mind the social context, the possible conflict between this position and that of those who stress the need to prepare young people for the world of work and the need to encourage specific work-related values. The conflict, therefore, is between those who stress autonomy and those who worry about the absence of socialization into the values which seem essential for social cohesion and economic well-being.

**Curriculum issues**

Possibly the advocates of autonomy win the educational argument. But we need, in pursuing this line of thought, to tread warily. There are specific issues which even the most enthusiastic advocate of autonomy would not want to see totally submerged under individual freedom. And, therefore, we see under the umbrella of individual autonomy a range of curriculum areas being promoted by schools. First (and who could gainsay this?), there is the emphasis upon health education. We must surely be concerned with the physical and mental health of young people. Balding raises, therefore, the questions that emerge from that concern. Similarly, we should be thinking beyond ourselves to those in less comfortable circumstances. A world perspective is required. Therefore, Stephenson has enlarged upon this. Furthermore, the dangers and morality of a nuclear future are understandably a focus of young people's attention, and Morrison addresses himself to peace education. There is a religious dimension to all this, and Priestley has shown how the advocacy of spiritual development can be reconciled with a broadly conceived sense of autonomy. Button and Plant have demonstrated how so much of this global concern can be translated into curriculum arrangements which, whatever the differences in belief, share a common faith in processes of reciprocal respect and interdependency. Perhaps there lies the key to personal development that seeks both to respect personal autonomy and to recognize the social and economic demands upon individual people.

Leslie Button worked extensively with groups of experienced teachers and placed great stress in his training programmes on the teachers experiencing the same activities that they would introduce with their pupils. Button comments that engaging in the same process of discovery and experience in a supportive training group is often reported to be as much value to the teachers as to the young people. Developmental group work provides a practicable training approach with a stress on process which has been shown to influence teacher style and attitudes. This is a hopeful sign for those looking for changes in the process of education. However, such training is intensive and therefore costly and requires a high level of commitment from the participating teachers. Such changes in teaching style are bound to have an impact in the wider institutional context and some of these reverberations were noted in Sue Plant's evaluation. Such influence is two way and the natural conservatism of schools can act to contain and neutralize these changes. Button feels that the difficulty is not in training teachers, but in ensuring that the methods are actually practised after the training programme is finished.

This also raises questions about how we prepare students in teacher training institutions. Do we encourage student-determined goals and student initiated and controlled learning, as Geoff Stanton suggested, in our teachers in training? Would we welcome the possible changes in relationship between student and institution which such emphasis on learning resulting in action would inevitably have? Whether individuals or institutions would be able to accept such changes, it is probably true that the move will probably be away from such approaches with the increase of interference from outside bodies such as the Inspectorate and CATE.

Another set of problems which needs to be tackled in this area are the attitudes of people outside schools, especially the parents. At times the personal and social education in schools is so arranged that it seems to be a genuine option only for the least academically able. Thus, unless part of a genuine core curriculum for all, PSMEd can be stigmatized as a low-status part of the curriculum. In addition, some parents may object to what they see as a distraction from the main enterprise of the school, namely instruction in examinable academic topics. Finally, and perhaps most seriously, there will be parents who do not see it as part of the function of the school to deal with sensitive personal and moral issues.

All these need to be taken into account and indicate a need for conscious approach to parental consultation and involvement. The families of children in the school are part of that wider community in which the lessons learned in PSMEd work in schools must be practised.

Particularly important at both school and home is the exercise of authority. Many of the contributors to this book accept the general aim of 'facilitation' of autonomy as an overall aim in this work. Can such autonomy be achieved in compulsory settings, such as school, where examination boards choose the content of the work and teachers decide on how they wish to teach? A question running through several chapters in this present book is whether our usual educational arrangements provide the conditions for the development of autonomy. Kutnick suggests that opportunities need to be provided for the young, even pre-school, child to experience genuinely co-operative peer relationships as a necessary step to later autonomy. He provides some empirical evidence about the efficacy of introducing physical trust exercises to young children in order to help create the appropriate conditions for such co-operative peer interaction. Similar work is being developed by class teachers in Exeter for the age range 7–13 years (Thacker, 1985) and is based on the work of Leslie Button. Button carried out his original work with adolescents but, as Kutnick comments, this can become a therapeutic exercise to *counter* existing relationships. Better surely to introduce similar work for children in the primary school, at an age when they need to experience co-operative relationships.

As the work is based upon the creation of a climate within the group where each young person can be helpful to his/her peers, the role of the teacher needs to shift to a greater level of partnership in order to put the young people in a stronger position. This shift in the exercise of authority is also seen at the level of the school as well as the individual teacher.

Several contributors in this book have pointed to the need for schools to provide opportunities to deal with issues of justice and fairness in the real life of the school, in issues which mattered personally to the pupils and which they would have a real chance of influencing. As Pring put it in his opening chapter, 'not playing at democracy or moral decision-making but "doing it"'. Schools need to examine the messages embodied in the way that the institution operates and the opportunities for pupils to participate in the school. This not only applies to the pupils, but also to the staff. It is difficult to see how teachers can develop such opportunities for their pupils if they themselves are denied a proper voice in the organization of the school and feel themselves powerless within an autocratic structure. On the other hand, a school staff which undertakes such an examination of the ethos and opportunities within their school – in an open, participatory spirit – are already embodying and practising those very qualities which they hope to show towards their pupils. The stress on teacher preparation in Button's chapter, and the awareness of school procedure in Morrison's chapter, add emphasis to this point and provide practical ways forward, as does Stanton's use of checklists, profiling and participative resource-based learning in curriculum matters.

We also need further research into the formative influences on children's personal, social and moral development, especially on the influence of the media in shaping children's attitudes and responses.

We need more research, too, on the perceptions of pupils on the role of school in PSMEd. Do they feel that schools can and should make a contribution? What are the changes that would need to be made to school structure and process to bring about improvement? It would be difficult to carry out such research without the pupils having first had experience of what such possibilities might feel like. Hence the importance of careful case studies where programmes are introduced or changes made in organization, as suggested in this book, and where such changes are evaluated for their impact on the pupils. It is only where young people are given a glimpse of how things might be different that they are able to comment from a position of knowledge.

# References

AINSWORTH, M., BELL, S. and STAYTON, D. (1974). 'Infant–mother attachment and social development: "Socialisation" as a product of reciprocal responses to signals'. In: RICHARDS, M. (Ed) *The Integration of a Child into a Social World*. London: Cambridge University Press.

ATKINSON, R.E. (1969). *Conduct: An Introduction to Moral Philosophy*. London: Macmillan.

BAIER, K. (1973). 'Moral autonomy as an aim of moral education.' In: LANGFORD, G. and O'CONNOR, D.J. (Eds) *New Essays in the Philosophy of Education*. London: Routledge and Kegan Paul.

BALDING, J. (1978). *Just One Minute*. Health Topic Questionnaire. London: Health Education Council.

BALDING, J.W. (1985a). 'The health related behaviour data bank', *Education and Health*, 3, 2, 29–45.

BALDING, J.W. (1985b). General Health-related Behaviour Questionnaire (Version 10). Exeter University School of Education.

BALDWIN, J. and WELLS, H. (1979, 1980, 1981, 1983). *Active Tutorial Work*. Oxford: Blackwell.

BELL, S.M. (1970). 'The development of the concept of object as related to mother–infant attachment', *Child Development*, 41, 291–311.

BLATT, M.M. and KOHLBERG, L. (1975). 'The effects of classroom discussion upon children's level of moral judgement', *Journal of Moral Education*, 4, 129–61.

BLOOM, B.S. (Ed) (1956). *Taxonomy of Educational Objectives*. London: McKay.

BREAKWELL, G.M. (1983). 'Moralities and conflicts'. In: WEINREICH-HASTE, H. and LOCKE, D. (Eds) *Morality in the Making*. Chichester: Wiley.

BRONFENBRENNER, U. (1974). *Two Worlds of Childhood*. Harmondsworth: Penguin.

BRYAN, J. (1975). 'Children's co-operation and helping behaviours'. In: HETHERINGTON, E.M. (Ed) *Review of Child Development Research*. Vol. 5. Chicago: University of Chicago Press.

BUTTON, L. (1971). *Discovery and Experience*. London: Oxford University Press.

BUTTON, L. (1974). *Developmental Group Work with Adolescents*. London: Hodder and Stoughton.

BUTTON, L. (1981). *Group Tutoring for the Form Teacher. Book I.* London: Hodder and Stoughton.

BUTTON, L. (1982). *Group Tutoring for the Form Teacher. Book II.* London: Hodder and Stoughton.

CARNIE, J. (1972). 'Children's attitudes to other nationalities'. In: GRAVES, N. (Ed) *New Movements in the Study and Teaching of Geography.* London: Temple Smith.

CARTER, R. (1980). 'What is Lawrence Kohlberg doing?', *Journal of Moral Education,* 9, 2, 88–102.

COHEN, B. (1975). 'Principles and situations – the liberal dilemma and moral education', *Proceedings of the Aristotelian Society,* 76, 75–87.

COHEN, B. (1981). *Education and the Individual.* London: Allen and Unwin.

COLES, R. (1968). *Children of Crisis.* New York: Delta Books.

COMTE, A. (1853). *The Positive Philosophy.* London: Chapman.

COX, H. (1969). *The Feast of Fools.* Cambridge, Mass.: Harvard University Press.

CRUMP, G.F. (1983). *Peace Education: Guidelines for Primary and Secondary Schools.* Bristol: County of Avon Public Relations and Publicity Department.

CUNNINGHAM, I. (1983). 'Assessment and experiential learning'. In: BOOT, R. and REYNOLDS, M. (Eds) *Learning and Experience in Formal Education.* Manchester: Direct Designs.

DAMON, W. (1977). *The Social World of the Child.* San Francisco, Calif.: Jossey-Bass.

DANCY, J.C. (1980). 'The notion of the ethos of a school', *Perspectives,* Exeter University School of Education.

DEARDEN, R.F. (1972). 'Autonomy and education'. In: DEARDEN, R.F., HIRST, P.H. and PETERS, R.S. (Eds) *Education and the Development of Reason.* London: Routledge and Kegan Paul.

DEARDEN, R.F. (1981). 'Controversial issues and the curriculum', *Journal of Curriculum Studies,* 13, 1, 37–44.

DEPARTMENT OF EDUCATION AND SCIENCE (1977a). *Education in Schools: A Consultative Document.* London: HMSO.

DEPARTMENT OF EDUCATION AND SCIENCE/HMI (1977b). *Curriculum 11 to 16.* London: DES.

DEPARTMENT OF EDUCATION AND SCIENCE/HMI (1979a). *Aspects of Secondary Education in England.* London: HMSO.

DEPARTMENT OF EDUCATION AND SCIENCE (1979b). *A Framework for the Curriculum.* London: HMSO.

DEPARTMENT OF EDUCATION AND SCIENCE (1980). *A View of the Curriculum.* London: HMSO.

DEPARTMENT OF EDUCATION AND SCIENCE (1981). *The School Curriculum.* London: HMSO.

DESAUSMAREZ, N. and PRIESTLEY, J. (1980). 'The existentialist theologian and the battery hen'. In: LEALMAN, B. (Ed) *Professional Papers 1.* London: Christian Education Movement, 26–31.

DEVON EDUCATION COMMITTEE (1982). *Personal, Social and Moral Eduction.* Exeter: Devon County Council.

DYKSTRA, C. (1981). *Vision and Character: A Christian Educator's Alternative to Kohlberg.* New York: Paulist Press.

ELIOT, T.S. (1963). 'The Rock'. In: *Collected Poems.* London: Faber.

EMLER, N. (1983). 'Moral charcter'. In: WEINREICH-HASTE, H. and LOCKE, D. (Eds) *Morality in the Making.* Chichester: Wiley.

EMLER, N. (1984). Differential involvement in delinquency: toward interpretation in terms of reputation management'. In: MAHER, B. and MAHER, W.B. *Progress in Experimental Personality Research.* Vol. 13. New York: Academic Press.

EVANS, D. (1983). 'Individual differences and autonomy in Personal, Social and Moral Education', *Educational Analysis,* 5, 1, 57–68.

EVANS, M., RICE, W. and GRAY, G. (1981). *Free to Choose.* London: TACADE.

FLAVELL, J. and BOTKIN, P. (1968). *The Development of Role-taking and Communication Skills in Children.* New York: Wiley.

FLEW, A. (1972). 'What is indoctrination?'. In: SNOOK, I. (Ed) *Concepts of Indoctrination: Philosophical Essays.* London: Routledge and Kegan Paul.

FREEMAN, J. (1969). *Team-teaching in Britain.* London: Ward Lock Educational.

FURTHER EDUCATION UNIT (1979). *A Basis for Choice.* London: DES.

GAJENDRA, V.K. (Ed) (1980). The Impact of Innovation. Vol. 1, revised edition of publications of the Humanities Curriculum Project, University of East Anglia.

GALTON, M., SIMON, B. and CROLL, P. (1980). *Inside the Primary Classroom.* London: Routledge and Kegan Paul.

GILLIGAN, C. (1982). *In a Different Voice.* Cambridge, Mass.: Harvard University Press.

GLIDEWELL, J., KANTOR, M., SMITH, L. and STRINGER, L. (1966). 'Socialisation and social structure in the classroom'. In: HOFFMAN, M. and HOFFMAN, L. (Eds) *Review of Child Development Research.* Vol.2. New York: Russell Sage Foundation.

HANNAY, A. (1982). *Kierkegaard.* London: Routledge and Kegan Paul.

HARE, R.M. (1964). 'Adolescents into adults'. In: HOLLINS, T.H.B. (Ed) *Aims in Education.* Manchester: Manchester University Press.

HARGREAVES, D. (1967). *Social Relations in a Secondary School.* London: Routledge and Kegan Paul.

HARGREAVES, D. (1982). *The Challenge for the Comprehensive School.* London: Routledge and Kegan Paul.

HARRÉ, R. (1979). *Social Being.* Oxford: Blackwell.

HARTSHORNE, H. and MAY, M.A. (1928–30). *Studies in the Nature of Character.* New York: Macmillan.

HEALTH EDUCATION COUNCIL (1984–86). *Initial Teacher Education Project.* Southampton: University of Southampton.

HIGHAM, A. (1982). In: BOLAM, R. (Ed) *School Focussed Inservice Training.* London: Heinemann Educational Books.

HINDE, R.A. (1979). *Towards Understanding Relationships.* London: Academic Press.

HOFFMAN, M.L. (1973). 'Child rearing practices and moral development: generalisations from empirical research', *Child Development*, 34, 295–318.

HOFFMAN, M. (1975a). 'Developmental synthesis of affect and cognition and its implications for altrustic motivation', *Developmental Psychology*, 11, 5, 607–22.

HOFFMAN, M. (1975b). 'Moral internalisation, parental power and the nature of child–parent interaction', *Developmental Psychology*, 11, 5, 228–39.

HOFFMAN, M.L. (1984). 'Empathy, its limitations and its role in a comprehensive moral theory'. In: KURTINES, W.B. and GEWIRTS, J.L. (Eds) *Morality, Moral Behaviour and Moral Development*. New York: Wiley.

HOMANS, G. (1951). *The Human Group*. London: Routledge and Kegan Paul.

HUDSON, W.D. (1969). *The 'Is/Ought' Question*. London: Macmillan.

HUDSON, W.D. (1970). *Modern Moral Philosophy*. London: Macmillan.

HUGHES, T. (1978). 'Myth and education'. In: FOX, G. *et al.* (Eds) *Writers, Critics and Children*. London: Heinemann.

*Humberside Agreed Syllabus of Religious Education* (1981). County Hall, Beverley, North Humberside.

HUSTON, T.L. and KORTE, C. (1976). 'The responsive bystander: why he helps'. In: LICKONA, T. (Ed) *Moral Development and Behaviour*. New York: Holt.

JOHNSON, D. and JOHNSON, R. (1975). *Learning Alone and Together*. Englewood Cliffs, NJ: Prentice-Hall.

KIERKEGAARD, S. (1945). *Concluding Unscientific Postscript* (trans. SWENSON and LOWRIE). London: Oxford University Press.

KIERKEGAARD, S. (1946). *Kierkegaard's Attack on Christendom 1854–55*. (trans. LOWRIE). Princeton, NJ: Princeton University Press.

KOHLBERG, L. (1974). 'Education, moral development and faith', *Journal of Moral Education*, 4, 1, 8–14.

KOHLBERG, L. (1976). 'Moral stages and moralisation: the cognitive-developmental approach'. In: LICKONA, T. (Ed) *Moral Development and Behaviour*. New York: Holt.

KOHLBERG, L. (1978). 'Moral education re-appraisal', Moral Education and Secular Humanism – a Symposium, *The Humanist*, 38, 6, 12–18.

KOHLBERG, L. (1979). 'From Athens to Watergate: moral education in a just society', *Curriculum Review*, 18, 8–11.

KOHLBERG, L. (1980a). 'Educating for a just society'. In: MUNSEY, B. (Ed) *Moral Development, Moral Education and Kohlberg*. Birmingham, Ala.: Religious Education Press.

KOHLBERG, L. (1980b). 'High school democracy and educating for a just society'. In: MOSHER, R. (Ed) *Moral Education: A First Generation of Research*. New York: Praeger.

KOHLBERG, L. (1981a) *Essays in Moral Development: The Philosophy of Moral Development*. Vols I and II. San Francisco, Calif.: Harper and Row; reprinted 1983.

KOHLBERG, L. (1981b). 'Moral development, religious thinking and the question of a seventh stage', *Zygon*, 16, 3, 203–241.

KOHLBERG, L. (1982). 'Recent work in moral education'. In: WARD, L.O. (Ed) *The Ethical Dimension of the School Curriculum*. Swansea: Pineridge Press.

KOHLBERG, L. and CANDEE, D. (1984). 'The relationship of moral judgement to moral action'. In: KURTINES, W.B. and GEWIRTZ, J.L. (Eds) *Morality, Moral Behaviour and Moral Development*. New York: Wiley.

KOHLBERG, L., HICKEY, J. and SCHARF, P. (1972). 'The justice structure of the prison: a theory and intervention', *Prison Journal*, 57, 3–14.

KOHLBERG, L., LEVINE, C. and HEWER, A. (1983). *Moral Stages: The Current Formulation of Kohlberg's Theory and a Response to Critics*. Basel: Karger.

KOHLBERG, L., SNAREY, J. and REIMER, J. (1984). 'Cultural universality of moral judgement stages; a longitudinal study of Israel'. In: KOHLBERG, L. *Essays on Moral Development, Vol. 2. The Psychology of Moral Development*. San Francisco, Calif.: Harper and Row.

KURTINES, W.B. and GEWIRTZ, J.L. (1984). *Morality, Moral Behaviour and Moral Development*. New York: Wiley.

KUTNICK, P. (1980). 'The inception of school authority: the socialisation of the primary school child', *Genetic Psychology Monographs*, 101, 35–70.

KUTNICK, P. (1983a). *Relating to Learning*. London: Allen and Unwin.

KUTNICK, P. (1983b). 'Moral incursions into constraints'. In: WEINREICH-HASTE, H. and LOCKE, D. (Eds) *Morality in the Making*. Chichester: Wiley.

KUTNICK, P. and BREES, P. (1982). 'The development of co-operation: explorations in cognitive and moral competence and social authority', *British Journal of Educational Psychology*, 52, 361–9.

LICKONA, T. (Ed.) (1976). *Moral Development and Behaviour*. New York: Holt.

MCCLELLAN, J.E. and KOMISAR, B.P. (1964). 'On deriving "ought" from "is"', *Analysis*, 25. In: HUDSON, W.D. (Ed) (1969) *The Is/Ought Question*. London: Macmillan.

MCPHAIL, P., UNGOED-THOMAS, J. and CHAPMAN, H., (1972). *Moral Education in the Secondary School*. London: Longman.

MEAD, G.H. (1964). *On Social Psychology*. Chicago: Phoenix.

MITCHELL, B. (1970). 'Indoctrination'. *The Fourth R*. London: National Society/SPCK, Appendix B, 353–8.

MONTAGU, A. (1968). *Man and Aggression*. London and New York: Oxford University Press.

MOORE, W. (1972). 'Indoctrination and democratic method'. In: SNOOK, I. (Ed) *Concepts of Indoctrination: Philosophical Essays*. London: Routledge and Kegan Paul.

MORAN, G. (1974). *Religious Body*. New York: Seabury.

MORAN, G. (1983). *Religious Education Development*. Minneapolis, Minn.: Winston Press.

MORRELL, D. (1966). Joseph Payne Memorial Lectures 1965–6.

MORRELL, D. (1969). Address to the Anglo-American Educational Alliance.

MUSSEN, P. and EISENBERG-BERG, N. (1977). *Roots of Caring, Sharing and Helping*. San Francisco, Calif.: Freeman.

NARAYAN, R. (1979). Quotation in *Guardian*, 12 August 1979.

OPEN UNIVERSITY (1981). *Education for Family Life*. Oxford: Oxford University Press.

PEPITONE, E. (1980). *Children in Co-operation and Competition*. Toronto: Lexington.

PETERS, R.S. (1974). 'Personal understanding and personal relationships'. In: MISCHEL, T. (Ed) *Understanding Other Persons*. Oxford: Blackwell.

PETERS, R.S. (1981). *Moral Development and Moral Education*. London: Allen and Unwin.

PFEIFFER, J.W. and JONES, J.F. (1983). *Reference Guide to Handbooks and Annuals*. La Jolla, Calif.: University of California Press.

PIAGET, J. (1926). *The Language and Thought of the Child*. London: Routledge and Kegan Paul.

PIAGET, J. (1932). *The Moral Judgement of the Child*. London: Routledge and Kegan Paul.

PIAGET, J. (1951). *Play, Dreams and Imitation in Childhood*. New York: Norton.

PIAGET, J. (1959). *The Language and Thought of the Child*. (1928 trans.) London: Routledge and Kegan Paul.

POWER, C. (1980). 'Evaluating just communities: towards a method for assessing the moral atmosphere of the school'. In: KUHWERKER, L., MENTKOWSKI, M. and ERICKSON, L. (Eds) *Evaluating Moral Development*. Schenectady: Character Research Press.

PRIESTLEY, J. (1981a). 'Religious story and the literary imagination', *British Journal of Religious Education*, 4, 1, 17–24.

PRIESTLEY, J. (1981b). *Bible Stories for Today. Vol. 1, The Old Testament*; *Vol.2, The New Testament*. Exeter: RMEP.

PRIESTLEY, J. (1985a). 'Towards finding the hidden curriculum', *British Journal of Religious Education*, 7, 3, 112–19.

PRIESTLEY, J. (1985b). 'It isn't true, is it Miss? It's only a story', *Resource* (University of Warwick Institute of Education), 7, 3, 1–3.

PRING, R. (1984). *Personal and Social Education in the Curriculum*. London: Hodder and Stoughton.

RHEES, R. (1984). *Recollections of Wittgenstein*. Oxford: Oxford University Press.

RICE, W. and GRAY, G. (1984). *Alcohol Education Syllabus*. London: TACADE/Health Education Council.

RICHARDSON, R. *et al.* (n.d.). 'Indicators of an international dimension', *Debate and Decision*. World Studies Project.

RUBIN, Z. (1980). *Children's Friendships*. Shepton Mallet: Open Books.

RUTTER, M., MAUGHAN, B., MORTIMORE, P. and OUSTON, J. (1979). *Fifteen Thousand Hours*. Harmondsworth: Penguin.

SCALLY, M. and HOPSON, B. (1980). *Lifeskills Teaching Programme*. London: TACADE.

SCHAFFER, H.R. (1971). *The Growth of Sociability*. Harmondsworth: Penguin.

SCHOLEFIELD, L. (1982). *Passover,* Exeter: RMEP.

SCHOOLS COUNCIL (1980). *Health Education 13–18 Project.* London: Schools Council/Health Educational Council.

SCHOOLS COUNCIL (1981). *Health Education 13–18 Project.* London: Schools Council/Health Education Council, R.14, R.15.

SCHOOLS COUNCIL (1982). *Health Education 13–18.* Schools Council/Health Education Council.

SCHOOLS COUNCIL/NUFFIELD FOUNDATION (1970). *The Humanities Project: An Introduction.* London: Heinemann Educational Books.

SEARLE, J.R. (1964). 'How to derive "ought" from "is"', *Philosophical Review,* 73. In: HUDSON, W.D. (Ed) (1969). *The Is/Ought Question.* London: Macmillan.

SELMAN, R. (1976). 'Social cognitive understanding'. In: LICKONA, T. (Ed) *Moral Development and Behaviour.* New York: Holt.

SELMAN, R. (1980). *The Growth of Interpersonal Understanding.* New York: Academic Press.

SHERIF, M. *et al.* (1961). *Intergroup Conflict and Cooperation: The Robbers' Case Study.* Norman, Okla.: University of Oklahoma Press.

SHIPMAN, M.D. *et al.* (1974). *Inside a Curriculum Project.* London: Methuen.

SIMON, S.B. (1972). *Values Clarification: A Handbook.* New York: Hart.

SIMON, B. and WILLCOCKS, J. (1982). *Research and Practice in the Primary School.* London: Routledge and Kegan Paul.

SKINNER, B.F. (1971). *Beyond Freedom and Dignity.* Harmondsworth: Penguin.

SLAVIN, R. (1984). 'Small group methods in teaching'. In: HUSEN, T. and POSTLEWHAITE, T.N. (Eds) *The International Encyclopedia of Education* Oxford: Pergamon.

SNOOK, I.A. (Ed.) (1972). *Concepts of Indoctrination: Philosophical Essays.* London: Routledge and Kegan Paul.

STAUB, E. (1978). *Positive Social Behaviour and Morality.* New York: Academic Press.

STAYTON, D., HOGAN, R. and AINSWORTH, M. (1971). 'Infant obedience and maternal behaviour: origins of socialisation reconsidered', *Child Development,* 42, 1057–69.

STERN, D. (1977). *The First Relationship, Infant and Mother.* London: Open Books.

SULLIVAN, H.S. (1953). *The Interpersonal Theory of Psychiatry.* New York: Norton.

SWANN REPORT (1985). *Education for All.* London: HMSO.

TAWNEY, R.H. (1938). *Equality.* London: Allen and Unwin.

TAYLOR REPORT (1977). *A New Partnership in Our Schools.* London: HMSO.

THACKER, V.J. (1985). 'Extending developmental group work to junior/middle schools', *Pastoral Care in Education,* 3, 1, 4–13.

VERMA, G.K. (1980). *The Impact of Innovation.* Paper No.9, EUA-CARE.

WARNOCK, M. (1971). *Ethics since 1900.* London: Oxford University Press.

WASSERMAN, E. and GARROD, A. (1983). 'Application of Kohlberg's theory

to curricula and democratic schools', *Educational Analysis*, 5, 1, 17–36.
WEINREICH-HASTE, H. (1979). 'Moral development'. In: COLEMAN, J.C. (Ed) *The School Years*. London: Methuen.
WEINREICH-HASTE, H. and LOCKE, D. (1983). *Morality in the Making*, Chichester: Wiley.
WHITAKER, P. (1984). 'World Studies: the learning process', *World Studies Journal*, 5, 2, 3–33.
WHITE, J.P. (1967). 'Indoctrination'. In: PETERS, R.S. (Ed) *The Concept of Education*. London: Routledge and Kegan Paul.
WILLIS, P. (1977). *Learning to Labour*. Farnborough: Saxon House.
WILSON, J. (1964). 'Education and Indoctrination'. In: HOLLINS, T.H.B. (Ed) *Aims in Education*. Manchester: Manchester University Press.
WITTGENSTEIN, L. (1961). *Tractatus Logico Philosophicus*. London: Routledge and Kegan Paul.
WRINGLE, S. (1974). 'Some problems raised by the Schools Council Humanities Project', *Journal of Curriculum Studies*, 6, 1, 30–43.
YOUNISS, J. (1980). *Parents and Peers in Social Development*. Chicago: University of Chicago Press.